FOOTPRINTS IN THE DUST

Nursing, Survival, Compassion, and Hope with Refugees Around the World

ROBERTA GATELY

PEGASUS BOOKS
NEW YORK LONDON

FOOTPRINTS IN THE DUST

Pegasus Books Ltd.
148 W 37th Street, 13th Floor
New York, NY 10018

First Pegasus Books edition October 2018

Interior design by Maria Fernandez

Library of Congress Cataloging-in-Publication Data is available.

ISBN: 978-1-68177-864-8

10 9 8 7 6 5 4 3 2 1

Printed in the United States of America
Distributed by W. W. Norton & Company, Inc.
www.pegasusbooks.us

To Sue, Marianne and Jim with love . . .

CONTENTS

INTRODUCTION

—◆—

Refugee—the latest buzzword, a word guaranteed to spark conversation and fuel emotion. There are more than twenty-two million refugees worldwide, and another sixty-five million who have been forcibly displaced from their homes, their villages, from everything they know.[1] But who are these people, these refugees that seem to slip into our conversations, our country, and even our lives with nary a chance for us to understand what they're all about? The scant news we have of them filters into our homes via dramatic satellite shots of distant, barely pronounceable villages in countries as foreign to us as any images of Mars might be. We barely have time to focus on the often gut-wrenching photos before the anchor is on to the next story, leaving us less enlightened and perhaps even a little more puzzled by what we've seen. It is in the seeing—the firsthand, close-enough-to-touch encounters—that the real truth can be found. It is my hope that by sharing their stories, their realities, I can provide a little of that truth here.

I am a nurse, a humanitarian aid worker, and a writer, and I've traveled to some of the most desolate lands on earth to deliver health care to persecuted, desperate people. But lest you think that this is some soul-searching, self-aggrandizing tome, let me assure you that the refugees with whom I've worked have done far more for me than I ever did for them. It is in this spirit that I share their stories as well as my own.

As a young (at least from my perspective some thirty years on) ER nurse in Boston, I'd been acutely aware of the intermittent refugee crises that gripped our world. These international disasters, appearing for brief moments in the media spotlight, invariably featured stark glimpses of big-bellied babies with empty, haunting stares, who invariably caught my eye and stopped me cold. And then, as if I'd only imagined them, they simply disappeared from the spotlight and I found myself wondering how this baby or that little girl had fared. Each new story sparked my interest a little more, and finally, in 1986, after a particularly gripping news story about Afghan refugees fleeing to Pakistan, I decided it was time to do something. I called the aid organization featured in the news story, and within two months, I was on my way.

I am by nature neither courageous nor adventurous, and though drama would weave itself throughout my days and nights delivering aid, it was neither a search for adventure nor a dramatic incident that served as the catalyst that finally drew me to aid work. For me it had been the right time and the right set of circumstances, and as an inner-city ER nurse well versed in the treatment of trauma and sad-eyed patients, I was sure I could help.

What happened, I'd always wondered, to people already living the hardest of hardscrabble lives when war and misery claim their land? For starters, they don't give up. They manage to go on and sometimes even to smile no matter their own suffering, much like Fatima, a young woman I met in Iraq not long after the US invasion. We'd gone to her small village to test the drinking water, and as expected, it was filled with bacteria and would require boiling before consuming. But Fatima saw possibility in that dirty water. Tucking a stray hair under her hijab, she smiled coyly and spoke to me in perfect English so that the watchful crowd of locals wouldn't under-stand her words. "My husband," she whispered, "is an old man and I am his second wife. My life is miserable, filled with sorrow." Her chocolate brown eyes scanned the horizon as if searching for something that was just out of sight. "I want to escape this place, and God willing, the dirty water will be the end of him."

And that brings me back to the beginning—who are these people, these refugees? Are they the desperate, doe-eyed children with hungry stares, or are they more like Fatima—searching for opportunity wherever it appears? The answer, I believe, lies somewhere in the middle. They are neither all saints nor all sinners, but perhaps a little bit of each. But without their names or their stories, all we can see of them are footprints in the dust, and even those will fade in time.

It is my hope that once you've read these pages, those footprints will linger in your thoughts and remain there—tiny, precious pearls that help to remind us that we are all more alike than we know, that whatever separates us, we are ultimately joined by the common thread of humanity.

PROLOGUE

———◆———

Iraq 2003

As I opened the door to step into the hallway, I heard a quick hush of voices and rustle of movement, and I hesitated.

"Step away from the door," a harsh, unseen voice commanded me.

My heart flapped furiously in my chest. This was not what I'd expected, not at all. "Can I come into the hallway?" I asked timidly.

Several rifles appeared, all trained on me. Other than the rifles, which seemed to glisten in the moonlight streaming in, the hallway was black, the men holding the rifles invisible. Bathed in deep shadow, their identities remained obscured, which made the moment all the more sinister. I hesitated, my breath catching in my throat, my lungs seizing up.

"Show your hands!" a voice demanded, and I put my now trembling hands into the air.

Motioning with their rifles, they directed me into the hallway . . .

Damn it, I thought. *What the hell am I doing here, anyway?*

I

AFGHANISTAN/PAKISTAN

1986–1988

First Steps

———•◆•———

The loudspeaker crackled to life. "The government of Pakistan has just announced that all foreigners must have an official entry visa for Pakistan." The stewardess cleared her throat. I felt my own throat tighten as her voice droned on. "Those without visas . . ." I'd stopped listening. When I'd left Boston, just twenty hours ago, a visa was not required for entry to Pakistan. I glanced through the smudged little window as the plane glided to a stop, the heat from the tarmac rising in spindly waves, almost obscuring the antiaircraft artillery that ringed the airport's periphery and the gun-toting soldiers who lined the narrow runway. As my eyes focused on the scene below, the warnings of well-meaning friends and family rang in my ears. *"Are you crazy? You'll be killed. You'll never make it out of the airport."*

My intentions had been pure when I'd signed up to help the Afghan refugees fleeing the Soviet invasion for the relative safety of Pakistan. It had seemed a romantic notion—the perfect struggle of good against evil, and I'd wanted to be a part of it. Like most Americans, I knew little about Afghanistan or the Soviet invasion there in 1979, but the scenes of stick-thin refugees clad in rags fleeing their homes and their country had moved me to action. I'd always wanted to be involved, but until then it hadn't been the right time, but there it was—the perfect spot for me. I'd had no doubt that I could do what was needed, and, with the images of starving children still flickering on my television screen, I'd picked up the phone and volunteered.

I'd been certain that friends and family would rally round to support me. But I was wrong. One after another chided me for what seemed, at least to them, a fool's errand. "Do you *really* think *you* can help?" I did. In fact, I was sure I could help. Finally, my aunt stepped into the verbal fray. "Are you sure," she asked softy, "that this is the right thing to do?" I nodded in reply. "And you're sure this is not some kind of death wish?" My jaw dropped. "Death wish?" I'd asked, perplexed. "This is a life wish. I want it to matter, someday in the very distant future, that I was here. I know I can help. I've never been more sure of anything." And once she was convinced of that, the angst surrounding my decision melted away. I would be fine. "I'm ready," I'd said confidently. "I've done a lot of reading." But as my face hugged the plane's window, I suddenly wasn't so sure.

I'd vaguely remembered President Carter's boycott of the Winter Olympics in 1980 in response to the Soviet invasion, but knew little else until my planned trip had thrown me into a reading frenzy. I'd learned that Afghanistan, a nation seemingly always embroiled in conflict, offered a harsh existence in the best of times. The preinvasion population of twenty-five million lived in rural villages, where they'd subsisted on small farms, eking out a living however they could. The simple resources that we take for granted—electricity, running water, plumbing—were rarely available beyond the city limits. Health care was limited as well, resulting in maternal and infant mortality numbers that were among the highest in the world. Sixty percent of all deaths occurred before age five, and overall life expectancy hovered around forty years.[1] In the best of times, life was hard, and in those worst of times, after the invasion, life was unimaginable.

The situation across the border offered at least some hope to the millions of Afghans who poured out of their own country to the relative safety of Pakistan. But, by 1986, they continued to languish in squalid camps along the border, and though they received food, education, shelter, and health care, their host country was resentful of the attention they received. Terrorist attacks were on the rise, and the refugees were blamed. Pakistan wanted to be rid of them and the problems they brought.

To avoid the rigid structure of camp life, at least a million more Afghans chose to live outside the camps, invisible to aid and to the world. If life in the camps was hardscrabble, then life just beyond was pure misery, especially so for women, who'd never been considered of any importance beyond the sons they produced and the chores they completed. The refugees there needed everything—food, shelter, medical care. You name it—they needed it. And it was there, to that border area and those people, that I was headed.

But first, I had to get out of the airport.

Until this trip, the farthest I'd traveled was a beach resort in Mexico, and I'd never traveled alone. As the first doubts about my mission began to bubble up in my brain, I held my breath, gathered my belongings, and stepped into a world more foreign than anything I could have imagined. The heat I'd seen rising in steamy ripples wove itself into my hair and skin and even my clothes. But it was the odors—the scents of food and spices and sweating bodies, all mingling in the heat to create a musky, pungent odor—that permeated everything. It was all so exotic, I might have just landed on the moon. Still, I tried to stand a little straighter and hold my head a little higher as I was shuttled, amidst one large chaotic crowd, from one long line to the next, but my sudden burst of bravado was short-lived. As others were allowed to pass through, I stammered my way through explanations for arriving without the necessary visa, watching as eyebrows were raised and soldiers moved in. My pulse quickened when a young soldier directed me to a small room, where three disheveled young European men sat, their feet tapping nervously, their eyes darting about every time someone moved. Drug dealers, I thought. And as that reality sunk in, my mouth grew dry. Shit.

As the minutes ticked by, I began to think I really might not make it out of the airport, but I was determined to somehow stay in this country and do what I'd come for. To give up now and just go home would be to admit defeat. I wasn't ready to do that, so instead I tried desperately to think of a way to reason with the soldiers. "I'm waiting for friends," I announced to the young soldier when he reappeared and motioned one of the young men to follow him. I'd been advised to keep my aid work a secret. "Pakistan is tired of the refugees," the aid recruiter had cautioned me. "Better to say you're a tourist." I'd stuck to that story though it had seemed implausible even to me. I heard the crack of a whip and shouts and another soldier returned and took a second man out. More shouts and sounds of a beating filled my ears. I could almost hear the acid churning in my stomach. Would they beat me, too?

But the young soldier had taken a shine to me and he brought me a cup of tea, smiling as he set it down. "Rafiq," he said, pointing to his name tag. I nodded. "Roberta," I answered with a hopeful smile. I settled in with my tea and prayed that the other members of the aid group would arrive soon and vouch for me. The third man was directed out of the room, and I sat alone. One, maybe two hours passed. Sweat pooled on the back of my neck. Surely, if they were going to beat me or arrest me, I reasoned with myself, they would've done it by now.

Finally, after what seemed an eternity, a handwritten sign rose above the crowd just beyond the small room, and my heart beat a little faster. Freedom Medicine, the fledgling NGO I'd be joining, had arrived to pluck me from the line, and I was free—with only a stern warning to get my documents straightened out. I nodded. I'd made it out of the airport.

As alien as the airport had seemed, the city of Peshawar in the North West Frontier Province of Pakistan was even more so. A tribal frontier town, Peshawar was the international epicenter during the Soviet invasion of neighboring Afghanistan. It had become an exciting, crowded, noisy city filled with refugees, spies, freedom fighters, foreign diplomats, aid workers, journalists, and those adventurers who had simply been drawn there, and now I was one of them. People and donkeys and dogs, and all manner of vehicles—buses, lorries, screeching taxis, tiny motorized rickshaws, horse-drawn wagons and even bicycles—filled every inch of space. Coupled with the noise of barking dogs, braying donkeys, squawking chickens, groaning motors, and the shouts of those caught in the middle, it was a place of absolute chaos, the sort of place a person might never adjust to.

For me and the others on my team—Ella, a nurse, and Tom, a medic, both from New England—Peshawar was just a quick stop, a place where we could acclimate a bit at the American Club, the brightly lit restaurant and dark, smoke-filled bar run by the American consulate, protected by security guards and hidden behind high walls. It was a place where the eclectic group of foreigners here could have a drink, flirt, begin or end an affair, and just let loose. Whether noon or midnight, it was always lively, always the place to be, but we didn't have time for more than a quick envious peek at the goings-on there.

The next stop after the club was the local bazaar, where Ella and I would pick up our new clothes—balloonlike pants covered by long dresses, and head scarves, all to comply with local customs and hide our evil feminine wiles. Men, on the other hand, were less restricted and allowed to wear their own clothes.

With those tasks completed, we set out for Thal, the small border village where FM was in the process of setting up a clinic and a medic training for Afghan freedom fighters. Once we left the city limits of Peshawar, the road narrowed, snaking through dusty villages where you could purchase a warm bottle of Coca-Cola, a bad-tempered camel, a newly polished piece of antiaircraft artillery, or, if you were so inclined, a bit of opium, fresh from Afghanistan's poppies.

These villages were miniatures of Peshawar—less crowded, less noisy, but still overflowing with donkeys, dogs, shrieking children, shouting men, and conspicuously absent—women. Hidden behind burqas or the mud-plastered walls of their own homes, they rarely ventured out. A sighting of any woman's face was rare, which made Ella and me the object of great curiosity. Were we—as some probably hoped—whores, or maybe just fools in a foreign land?

Hours later, we arrived at the Freedom Medicine compound in Thal, situated on a paved stretch of road on the way to nowhere. The surrounding landscape was bare—dust and an occasional bit of scrub or a lone stray dog were all that I could see. FM, hidden behind high mud walls, was a series of one-story brick buildings with plastic sheeting for windows and doors. The living quarters, a cluster of tents, were nestled behind those buildings.

Ella and I would share a raggedy old UN tent that housed two bare cots and countless bugs, some the size of small animals. There were no amenities—no electricity, two simple outdoor showers, and two doorless side-by-side latrines (no toilets here, just simple no-nonsense holes dug deep into the ground) separated by a brick wall. A roll of toilet paper (Chinese and very scratchy, I'd later learn) lay in the dirt.

A fresh bead of sweat tracked along my forehead. Before I'd volunteered, I'd never even gone camping. My idea of roughing it had been no room service after ten, and yet, I was sure that my experience at the airport had somehow toughened me. Or so I hoped. But, in all my planning, I'd somehow never imagined what it would be like to actually be here—the scents, the noise, the desolation—and that was only here, in the FM compound. I'd only imagined myself cradling desperately ill babies or tending to fresh wounds, and so far, it wasn't like that at all.

Ella, a seasoned aid worker who'd most recently volunteered at a Cambodian refugee camp in Thailand, unpacked quickly, as she filled me in on her work there, regaling me with her memories of the work she'd done. "Mostly in the morgue," she announced matter-of-factly. "I was in charge of public health, and when the rains came and the camp flooded, there was a big problem with what to do with the bodies, so I worked on that." I sighed and hoped that the work here would be different. Ella barely noticed my chagrin. She pulled out a blue nylon nightgown before plopping herself down on her cot. "So, tell me about yourself," she said, a quick smile draping her lips.

There wasn't much to tell. Until a few hours ago, I'd been an opinionated, maybe slightly overconfident ER nurse, but now, I wasn't even sure of that. Ella sensed my unease, and she literally took my hand as she walked me to the latrine and the shower and demonstrated the basics of third world life.

By the time I fell onto my cot (still in my clothes, since I'd inexplicably decided that bringing a nightgown might be seen as too prissy), I was certain sleep would come quickly. And it did. For Ella.

For me, it was a different story. I lay awake, my mind still racing—so much to learn, so little time, my confidence ebbing away with each passing minute. Just as I felt myself start to drift off, I was startled by the sudden rumble and whistle of distant artillery. I sat bolt upright, my eyes wide open. "What the hell is that?" I whispered. Ella's only reply was the soft snoring that punctuated her sleep. I wanted to shake her awake, to make her sit with me, but she remained blissfully wrapped in her dreams. I curled up, covered my head with my pillow, and tried to sleep. And, as the artillery rounds tapered off and the sun began to poke through the tent's flap, I finally drifted off.

Not much later, I woke to find Ella, already dressed, swiping a line of blue eye shadow across her eyelids. I sat up straighter. "Ella, makeup?" I sighed. "I am *so* impressed."

"Oh honey," she replied, finger-combing her tousled curls, "you've got to look good, you never know who you're going to meet."

My pencil eyeliner and lipstick had already melted in the sticky heat, but I was learning. After that, I never left home without sturdy lipstick, not to mention real sleep-wear. Ella was right; even if you are without water and haven't washed your face in days, a swipe of color across your lips and you feel better, renewed somehow.

Lipstick, even in Afghanistan, or perhaps especially in Afghanistan, makes a world of difference.

Thal

———◆———

Summer 1986

Our first days were spent organizing the medicines supplied by the UN, and writing protocols and procedures for the medic training program. There were still no babies to soothe, no wounds to tend. We didn't even have a clinic yet. We watched as Mike, an American construction worker, and his crew quickly crafted a rustic structure—a mud-and-grass roof, a floor of swept dirt, and walls made of canvas sheeting strung from ropes laced throughout the clinic. The furniture consisted of old army cots for patients and simple metal tables where we could write.

It wasn't until the second week that we were able to see patients, and the work, once we began, was challenging. The refugees were a bedraggled group dressed in tattered, threadbare clothes, many of them gaunt and hollow-eyed and desperate for help. It is one thing to see refugees on television, but it was heart-wrenching to see them in person, and I wondered if I could really make a difference here. I had been so sure that I would know what to do, how to help, but in those first days, I lost that cocky confidence and sometimes felt paralyzed by what I was seeing. And who was I anyway, to think that I could really help? Those sad-eyed babies with big bloated bellies that had so moved me already had worried mothers to soothe them. But, I was there. I had to do something.

FM had only one physician, a Brit named Daniel, a thin, quick-witted man who guided the rest of the medical team through the assessment of so many foreign diseases—malaria, typhoid, malnutrition, dysentery. Within days, we were doing what had seemed unimaginable only days before—diagnosing dysentery and worms and occasionally malaria—each of us clutching our handbooks as we plowed through the list of waiting patients. As each day passed, my confidence grew. It would be okay. I would be okay.

And I proved that to myself one bright morning when I was summoned for an emergency. "Miss! Come here, miss!" One of the Afghan medic students frantically waved his arms and motioned for me to follow him. I adjusted my head scarf and hurried after him to the entrance. Already, I could see a crowd hovering there. A baby's cry rose above the din, and as I approached, a sudden hush fell over the scene. I moved closer and the group parted, revealing a young man holding a baby out to me. The baby, from what I could see as I quickly cradled him, had a large, gaping head wound, with blood and gray matter that seemed to be spilling out from his skull. The father was speaking quickly, the student trying to keep up. "He fell," the father cried as we rushed to the back of the clinic.

As I stopped and leaned down to place the baby on the cot for a better look, the lump of gray matter fell to the dirt floor. My heart stopped. The baby cried, and his father reached for the tissue in the dirt.

"No," I shouted. "Leave it." I knew we couldn't replace it in the baby's skull. I didn't want this distraught father to try. He seemed not to have heard or understood me. Gripping the gray squishy lump in his hand, he reached for the baby's head. Still holding the baby, I turned away. The baby screeched and flailed about. It was then I saw a long gash in his scalp that surely needed stitches, but there was no evidence of a more serious injury, and no sign that his brains had leaked out. The wound was superficial. I rocked the baby and turned questioningly to the medic, who was laughing.

"*Che ast*?" 'What is it?' I asked.

The father held the gray hunk out for me. "It is the liver of a goat. We put that on a wound to keep it clean and to stop the blood. "*Famidi*? Understand?" the medic asked.

I didn't really, but in a way, it made sense. The blood's clotting factors are produced in the liver. The animal liver may have helped stem the bleeding, and at least protected the wound from the dirt that was all around us. We irrigated, cleaned, and sutured the wound the only way I knew—with saline and stitches and bandages.

"*Tashakore*," the father said as he lifted the baby into his arms. He slipped the little envelope of antibiotics we'd prescribed into his shirt pocket and turned to leave.

"Come back," I cautioned, "if there are any signs of infection, and in seven days, we want to take those stitches out. Understand?"

The father ignored me. I had done what was needed, and now I was just a female again. The Afghan medic repeated my instructions, and the father nodded. The baby squealed, delighted to be done with us, and I heard his laughter as father and son were on their way back home, but home was a worn and dingy tent with a dirt floor. We had yet to develop a record-keeping system, so we never got the family's name, and I knew it was likely we'd never see them again. This baby and his father were blunt lessons in understanding the realities and limits of delivering health care amidst chaos, especially as a woman in a land where women were not to be heard or seen.

Our days were full. Refugees and locals walked for hours just for the hope of medical care. For others, who really weren't sick, a visit to the clinic provided a break from the hellish monotony of life in the camps. For the women, each day was filled with reminders of all they had lost—their homes, their husbands, sometimes their children. Once surrounded by large, extended families in thriving villages, they were now forced to live in small tents or mud houses with their remaining family members. A visit to our clinic allowed them a glimpse of foreigners and provided gossip for days to come. I could see the women, hidden by their veils, their shoulders shaking with laughter, as I fumbled with my head scarf or the baggy pants I wore under my dress.

Asma was among them, an older woman who'd walked to our clinic one day, not because she was sick but rather because she'd heard about the foreigners in Thal and wanted to see us for herself. She wore a threadbare dress, a grimy head scarf, and plastic sandals. She took a number, and when I called her in, she rose, leaning her thin frame on a crooked wooden stick. She followed me into the clinic and sat heavily on the old cot.

"*Salaam-aleikum, chetore asti? Khoob asti? Jon 'a jurast?*" I greeted her. 'Hello, how are you? Are you well?' I'd been learning Dari, enough that I could sometimes get by on my own.

She nodded and shrugged her shoulders. "*Waleikum-salaam. Khoob astam.*"

"*Che taklif em rosa?*" 'What is your problem today?' I asked, reaching for my stethoscope.

"I have no problems," she said haltingly in a mix of English and Dari.

"You speak English?"

"*Kam, kam*, a little." She swiped the end of her head scarf across her brow. "I am Asma," she said. "I am from Afghanistan, a beautiful place. Not like this," she added, casting a scornful eye around the clinic. "I am here for a short time. You understand?"

I nodded and set my stethoscope back down.

Asma smoothed her dress and wrinkled her nose. "This dress," she said, tracing her finger along the worn fabric and what remained of the fancy beads sewn into it, "was new not so long ago. It was my best dress, the one I wore for Eid and other happy occasions, but now it is only a rag. Ours is a hard life. You understand?"

And I nodded again, though I couldn't even imagine how hard it must be for these women who had been forced from their homes, from everything they knew. Their children—if not injured or sick—were hungry, their husbands at war, their land lost, their homes destroyed. How could I, how could any of us, who would all eventually go home to warm, safe homes, ever really know the extent of their suffering?

Asma looked me straight in the eye and continued. "I had a trunk full of fine clothes once. I had a garden and flowers and a fine house, and now I have nothing. My husband is all I have left, and even he is not the same. *Famidi*? I was somebody important." She dropped her gaze to her hands and sighed. I reached out and pressed my hand on top of hers, a display of understanding, I hoped.

"Why are *you* here?" she asked me, her eyes suddenly flashing. "Why would you, why would any woman, leave her home to come to a country of strangers? Are you rich? Or maybe bored?"

I pulled my hand away and tried to explain that I was a nurse at home, that I came here only to help. And contrary to being rich, this trip—at my own expense—just might break the bank, but already, I knew that I loved being here, that this work mattered. "I'll have to work twice as hard when I go home to save up so that I can do this again. Understand?"

She smiled—finally—and reached into a pocket, her fingers fumbling for something, and when she found it, she rolled it into the palm of her hand and held it out to me. "Chickpeas," she said proudly. "For you. It is all I have to say thank you."

A flush rose to my cheeks. We had food here, and though we all complained about the beans and rice and occasional chicken that had seemed to die of starvation, it was still food. I'd never known real hunger, and I hesitated. "I . . . I can't . . ." I started to say until a cough interrupted me. It was one of the interpreters who had happened by. "You must take them," he whispered. "To refuse is a terrible insult."

Chastened, I held out my hand and Asma dropped the peas there. "Can I do anything for you?" I asked, my fingers closing over the gift.

She shook her head. "The only thing I need now is to go home, to work in my garden again, and to die in my own land." She adjusted her head scarf and stood, pulling her stick close.

"I would help you if I could, but I hope you know I won't forget you," I said.

"I think you will forget me," she answered matter-of-factly. "You will go home and *inshallah*, I will, too," she said softly as she hobbled out and away.

But I haven't forgotten her, and I've always wondered if she made it home before she died, if she had a chance to work in her garden and feel the sweet soil of her own land in her hands once again.

And there were so many others, too—hungry babies, exhausted women, war-weary men and boys—none returned for follow-up. I worried about them all—the baby with the head wound, the old man with the worrisome cough, the young woman with five tiny children in tow who'd left the clinic before we had a chance to speak with her—and the rest we'd seen so quickly in our clinic. Although I'd barely had a glimpse of most of them, they'd all made a lasting impression.

My four weeks here had passed in a rush of long days and longer nights. The sounds of war, of mortars and Kalashnikovs, had taken some adjustment, but I was already sleeping through most of it. I was still relieved to hear the gunfire and missiles and mortars during the daylight hours; it was fast becoming almost normal background noise, and it made it less likely that they would fight again that same night, meaning a peaceful sleep for me. And although the echoes of war were distant, I had learned to distinguish the difference between the sounds that marked incoming and outgoing missiles and rockets. Incoming was characterized by a whistling sound, while outgoing was signaled by a bang and a whoosh. And luckily, none ever came close to us.

When I left Thal and returned to Peshawar on my way home, I learned that I would now need exit papers to leave Pakistan. God, what a country this was. I didn't know why they couldn't just make one set of rules and leave it at that. The procedure to get exit papers was long and involved, and at the American Club, with the courage of several glasses of wine under my belt, I said the hell with it. It seemed a brilliant decision at the time, but as soon as I got to the airport and saw the fierce men stamping passports, I regretted my alcohol-fueled show of bravado. I was determined though to get on that plane, so I hung back and watched the process. I'd learned enough in my four short weeks to know that surely not all of these men could read. I watched until I noticed one man who seemed not to be reading the documents or papers, only glancing quickly. I scurried into his line and when my turn came, I smiled broadly, chattered away in English, and gave him every paper in my possession, including my FM curriculum, TB treatment guide, and more, and I watched warily as he shuffled through. Finally, he gave up, stamped my passport, nodded and pointed the way toward the departure terminal. I could have shouted with joy, but instead, I smiled. I'd outwitted the airport rules, not once but twice. I was feeling pretty cocky once again.

I returned home forever changed—more confident and yet less sure of the direction of my own life. Supermarkets and malls were too crowded and offered too much of everything and too many choices. At work, I was distracted—wondering about Asma and the others, and how they were doing. I spent hours writing to politicians and speaking about the refugee crisis in Pakistan. There was something so honest, so pure, about those refugees, who, though they had nothing, lived with a kindness and courage that was life-affirming. I knew I'd go back, and though it was difficult to explain to family and friends—who still lamented my crazy decision—I was hooked. I couldn't convince others how right it had felt—I'd already seen their eyes glaze over the few times I'd talked about it—so I avoided the conversation altogether save for one old boyfriend, who understood. "You're never so alive as when you're living on the edge and risking it all to help," he said, referring to his own time in Vietnam at the end of that war. "You can feel it in your bones, right?"

And that was it—in a nutshell. I'd never been more alive than I'd been with the refugees. John had put into words everything I'd felt.

At last, someone understood.

I saved my money, paid my bills, was allowed a little extra vacation time, and finally, I was able to make arrangements to return to Pakistan right after Christmas. And as I packed, my pulse quickened and butterflies flapped in my stomach, and I realized that, for me, going back to the refugees was a little bit like falling in love. How could I ever say no to that?

———•◦•———

Winter 1987

When I returned to Thal in winter, a living compound had been built across the road. I would share a real, though very bare, room with Ella, and a Western bathroom with everyone else. Real toilets and showers with doors had never looked better. And a hospital with six inpatient beds, an ER, and an OR was almost done. There were two new additions to the staff—both Afghan physicians. The medic students were coming along nicely. They were halfway through their six-month course and already were suturing wounds, treating dysentery, and learning to start IVs.

I slid easily into my old role in the clinic, where one of my first patients was Rahima, a young woman who, like so many others here, had no idea how old she was. She'd only shrugged her shoulders when I'd asked. Few of the refugees, and fewer still of the locals, seemed to know their exact age. They didn't celebrate birthdays and found it funny that we did. When pressed, they could guess that they were about a certain age, or that they'd been born in the year of the flood or a drought, or during a crop failure, or maybe during an especially full moon. Beyond that, they simply didn't think about it and couldn't imagine why it mattered. They were puzzled when we pressed them for an age. You were either old or not, what else mattered?

Draped in the folds of a heavy burqa, Rahima sat quietly, only lifting her veil away when we were alone and there was no chance of a man catching a glimpse of her. Her face was all angles and hard edges. She had deep onyx eyes lined with black kohl, eyes that should have sparkled and shone but instead were as flat and dull as the landscape. I introduced myself and asked what her problem was. She lifted her eyes to me and spoke in a rush of words, too many and too quickly for me to follow. Her list of complaints seemed endless. When I rose to fetch an interpreter, she wagged her finger at me. "*Nay, nay,*" she said. She somehow knew that our interpreters were men and, as I'd soon learn, she was embarrassed that a strange man would know what it was she'd come about.

"*Balay,* yes," I said, calling for Halim. "Otherwise, I'll never understand what you need. He'll stay just outside. He won't see you. *Famidi*?"

She nodded and we began, Halim translating her every word.

"I am married," she said softly. "It has been five years now and . . ." Her eyes darted to the doorway, checking to be sure that Halim could not see her. "And, my husband is unhappy with me." Her eyes filled up, her lips quivered.

"*Aacha*, it's okay," I said, encouraging her to go on. "You're safe here."

Her shoulders slumped. "We have no babies," she said. "I have not been with child, not ever, though my husband and I have been together in that way many times. Do you understand? In my culture, this is very bad. This is why men take second and even third wives, and the first is all but left alone, shamed and untouchable."

I'd heard this rumor before—women were only as good as the babies they produced, and the more sons, the better. For Rahima, even a daughter would be a blessing.

"I've come here today because I know you can help. Foreigners have special ways. I've heard it whispered that you can help me to get a baby to grow in there." She patted her flat belly as she spoke. "Will you help me?" Her eyes were pleading when she spoke.

I swallowed the sorrowful lump in my throat. We could provide only the most basic of care here in Thal. I could suggest that maybe Peshawar or

Islamabad could offer those services, but it seemed unlikely that she could afford the cost even if they did. In as gentle a manner as I could, I explained that even when our hospital was open, we would not be able to provide the special services she would need.

"Not ever?" she asked.

I shook my head. "Not ever. But don't give up—"

She stood, hastily pulling her burqa over her face. "I must go," she said, her voice cracking, and I understood what she already knew—that she'd be the forgotten first wife reduced to cooking and cleaning for whoever followed her into her husband's house as his second wife. And that was only if she was allowed to stay. Some first wives were cut off, forced to return home to families who'd have to bear the shame of an abandoned wife under their roof. She would be unmarriageable, an embarrassment and a burden on her family. And there was nothing that I could do to save her.

It was a heartbreaking encounter—for each of us.

The winter was cold, the air especially bitter in Afghanistan, and for a time we were inundated with war-weary young men, with frostbite wounds to their feet. Plastic sandals were the standard footwear in their country, and though the lucky ones had socks, the snow and ice eventually seeped through, freezing the tissue until it blackened and died. When they hobbled into our clinic, many with deep infections in the necrotic flesh, we could only debride the wounds before sending the men on to Peshawar, where many would undergo amputations. As with most of our patients, we'd never see them again, but one young man, a first-time visitor to our clinic in Thal, helped us understand what might have happened with many of them.

Abdul was about twenty when he came to our clinic complaining of leg pain.

"For how long?" Ezat, an Afghan doctor new to our team, asked as Abdul settled himself on the cot. "Since they cut it off," he said, wincing as he pulled his pant leg up to reveal a vinyl leg that reached to his thigh. He pointed to the area where the prosthetic met his stump. A dirty strap and old ACE bandage held it in place. The odor of old sweat and unwashed skin filled the small room.

"When was that?" Ezat asked as he reached to undo the straps and wrapping that held the stump to the artificial leg.

"No!" Abdul shouted, pulling his leg back. He grimaced with the sudden movement. "Don't touch me. Just take the pain away."

Ezat tried to explain that we had to see the stump to understand why he had pain.

Abdul crossed his arms and shook his head. "I haven't taken my leg off since they put it on in Islamabad two, maybe three years ago."

"Why?" Ezat's brow wrinkled.

Abdul's expression softened. "I stepped on a land mine in Afghanistan, and in a moment, my leg was gone." He straightened his vinyl leg. "This is all I have now, and without it, I cannot even walk by myself. Do you understand? Without this, I am nothing. With this, you might see me and never notice that I am different. Understand?"

Ezat nodded. "But if you never take it off, if you don't let me take it off now, you might lose even this. Understand? Things could get worse for you if your stump is unable to support a prosthetic."

Abdul finally relented and allowed Ezat to remove his artificial leg. Two large skin ulcers marked the end of his stump, the area that bore the pressure of his prosthetic. "You see this?"

Abdul's eyes avoided the stump. "Can you just fix it?" He looked at me and not at Ezat. It was Western medicine he was looking for, not the same old care he was used to.

I glanced at Ezat, seeking the approval I would need to answer. He nodded and I turned to Abdul. "We can give you antibiotics and ointment to soothe those ulcers, but you must remove your vinyl leg and wash your stump, at least once a day. It's important. Do you understand?"

He looked, finally, at his stump and shrugged. "*Inshallah*," 'God willing,' he said as he adjusted his prosthetic, pocketed his medicine, and shuffled away.

And, with little time to think about what might happen to Abdul and his vinyl leg, I was on to my next patient—a tiny little girl named Mariam, who was carried into the clinic by her father. Her mother, hidden in the folds of a faded burqa, remained in the shadows. Only her hands—balled into tight fists and pressed together—gave away her worry.

"She is sick," her father said, running his fingers through the coarse, dry strands of the little girl's hair. He unwrapped the small, dingy blanket that covered her, revealing a mere wisp of a child. Mariam was stick-thin with translucent skin, and her fragile bones looked as though they might snap at my touch. Her father lifted her shirt and I caught a glimpse of her bloated belly. She let out a shriek as I leaned in to look in her eyes, the membranes there a pale, almost white hue instead of the healthy bright pink of a well-nourished child. She wasn't just malnourished; she was starving, and there was little I could do for her. In those days, we had no nutrition programs, no way to feed the hordes of starving here along the rural edges of the Afghan border. Food was provided by the World Food Programme (WFP), and only to those refugees who'd registered with the UN or were living in one of the crowded camps.[1] The rest, afraid to register as refugees and be sent to crowded camps, were on their own. Mariam was, and remains, the hardest kind of patient to see. I had medicines aplenty, but this little girl needed food and I had none to give. Food was available in Thal and throughout Pakistan—for a price—so the starvation here was due more to a lack of money than to a lack of food. Aid agencies weren't allowed to distribute food—only the WFP had that authority. Therapeutic feeding programs for malnourished babies were only then in the planning stages. At the time, all I could offer was a few rupees, but I would be gone soon, the money would run out, and the problem would only get worse, especially here in the deep freeze of winter, when even hope was in short supply.

In those early days, we didn't track disease or even malnutrition numbers. We had no epidemiologists on staff, we only had anecdotal evidence to guide us. We flew by the seat of our pants, reacting to situations as they arose. All of that would change in time, but not soon enough for Mariam and so many others.

I knew that I had to come back, if only to figure out a way to help the Mariams of the world. I flew home, and without much planning, I arranged to quit my job and work per diem by early summer. I kept the news to myself. People already thought I was nuts. Why throw fuel on the fire? I knew I'd return to Pakistan again as soon as I had saved enough money to cover my bills and maintain my apartment. For someone who'd always been reluctant to do anything on my own, I'd found that I liked relying on myself. There was something affirming about being a solitary traveler through the world's grittiest spots. I was an aid worker; I could handle anything.

At least, that's what I told myself.

— ◆ —

Summer 1987

I returned to Pakistan in the summer of 1987. This time, I would spend the summer, my longest visit yet. My love affair with aid work continued.

On the ride from the airport to the FM house, I noticed, not for the first time, how the crowded streets were filled with beggars. Many of them—just skin and bones and tattered clothes covered with years of dirt—held out their hands and boldly begged. It wasn't really a shock; we had plenty of our own homeless in the United States and they begged, too, but here it was their only means of getting money. Pakistan didn't have the government programs we have in the United States. There was no safety net. Many of the beggars here had handicaps, making witnessing their plight all the more disquieting. Those who couldn't walk dragged themselves around by their arms. If they were lucky, they had a little platform on wheels and they could sit and use their hands to propel themselves. I knew that the best response didn't involve money, but it was all that I could offer.

On this ride, I saw a withered, dirt-encrusted woman dressed in thread-bare rags, dragging herself on stumps of legs through the street. A filthy rag tied about her neck held a sleeping baby. She was a beggar and I asked that we stop so that I could give her money. The Afghan driver reluctantly stopped and let me out. The woman gazed up at me with empty eyes when I handed her the rupees. "*Shukria*," 'Thank you,' she whispered as she crawled away. The driver shook his head. "Not good," he muttered. I knew he was right, but how could I just walk away?

I headed out quickly to Thal. The team had changed and now included Rick, a Special Forces medic who bore an uncanny resemblance to Kevin Costner. Tom and the earlier team members had all left; Rick had joined Ella, and until I arrived, they were the team. Others—medical visitors—would come for a very short time, leaving the rest of us little chance to get to know them. Once I arrived at Thal, Ella and Rick each took their Afghan para-medic students into Afghanistan for real-time training with real patients and real injuries, right where they would all eventually be based. I was left in charge in Thal, but it would be the newly constructed OR and ER that would occupy my time. And though the ER would be my home turf, the place I would be most comfortable, it was also the place that moved most quickly, allowing me little time to get to know my patients.

We now had an Afghan surgeon, Majid, on staff so we were able to take some cases to the OR. It meant, too, that more wounded would be brought here, and though we were better equipped than we had been, we didn't have blood transfusion capability. If someone was bleeding to death, we were helpless. It made me, made all of us crazy. I looked around our storeroom one day and found blood bags and filtered tubing, all necessary to administer blood, but we had no blood-typing equipment, so we were still unable to give blood. I thought about it often. I knew there had to be a solution to this dilemma. I just didn't know what it was.

One evening, the emergency siren went off and Majid and I rushed to the ER. Our patient was a twenty-year-old male who had been stabbed in the chest during a fight in a nearby refugee camp. Even in war, people argue and fight among themselves. We didn't need an X-ray to know that he had suffered a collapsed lung and was bleeding into his chest. His blood pressure was dangerously low and his pulse dangerously high, meaning serious blood loss. Without a transfusion, he would continue to bleed and he would die. The surgeon prepared to put in a chest tube to drain the blood and reinflate the lung. Back at home, we would collect the patient's own blood from the chest tube and transfuse him with his own blood. It is called auto-transfusion and was, and remains, a common life-saving procedure around the world. Majid asked if we could give it a try for this patient.

I nodded and inserted two large intravenous lines into our young patient, then gathered the blood bags and tubing from the storeroom. I cut the filters from the tubing, connected these filters to each other, and then connected this to a donor bag with tubing. When Majid inserted the chest tube, I hooked my lengths of tubing to the end of the chest tube and laid the blood bag on the floor. Gravity and our makeshift equipment worked! Majid, the patient, and I watched in amazement as blood from the chest tube began to drain into the bag. As it flowed, I set up another group of filters and attached this to another bag. To transfuse our patient, I simply connected the filled blood bag to a double-filter and blood tubing and attached that to his intravenous line.

We auto-transfused our patient with three bags of his own blood. We kept him in our small hospital for several days, and then discharged him back to his tent, a little worse for wear, but alive. Although it had been exhilarating to have succeeded, it would turn out to be just another emergency in a summer of so many. There was no time to pat ourselves on the back.

One morning, just as the sun was rising, the siren sounded and we found five patients in our ER. All had been victims of a brutal attack in one of the nearby refugee camps. Rival gangs or Soviet-backed thugs (we were never sure which stories were true) had attacked in the night and hacked away at the residents with knives and machetes, killing many. Those who had survived had hidden until it was safe to escape, finally reaching us just as dawn broke.

My first patient was Aziza, a thirty-something-year-old woman whose husband, we learned, had just been killed during the assault. She had been viciously attacked and had suffered many wounds, the most serious of which was a left arm that was slashed to the bone, her blood seeping into the once faded red dress she wore, now vibrant with color again. Her skin was pale, her lips drawn, her eyes a dull gray. She spoke little except to reply "*balay*" when asked if she had pain. A man, his hands coated in the stain of old blood, and suspiciously without wounds of his own, insisted on staying in the ER with her. I was wary, concerned that maybe he was one of the attackers, so I asked him who he was. "I am her husband," he said, an unmistakable arrogance in his voice.

I knew her husband had just been killed, but I wasn't at home in my own ER. I couldn't call security to come and haul him out, so I turned to Aziza. "Who is he?" I whispered.

"He is the brother of my dead husband," she replied softly. I knew that, according to Afghan culture and tradition, he was now her husband. It was a custom intended to protect the woman and her children, but I found it unsettling. Aziza, however, though wounded physically and emotionally, was resigned and calm; I was the one who needed convincing, and I reminded myself that at least she and her children would not be on their own, a far worse fate in this dangerous land.

We worked over our victims for several hours, finally taking Aziza to the OR for repair. Although she probably needed complex neuro-vascular repair, it wasn't available here. To refer her to Peshawar would mean losing valuable time, which could ultimately cost her the use of her arm. We did the best we could—cleaning, debriding, and closing the wound before discharging her home the next day. She never returned for the follow-up we suggested, and we never learned how her wounds had healed or how her life turned out. Like so many others, she simply disappeared from sight, but not memory.

Weeks later, Rick and Ella returned to Thal just in time for Eid, the Muslim holiday. Out of respect, everything would be closed, including our clinic. We three traveled to Peshawar, noticing along the way how quiet the roads were. In Peshawar, every shop, every business, every stall was shuttered, but we were headed to the American Club for wine and cheeseburgers, or so we thought until we arrived to the dark and empty club. Damn. The club was closed, too.

Our plans awry, we turned and headed to the FM staff house, and there, Ella and Rick, eager for a drink, searched through the house, coming up empty until Rick happened upon the boss's secret stash of whiskey. He held it up. "Success," he exclaimed. The three of us—in the house alone and without assigned rooms—decided to pull out mattresses, arrange them in a circle in the living room, and have an adult slumber party. I took a sip of the hard stuff. It burned through to my gut. I shuddered and passed it back, shaking my head at the next go-round. We stayed there, laughing, drinking, and carousing until, one by one, we drifted into the deep sleep that whiskey brings.

In the morning, it wasn't the sliver of sunlight seeping through the curtains that woke us; it was the boss's angry shouts. "What the fuck?" he yelled, an angry flush rising from his neck. He'd discovered the almost empty bottle and the three of us stretched out in the living room. We blinked our way awake while he shouted and threatened. "Who opened my bottle?"

We caught each other's eyes, smiles sparkling there. His anger would wear off. And so we waited and listened until he quieted down and the usual pasty color returned to his cheeks. He mumbled something and left, and the three of us headed to the club for breakfast and Bloody Marys and laughs.

I returned home, even more appreciative of everything that I have here, a place to call home, electricity, a bed, a bathroom, a washing machine, a glass of wine, no one to shout if someone opens a bottle of whiskey. All of it.

But, even with all of that, there was an empty space in my heart when I was away from refugees. It was not unlike that same longing for an old lover, and the separation only made me miss them all the more.

Chitral

———◆———

Fall 1988

Ayear passed before I was able to save enough money and return
to Pakistan to volunteer again with FM. I'd bought a condo,
which had obliterated my savings account but had given me a real
home, a place to always call my own. I needed that sense of security and
belonging—I'd become an unintentional outsider, working per diem, my
ears tuned only to the world news, my heart with the refugees, my focus
on getting back to a place that needed me.

I arrived back in Pakistan as a seasoned aid worker. I carried a sturdy
lipstick, scrubs for sleep, and what I felt was a wealth of experience. The
team here now was entirely new; even Ella had left and joined another
NGO based in Quetta along the southern border of Afghanistan and

Pakistan. I was asked to go to Chitral to staff a small outpost clinic in the northern mountains. The village of Chitral was a small border town in the northeast corner of Pakistan, a lush green area nestled between several mountains with a small, muddy river snaking through the valley. The surrounding landscape was exquisite and tranquil, but the village, and nearby Garam Chesma, were the staging areas for freedom fighters and refugees returning to or coming out of Afghanistan. It was the first stop, too, for those who had left Afghanistan injured or ill and in need of medical care. Freedom Medicine ran the only clinic in the area, and I would work alongside an Afghan medic, Noori, whom I had trained on an earlier trip. It would be just the two of us providing whatever care we could.

Our small compound was primitive by any standard. Located just outside the village center, a small mud and plaster clinic building and a cluster of tents stood at the edge of a rickety old airport, the runway a collection of rocks and ridges, where, once every few days, a small, sleek plane would land, carrying UN supplies, locals who could afford the cost of the flight, and, inexplicably to me, the occasional tourist.

I shared the compound with the medic, several bodyguards, a cook, and occasionally some freedom fighters—all of whom treated me like a sister. I had a tent to myself; my only furniture was a cot, my only light my flashlight. I did have my own "bathroom," a small plaster room that I shared with countless croaking, slimy frogs that slithered and jumped about endlessly as I tried to wash or squatted in this indoor latrine. I rose about 5:00 A.M., breakfasted on strong, black, instant coffee and smoked a cigarette, "my American breakfast," I told them. The Afghan staff ate the traditional flat bread and drank green tea filled with sugar, and after a while they added my cigarettes to their daily fare. The scant two cartons I'd brought didn't last long, and when I ran out, I went to the village bazaar and bought American cigarettes that the Afghans had hijacked from Russian supply trucks and then sold to help support the resistance. When the bazaar ran out, I was forced to smoke Chinese cigarettes. They tasted and burned as though they'd been dipped in gasoline. It wasn't long before the Afghans lost interest in sharing my cigarettes.

Aside from my cigarette woes, my routine was simple. Since I washed at night and slept in my clothes (this time, it really did seem prissy and impractical to wear a nightgown), I had only to splash water on my face and I was ready for the day. My night routine consisted of washing my face, my feet, and my underarms. I would take off my socks, shake the dirt off, and turn them inside out. Once I put them back on, I felt clean and fresh again. There wasn't enough water for more than a weekly bath, and there wasn't much need. The mountain air was cool and refreshing here, not the sweat-inducing heat of the south.

Patients began arriving at the clinic early and were given numbers to mark their place in line. By 8:00 A.M., we were seeing our patients. The medic saw the men and I saw the women. I had picked up and remembered enough of the language to do most of the exam and history on my own. Those vital Dari words and phrases would stay with me, tucked away and hidden in the deep corners of my mind, and when, years later, I returned to Afghanistan, so did the easy feel of the language return to my tongue.

When I called "*yak*" for number one, the first patient or family of women and children shuffled into the clinic. The exam table was a small, canvas-covered army cot, a leftover from our very first clinic in Thal. The patients and I sat together on the edge of the cot and tried to sort out their problems. "*Che taklif dori?*" 'What is your problem?' I'd ask.

Just as in Thal, the complaints were varied—sore throats, earaches, minor skin infections, headaches. Equally common and familiar now were the complaints of tuberculosis (TB), malaria, intestinal parasites, dysentery, and, always, the terrible malnutrition that complicated all of their other problems.

The clinic was supplied with an abundance of medicines, chloroquine for malaria, Flagyl for the intestinal parasites, antibiotics for most other infections, including TB. Still impossible to treat was the malnutrition. Though there were refugees in Chitral, there were no UN camps, no way for them to register for rations from WFP. I could provide vitamins, but without a proper diet to guarantee absorption, they were useless. The refugees however, believed that vitamins, or any pill, would help, so I gladly handed them out.

Almost daily, we saw one or two patients in our emergency area. The war between the Soviets and Afghans, though reported to be winding down, in fact still raged on, and our small outpost clinic provided the first chance for medical care for many of the young fighters and refugees. But refugee life was hardest on the children, and for Noor, it would cost him his life.

He was tiny—maybe six years old and suffering from horrific second- and third-degree burns to both legs. His family had fled the brutal Soviet advance in Afghanistan and had settled deep in the mountains of northwest Pakistan, not far from Chitral. There, they eked out a living, working the fields and doing whatever odd jobs they could find to survive.

Every family member worked at something. It was Noor's job to gather dung for fuel, to watch over sheep for local farmers, and to collect water from the streams. There was little time for anything else, but one afternoon in a cherished moment of childish abandon, Noor ran and shouted and played like the child that he was. While racing his friends through the village, he looked back to see if they were gaining on him, and at that moment, an open tandoor oven loomed. A tandoor oven is dug into the ground, a searing fire is always ablaze at the bottom, and a metal cover is fitted over the hole to maintain the high heat. But that day, there was no cover, and Noor's eyes were on his friends. He never saw the danger until he fell into the blazing open oven.

His screams alerted the villagers, who quickly pulled him out, but the damage had been done. Third-degree burns covered both legs right to his hips. The fire had literally seared and torn the skin and muscle from his legs, but there was no medical care in the village and nowhere else to go. His family kept him at home, where his wounds festered and became infected. By the time a Medecins Sans Frontieres (MSF) nurse came upon Noor, he was septic and dying. His family was terrified of going to Peshawar for care; they were true rural dwellers and simply did not trust big-city medicine. They did agree to bring him to our clinic for dressings and medicines.

He was carried into our clinic by his father, who was accompanied by a harried French nurse from MSF. "You must see this boy. Understand?" Her French accent was heavy, her words rushed. Her head was uncovered, her hair a wild, unrestrained mop of black curls, her cheeks flushed from the crisp mountain air. When she pulled a cigarette from her pocket, lit it, and took a long, slow drag, the men watched her in wonder. Although I smoked, I kept my head covered and wore the traditional clothes of Afghanistan. The French nurse wore jeans and a long shirt. She seemed not to care what they thought.

Her eyes darted around the room until she rested her gaze on me. She gave me hasty instructions on Noor's wound care as she pointed to his legs, both wrapped in heavy layers of gauze. He let out a screech when she pulled off one of his dressings to show me the raw flesh underneath. "The others are clean. Just re-dress this one today, and if you have any questions, you must send him to Peshawar. Understand? His father will not let him go, but you must insist." She shook her head, her lips curling down as though she'd just eaten a sour fruit. And, with that, she was gone.

Noor pulled away when I approached. "*Aacha*," I whispered. 'It's okay.' I gently reapplied his dressing and sent him on his way, his father promising to return twice a week.

Days later, he reappeared, the heavy gauze sticky with drainage that had seeped through from his wounds. I took a deep breath. Pulling off the gauze would be agonizing for Noor. We tried everything to minimize the pain—we medicated him, soaked the dressings so that they would ease away from the tissue, but still his anguished screams pierced the air. I remember even now how excruciatingly sorrowful were those sounds, how I hesitated with each pull of the gauze, and how frightened his eyes were when he caught my gaze.

His dressings and wound care took hours, and every second was agony for him. This poor boy had suffered beyond anyone's capacity to endure, and without skin grafts and advanced care, he would never recover. We tortured him every time he came to the clinic, and he came once or twice a week. His father held him tightly while we tended to the boy's wounds, and he carried him away quickly when we were finally done. There was so little we could really do. I dreaded his visits as much as he likely did.

Though many patients had affected me, Noor was the first one to bring me to my knees with grief. I wanted to give in to my sadness and anger for this little boy. But I didn't have that luxury. As an ER nurse, I knew I had to distance myself. Noor and so many others didn't need my self-absorbed melancholy. They needed me to help, and to do that, I had to be fully present. I'd have time enough for sad reflection when I returned home.

When I hadn't seen Noor for a few weeks, I knew that mercifully, his suffering was over. His one moment of joyful play had cost him his life, a lesson that the other boys in his village would surely long remember and I would never forget.

Just as in Thal, we also saw many others—babies, children, and adults—all suffering from severe malnutrition. One of these children was a tiny, malnourished girl named Laila, who was tenderly carried into our clinic by her equally malnourished father. Laila was about two years old but looked about one. With her big belly, loose skin, haunting eyes, and wispy hair, she reminded me of Mariam. When I examined her, she made none of the squeamish moves normal for a two-year-old; she had no reserves left, no more fight. It took all she had just to keep her eyes focused on me, and she watched me with the wary eyes of a child who had suffered plenty in her short life.

There was little we could offer—a small amount of food and a few rupees to purchase a little more. The terrible reality was that Laila was dying and there was little we could do. We had no nutrition program, though it was clear we needed one desperately. FM's grants only allotted money for training freedom fighter medics, as well as our two small clinics in Thal and Chitral. There was no leeway in our spending.

Sadly, there were still hundreds of thousands of equally malnourished Lailas and Mariams in the refugee camps along the border. They were still the most difficult patients. We could not fill their bellies; the best we could do was to share our midday meal. Though many took us up on that offer, it was precious little to children who needed so much more, but perhaps to remember them even now and to keep them alive in stories honors their short, brave lives in some small measure.

Into all this sadness, a Chevy station wagon arrived at our compound late one afternoon. Two men emerged, clad in jeans, plaid shirts, and heavy boots, one carrying a paper bag under his arm. The Afghans watched in wonder. "Hey y'all," one of the men said, "Mike told us to drop in and see how you were doing."

I smiled. Mike had been the construction and all-around whatever-needed-doing guy in Thal, who'd always hinted at mysterious connections. These men were clearly CIA. Who else would drive around this border—dangerous not just for the explosives buried here but also for the roads, which were equally, or maybe even more, treacherous.

"Y'all gonna invite us in? We got something for ya." He pointed to the bag he was cradling under his arm.

The Afghans' eyes drifted from our visitors to me. It was imperative that I be seen as a good and honorable woman. Once these men left, there couldn't be any rumors that might endanger me. I hesitated. "I . . ."

"Well, just show us your tent then," one said, sensing my discomfort. "We got some good old American tea for you right here." The Afghans nodded in understanding. Tea was okay; in fact, tea was good.

The men followed me to my tent, the Afghans drifting away but likely still watching. I left the flap open so there'd be no doubt that this was an innocent visit. We sat cross-legged on the floor and introduced ourselves, though they already knew who I was. Jack opened the bag, drew out three cans of beer, and passed one to Gary and one to me. "Open it," Gary said.

"I don't know." I cradled the warm can in my hand. "I have to be careful. I can't have any rumors getting to the local mullahs."

"Well, just have a sip then. We'll leave the rest for you."

The offer was tempting, enormously so, but the risks were greater. These men would drive off shortly and I'd be left here to deny any wrongdoing.

It seemed best just to avoid it altogether. I shook my head and slid the beer back. "I would love to drink this," I said, "but I'll just have to wait for the American Club. Maybe I'll see you there?"

Gary and Jack finished their beers and stood to leave. "Y'all be careful up here, ya hear?" Jack said as they piled into their car. I stood and watched as they maneuvered that old Chevy back through our gate and along these rocky roads, hoping I'd get to really share a beer with them at the club.

Before I left for home, I flew to Quetta, in southwestern Pakistan, to see Ella. She was working there with another American NGO. Quetta was a squat and squalid city, dotted with colorless one-story buildings, the scene unbroken by grass or trees. It was also a deeply religious city and the city to which, we all later learned, Al-Qaeda funneled money for religious indoctrination and terrorist training in the late 1980s. Ella was working in a local hospital, teaching nursing. The hospital was a short distance from the house she shared with other members of her team. There were several religious schools, called *madrassa*, for boys, located between the team's house and the hospital. I had noticed the schools along the road but had never given them much thought. I had become that confident, cocky ER nurse once again. I felt safe in one of the most dangerous places on earth, and that sense of safety made it all the more perilous for me.

One afternoon, as I walked alone from the hospital to the NGO house, I passed a school just as scores of young men and boys were being released for the day. I was dressed not in the full veil and covering I had worn in Chitral but in long, loose pants, a large long-sleeved shirt, and a lacey scarf to cover my hair. It was typical expat attire. I also had my sunglasses on as I walked in the heat of the midday sun. Although my clothes were respectable, it was clear that I was a foreigner, something I hadn't even considered until the boys began to pour out of the gate. I stood in stark contrast to local women, who would have covered up under the full cloak of the burqa if they'd even dared to venture out alone.

The road home was long and isolated, no shops or cars or people about, just empty expanse. As the young men's footfalls sounded behind me, I felt the first stirrings of fright. They began to laugh, and then moved closer, taunting me. The air crackled with tension. Finally, I felt the sting of a rock hit my back and I came to a full stop. The group was suddenly silent. The only sound was the frantic throbbing of my own heartbeat as it pounded in my ears. I couldn't seem to catch my breath, and my skin felt clammy and cool even in this miserable heat. My thoughts raced in a confusing maze as I tried desperately to simply think. There was no hope of rescue; I was well and truly on my own. I knew my options were few. There were too many boys and I couldn't risk inciting them further. I never turned to face them; instead I resumed my steps and gauged the distance to the NGO house.

And with those first steps, the rocks began to fly in earnest, many finding their mark on my back. As the distance to the NGO house closed in, I began to run. My fear gave me wings. I was a runner at home, and I knew I could make it. Breathless, I flew around the last corner and quickly opened the gate to the house and jumped in. I slammed the gate and hurried to lock it. As the bolt slid into place and I slid to the ground, I heard the crowd of thugs reach the gate. They shouted and threw their remaining rocks at the impenetrable walls. My tearful sobs were great gulps of empty silence as my tormenters milled about just feet away. They lingered for only a moment and then moved on, never aware that I hugged the other side of the gate, afraid to move, tears stinging my eyes.

I had learned what it was to be an outsider.

I shared my experience in Quetta with only Ella and her housemates. They at least would understand the situation. People at home never would. It just seemed best to keep that incident to myself. And, as I reminded myself, I'd survived to tell the story. It was best not to make a big deal of it.

Intervening Years

---◆---

By 1989, the Soviets had left Afghanistan. The nation spiraled into further chaos, the freedom fighters trying to wrestle control from the Communist government and each other. The United States pulled out all aid in 1991, but it was in late 1990 when Freedom Medicine closed. They'd been a small organization focused only on Afghanistan, and without that focus, they simply closed their doors and went home.

Pakistan was still trying to send refugees home, but with civil war raging in Afghanistan, they refused to go. In 1992, the freedom fighters ousted the Soviet-backed government and took control, but the country was in dismal shape and ripe for exploitation by men who made promises they'd never keep. The Taliban emerged in 1994 and fought viciously to wrest control of the nation. In 1996, they took Kabul, and the rest of the nation soon fell. The Taliban ruled with an iron fist. There was scant information coming from that besieged nation, and though I scoured the news, there was little to learn. Few aid groups remained, though one or two had managed to stay. Though the Taliban tolerated some aid groups, Americans were not welcome. It seemed that my dream of returning there was all but lost.

I was still determined to volunteer again, if not in Afghanistan, then somewhere that needed me. In 1993, I called Americares, an aid group based in Connecticut that I'd seen on the news. After an interview, they offered me a position in Kenya in a new refugee camp built to accommodate the thousands fleeing the civil war in South Sudan. I would help get their medical clinic up and running as long as I could get the time off from work.

I was back in the ER full time by then, but my generous manager agreed to a one-month leave so that I could go. I checked my vaccines, made a list of things I'd need, and began to pack. Days before my expected departure, Americares called me to say there was a problem in the camp and aid workers had been evacuated. "You'll still be going," the caller reassured me, "but you'll have to stay in Nairobi until we're sure it's safe."

"For how long?" I asked.

"Not more than three weeks, probably less."

Damn it. I didn't have enough time off to sit in Nairobi and wait. "I won't be able to go," I said, my voice cracking. "I only have a month of leave."

"Oh," he said, sounding as disappointed as I felt. "You'll give us a call if that changes, won't you?"

I nodded and quietly hung up, afraid that aid work was somehow out of my reach. But cable news, just as their commercials promised, had ushered in a whole new way for news junkies to see what was happening around the world. The internet added yet another outlet for my curiosity. I followed the news of Afghanistan online and scoured the internet for available aid assignments. Every time I saw a humanitarian crisis reported on CNN, I was desperate to go, but I'd just bought a house and rented out my condo, which brought a whole new level of financial responsibility into my life. Aid work was still my goal, but it wasn't in my immediate future. I spent my time falling in and out of love and trying to coax grass seed to sprout in my yard. I had better luck with the grass than with my choice of men, but I still had a dream—that I'd return to Afghanistan and aid work once again.

In the meantime, I left the ER that year and took a position in a fancy uptown law firm working on medical malpractice cases—no weekends, no night shifts, and better pay. And by 2000, I'd saved enough money and was finally able to make those plans to return to aid work. By then, aid work had become increasingly businesslike—far more technical and targeted, and driven by sophisticated grants overseen by government agencies and private donors who doled out money based on fact-based research, and stringent goals and objectives. Gone were the days of throwing money at problems and hoping for the best. I wasn't sure I'd be considered experienced enough, but I threw caution to the wind and applied anyway.

MSF (also known as Doctors Without Borders) was an NGO that had always interested me. I had never forgotten that harried French nurse who had brought Noor, the tiny, badly burned boy, to me in Chitral. IRC, the International Rescue Committee, was another NGO that I had seen in Pakistan and had admired. IRC is recognized for its planned and thoughtful interventions in the bleakest corners of the world, where they strive quietly and diligently to deliver aid to the world's forgotten and dispossessed. Both are very impressive groups and I was excited when they each responded quickly to my applications.

I flew to New York City for interviews—the first with MSF. Once it was clear that I met their requirements, they began to ask where I would be willing to go. "What about Afghanistan?" I asked. I'd learned that life there under the despised Taliban had gone from bad to worse.

Bendu, the Liberian woman who interviewed me, looked at me sternly and shook her head. "No way, no Americans. Too dangerous." My face fell. She leaned back in her chair, nervously clicking the pen she held in her hand. "If you have a passport from another country, though," she added, "we can consider you."

"Another passport?" I asked, intrigued by the possibility. "Do you know how I can get one?" She shrugged in reply, perhaps already regretting her suggestion. But it didn't matter. I was determined then to somehow get a foreign passport and get back to Afghanistan.

In late winter, IRC offered me a three-month posting to a refugee camp in Africa, to the same camp I had been headed to some seven years earlier. It seemed that fate meant for me to be there. I took a leave from my job, and I was on my way in March of 2001, but not before the Irish consulate in Boston confirmed that I was eligible for an Irish passport as long as I could gather the necessary documents from Ireland and Boston. Before I boarded my plane, I made arrangements to get my grandparents' birth certificates from Dublin.

I was headed to Africa, but Afghanistan was still my goal.

II

AFRICA

2001

A War-Torn Continent

———•◆•———

I n the midst of a late winter blizzard, armed with a sturdy, heat-resistant lipstick and a new tropical medicine handbook to help me through the diseases indigenous there, I set out for Africa. From Boston, I stopped in Amsterdam and then flew on to Nairobi, Kenya. I arrived exhausted and late at night, so I just fell into bed at the IRC guest house in Nairobi. The unmistakable sounds of the third world, the barking of several dogs, the crunch of feet on gravel beneath my window, foreign voices carried on the warm night air, the hum of birds and insects, mingled with the peculiar local scents, and all of it soothed me into sleep.

The camp to which I would head was called Kakuma. Located in north-west Kenya, close to the border with Sudan, Kakuma is a UN-sponsored camp of sixty thousand, providing refuge for those fleeing war and crisis in neighboring Sudan, Ethiopia, Somalia, Eritrea, Burundi, Rwanda, DRC (Democratic Republic of Congo), Uganda, and Angola. In 2001, Kakuma

resembled a multinational African city. Each ethnic group had its own section in the camp—the Sudanese, for whom the civil war in their nation
still raged, comprised 80 percent of the camp population and were housed
in one area, Ethiopians were in another, Somalis in yet another, and so on.
The groups had little in common, I was told, save that they had all escaped
desperate conditions and were now in competition for the scarce resources
the UN could provide.

Several days after my arrival, I flew in a rickety old commuter plane to
Lokichoggio, the border town that was home to all of the UN-sponsored
programs in Sudan. The town was dusty, dirty, and crowded with so many
NGOs and aid workers that local entrepreneurs had opened a restaurant,
a rooming house, and a small shop selling trinkets. Sleek UN and World
Food Programme (WFP) jets floated momentarily in the sky before slipping
through the high clouds and gliding to a landing on an airstrip ringed on
one side by a village of simple mud and grass huts, and on the other by miles
of scrub and dirt. The roar of the jet engines and the crush of road traffic
created a fog of swirling dust that almost obscured the villagers who came
out to watch, but they stood firm amidst the fog. Those planes and vehicles
carried supplies and people and the promise of new life in this place with
little greenery and less hope.

I was headed to an even more desolate area. Kakuma was a two-hour drive
from Lokichoggio along a dusty, bandit-infested road. The desert landscape
was occasionally broken by bursts of lush green and primitive grass shacks.
The villagers, some so poor they had only pieces of faded and threadbare
fabric to cover their skin, walked slowly, shoulders hunched, heads down.
They acknowledged our passing by turning away from the veils of dust our
car generated. We had more attention from the animals—camels, giraffes,
donkeys, zebras, horses—all living in the wild and somehow thriving in this
land of drought and dire need. They occasionally paused in their feeding
and gazed as we passed, some even racing alongside our car for a while.

Finally, after a long, hot, and dusty ride, we arrived at Kakuma. The refugee
camp was a sprawling compound of mud and grass huts and small sturdier

buildings that housed medical clinics and warehouses and administrative offices, all arranged in neat rows that wound through the camp's dusty roads.

I arrived in the afternoon and was assigned a room in the dormitory-like staff compound located on the periphery of the camp. The area housed Kenyan staff and the only other expat with IRC—Aimée, a French nutritionist who spent as much time as she could manage with her boyfriend, who was working back in Loki, the shortened name we used for Lokichoggio. My narrow room held a metal frame bed topped by a thin sleeping pad, with an unyielding slab of stiff foam for a pillow. There were also screened windows and, when there was electricity, a floor fan. It looked like heaven to me, much more than I had expected.

The bathrooms, housed in a separate small building, were another story. Combination squat toilets and showers in one tiny, closet-sized space. The shower water was drained off through the latrine-toilet. The overhead shower piece did not work, but the tap coming out of the wall at waist level worked fine. I always shared my shower with lizards, frogs, beetles the size of my fist, and other unknown insects, all of them scurrying feverishly at my feet. The sinks were outside and were awash with more large insects not eager to share their space with me. I had to jockey for position and hope for the best when I turned the water on. At home, I would surely be horrified and shouting for an exterminator, but here there was nothing I could do. I had to learn to coexist with my new roommates and keep my complaints to myself. The last thing I wanted to be was a whiny self-absorbed pain in the ass. The cockroaches, beetles, bugs, and frogs would be here long after I was gone. This, after all, was their turf, not mine.

More than the logistics of life here, it was the endless waves of heat that would take some getting used to. I took a deep breath; I'd survived worse, though this time, there'd be no American Club, no place to really unwind or feel the cooling breeze of an air conditioner on your skin.

The six clinics covered a population of sixty thousand. They were spread out to ensure reasonable proximity throughout the camp so that no one would have to trek for very long distances in the blazing sun.

The hospital included several whitewashed, one-story buildings throughout the main medical area in the center of the camp. A large tent housed the pediatric ward. The tent had a bed capacity of about forty, but there were often many more patients than that. To accommodate the number of sick babies and children, they shared beds. Mothers and siblings also stayed with the patients, so the ward was usually very crowded; sometimes it was hard to know which ones were the patients, though family members usually slept on the floor.

The maternity and male and female wards were small, separate buildings and were often covered in dust and dirt. The infectious ward was housed in a tent away from the central hospital and was surrounded by a fence to protect the camp from the communicable diseases and infectious patients housed there.

The next day, I started in the hospital-based clinic, and just as I did with the Afghan refugees, I followed the standard protocols for diagnosis and treatment of so many familiar and unfamiliar diseases—malaria, diarrhea, skin infections, and dysentery. But Africa also had her own particular diseases and dangers for the population here. Exotic maladies like kala-azar (leishmaniasis), caused by the bite of a sand fly; filariasis, caused by infected blood feeding black flies and mosquitoes that transmit worms with their bite; and trypanosomiasis (African sleeping sickness), caused by the bite of a tsetse fly, all unusual diseases with similar initial presentations—fever, fatigue, headache, enlarged liver.

That first day, an old man from South Sudan, tall and bent, limped into our clinic complaining of swelling to both lower legs. "It's filariasis," a young Kenyan aid announced, pointing to the man's legs. "See here," he said, directing my gaze to the tiny undulating worms that were evident just under the elderly man's skin. The old man nodded. He'd had this before. He knew what the treatment would be, and we both watched as the experienced clinic staff made several small incisions just over the worm sites. These would be routes to allow the worms to migrate out.

His wounds were loosely wrapped and he was instructed to return so that we could monitor the worms' progress, and though he lived right here in the camp, he never did return, much like the Afghan refugees. I also saw several patients suffering from trachoma, an eye infection that, if left untreated, can result in permanent blindness. The swelling, the drainage, the pustules that cover the eyes and lids all render the victim essentially blind with disease. It was frightening for the patient, and difficult for us to convince them that if they adhered to the relatively simple treatment of antibiotics instilled into the eye and taken by mouth, they would be fine. Until I saw the dramatic improvement myself, I was a little skeptical as well.

As busy as my days were, my evenings were filled with the simple beauty that was Africa—the sunset a glow of embers on the distant horizon before finally giving way to the deep wash of stars that blanketed the night sky. Pictures will never do it justice. It has to be seen to be appreciated.

Within days of my arrival, the rainy season started in earnest. Great sheets of water fell from the sky. It barely cooled the air. Worse, it created rivers and streams of standing water throughout the camp, and that brought out the scorpions and camel spiders, whose bites were painful and had the potential to be life-threatening to an already fragile populace.

Dear God, I thought, clutching my tropical medicine handbook, I had a lot to learn. But at that moment, even with everything there was to learn and the bugs scurrying by, I was certain there was nowhere else I'd rather be than right there with the refugees.

Grace's Story

———•✦•———

As preoccupied as I was with the heat, the rain, and all of the new diseases, it was the women here, both staff and refugees, who took notice of my insecurities and tucked me under their collective wings. They began by calling me "sistah," not in the slick and almost meaningless way we so often hear at home but in the honest, sincere, and deep-from-the-belly way of African women. Hearing "sistah, sistah" ring like music through the air always made me smile and made me feel a real part of this place.

One among them—Grace—became a good friend.

It was at the camp's pediatric hospital—a large, open-ended burlap tent, the dirt floor lined with metal cots and cribs, where the most malnourished and sickliest of the children were housed—that I first met her. She guessed her age at about thirty-four, though she couldn't be certain, and it didn't matter anyway. There were no age-related health screenings, no pap smears, no mammograms. The camp provided only the most basic health care, and only when you were sick. There were neither the resources nor the staff to offer anything else.

Grace, a widow whose husband had been killed in the vicious civil war in South Sudan, had been pregnant, with three small children and a mother in tow, when she'd arrived in Kakuma the year before. She'd had something of an education in Sudan; she could read, and she spoke some English, all of which set her apart from so many of the other refugees who could neither read nor write and often spoke only their own pidgin dialects.

Tragedy seemed to follow Grace, but at almost six feet tall, she carried herself, as her name suggested, with an easy grace and quiet calm despite the chaos swirling about her. As a Dinka, one of the tribes of Sudan, she adorned herself according to their particular customs. The women, and sometimes the men, cut their faces in fancy lines and patterns intended to produce decorative scars. She'd become a mother and then a refugee before she'd had the opportunity to follow that custom, and as a result, her skin, the deep black of a starless night, was smooth and unlined. Her teeth were long and almost stark white, the latter the result of vigilant cleaning with small sticks of wood. Her fingers were long and tapered, her hair close-cropped, but it is her voice I remember best. She spoke in an almost whisper, her words spilling out in a rush when she was excited, or slipping softly from her lips when she felt unsure of herself.

Each day, she wore one of the two dresses she owned. Her dresses were old and well scrubbed, and in another time they might have been worn by the Beaver's mom—June Cleaver without the pearls. The dresses had been donated, and she was lucky to have two; one to wear and one to wash.

Not long after arriving in Kakuma, Grace gave birth to twins, whose date of birth, unlike their mother's and siblings', had been officially recorded and would always be known to the exact minute. The twins, a boy and girl, were never really healthy; they suffered from chronic malnutrition and were enrolled in IRC's supplemental feeding center based in the pediatric ward. Here in this established camp, nutrition programs were available for starving babies and children, and I was overjoyed at the prospect, assuming that all babies would be saved.

It was there that Grace's babies received nutritional support and medical care for their repeated bouts of pneumonia and malaria. They'd just been hospitalized with pneumonia when I met Grace and her babies. Just six months old at the time, the boy was always sickly and irritable, the tiny girl the polar opposite. Even when feverish and barely able to feed, she craved attention and cuddling, and cooed with delight when anyone picked her up.

Grace's older children were dressed in literal rags, clothing so worn and ragged, their bony frames poked through. Her oldest daughter had acquired a discarded man's wool blazer, torn and fraying at the seams, but even on the hottest days, she never removed it, worried that if she did someone would snatch it from her. Even though this tiny girl was lost in the jacket, it gave her an air of authority, which she wore with a charming pride and a wide smile.

Once Grace and I met, I often sat with her as the babies were weighed and measured before the precious supplements were doled out. After one particularly long wait to be seen, Grace sought me out. "Will you come home with me today?" she asked, her face drawn, her shoulders sagging. She'd asked me before, but I'd always seemed to be in the midst of a hectic day and had never been able to find the time. But today she was different—subdued, less energetic.

"Is everything okay?" I reached for her hand, her fingers curling up tight against mine. She sat up straighter and nodded. "I'd like you to see where I live, and maybe share some tea. Yes?"

I nodded. "I'll finish up in an hour, but will you meet me?" I knew the area where she lived, but I had no idea which of the hundreds of look-alike huts was hers. We decided to meet at one of the little refugee-run kiosks that sold soda, sweet biscuits, gum, and cigarettes, along the camp's main road. I searched in my pocket for the loose change I seemed always to have and smiled. It would be enough to buy at least a packet of biscuits.

Grace was waiting for me that afternoon, one baby in her arms, the other lashed to her back in a kind of sling. She raised her hand when she spied me on the road. "Sistah!" she shouted as I approached. We stopped to buy a small packet of vanilla biscuits, then I followed her through the paths between the huts to the one she called home.

"Here," she said, motioning me to one of the thousands of look-alike shelters that filled every available space in the camp. Hers was tiny—a windowless, grass-roofed mud hut with a sheet of plastic billowing from the entrance. Two lawn chairs, a large cooking pot, and a container of water were arranged out front. She smiled, pulled back the plastic sheeting, and invited me to have a look.

"See," she said proudly as I peered inside, squinting to adjust my eyes to the dark. The quarters, though tiny, held two small beds pushed together. "My mother, my sister, my babies, and I sleep on the beds," she said, pointing to the measly straw mattresses covered in simple cotton ticking. Her three older children, she explained, slept on the ground outside, but in the hut, every square inch of the floor was covered with their belongings, clothes, bowls, and food, some pushed under the beds so that you could make your way in. It was there, on the floor, that a puddle of water caught my eye. I looked up and saw a tiny bit of sun poking through the flimsy roof. If the sun seeps through, surely the rain did as well. I looked back to Grace, who answered me before I had a chance to ask.

"The rain comes in," she said, nodding her head. "I try to catch it in my pots before it makes everything wet. See," she said, placing a pot just so on the mattress. "And, if we collect enough here, the children won't have to haul so much from the tap."

I knew that Grace and the others collected water twice a day in great pots and plastic cans from tap stands located throughout the camp. I'd seen her balance those containers on her head, her older children at her side, lugging the heavy jugs, their stick-thin arms dragging the heavy containers along the road.

Food was rationed and distributed every two weeks in fifty-kilo burlap bags, rice or corn meal, tea, sugar, and cans of oil, which she and her children dragged home or, when they were lucky, piled into a borrowed wagon and pulled home. It was, at best, a meager existence that required daily drudgery simply to survive. Latrines were also placed in areas throughout the camp, although many refugees just squatted anywhere.

Setting first one sleeping baby and then the other on the bed, Grace motioned me to the plastic chairs just outside her little hut. She sighed and sat heavily next to me. "What is it?" I asked.

She threw her arms wide. "I want to go home," she said softly. "I want to smell the clean air, feel the sweet soil under my feet, and sleep under the stars. I want my children to know that, to run free, to know a place where they belong." Here in the camp, children were restricted to playing just outside their huts; to venture further was likely not safe. Even in a refugee camp, there was crime. When people have nothing to lose, everything is fair game.

But Grace was realistic about starting life anew in Sudan. "It was never easy, there was always work to be done, food to cook, mouths to be fed," she remembered, "but it was home, at least it was that. Here, there is nothing, and I have nothing." She threw her arms wide. "The UN owns all of this, and they are the ones who decide where we'll live, what we'll eat, even what we wear. We are prisoners here."

I could only nod. She was right. It was the first time I'd realized that being a refugee meant that even the smallest decisions about one's own life were taken away. She lived where they assigned her, ate whatever they provided, and wore what they gave her. She'd traded one kind of misery for another—a life of absolute dependence.

She clasped her hands together. "I don't mean to be ungrateful. I just want to go home. You know?"

There was nothing I could say or do. Just as with Asma and her longing for her home in Afghanistan, I was powerless to help. I gripped her hand. "I know," I lied, though I really didn't know at all. Wherever I volunteered, it was for a specific time frame, and in the end, I would always go home—to a familiar place, to good food, warm baths, clean clothes. It was the first time I began to understand what it must be like to face the prospect of never going home again.

Right before Easter, fighting broke out among the young Sudanese men, many of whom were from competing tribes. The unrest erupted, we learned, in the same small area where Grace lived with her children. Aid workers and staff were not allowed into the camp once the fighting escalated, so the refugees—all of them, not just the Sudanese—were deprived of vital services. There were no clinics, no food distribution, no garbage pickup, nothing. The UN staff thought the fighters were perhaps "plants" sent in by the Sudanese government to create chaos and enmity among the Sudanese refugees and thereby dull the rebels' war efforts against the Sudanese government. Though it was only a theory, the result was cruel torture of one another and indirectly of all of the refugees throughout the camp, whose very lives were so affected during the turmoil.

One young Sudanese refugee worked with an animal husbandry program and was very concerned that his small rabbits would starve. He left his own mud shack in the dark of night and went secretly to check on his rabbits. He was caught by a rival tribe and tortured mercilessly with machetes and spears until finally his throat was slashed. His body remained in the road where he had died, since no one could get in to move him or give him a proper burial. His was one of fifteen eventual deaths reported to the UN over the next days, all horrific. The fighting and killing raged for four long days. Word trickled back slowly, and every day, I listened for any word of Grace, but there was none.

It was days later, as I sat in the small van that delivered staff to hospitals and clinics scattered throughout the camp, that I spotted Grace on the road. She carried one baby in her arms and the other on her back, and she walked with a stooped, almost defeated posture so unlike the tall, confident woman I'd come to know. But she was safe, and at that moment, that was enough for me. I cranked the window open, pushed my head and arms through, and called her name. "Grace!" I shouted. Her head popped up, and when she saw me, she smiled and waved. My arms flailing about, I waved wildly back. "I'll come by later. Okay?" She nodded. I watched from the window, craning my neck as we rounded a curve, until she faded from sight.

Later, she told me that the fighting hadn't really touched her family. "We knew about it. We were warned to stay close to home and we did. But we knew the trouble would pass. Here, there isn't so much to fight for. You know?"

Within days, calm had descended on the camp and life returned to what passed for normal, but each of us still silently held on to a bit of unease about how quickly things here could spiral out of control. One afternoon, as we sat outside her hut, Grace, who'd been cradling one baby while her eldest held the other, cleared her throat and shooed the children away. She leaned toward me, her bony knee brushing my own. "Please, when you leave," she said haltingly, "take her with you." She slid her baby into my arms. "There is nothing here for her; you can see that for yourself. With you, she could have a better life and grow into a strong woman." Her back seemed a little straighter as she spoke.

The baby cooed softly in my arms, her eyes sparkling as though she knew what her mother was proposing. I pulled my own eyes away and locked my gaze onto Grace's. "Oh God, Grace," I said, my voice cracking, "I would love to take care of this baby for you, but I can't, and what she needs most isn't me. It's you."

Grace paused and took a slow, deep breath before nodding her understanding. My heart broke for her as she squeezed my hand, stood, and walked away. I sat there for a while rocking the baby, lost in my own thoughts, wishing I could bring this fragile baby home with me. Grace returned not much later. "I had to ask," she said softly, and she never brought it up again, though the thought lingered between us, an unspoken promise that maybe one day . . .

That one day never came, but once Grace had asked, many other mothers approached me with the same request, each hopeful that I would change my mind, and with each request, my heart broke again.

Before I left Kakuma, Grace presented me with a delicately hand-embroidered bedcover, "So you won't forget me," she said.

Tears rimmed my eyes. "Oh Grace," I sighed, "I will never forget you, never."

Peace and independence finally came to South Sudan for a time when the country gained its independence in 2011. Many Sudanese left the camp for home, but fighting, drought, and starvation found their way back to that brittle piece of land. I often wondered if Grace managed, even for a time, to feel the sweet soil and breathe the clean air of her beloved South Sudan, but there was no news, no way for me to know how things had turned out for her and her family. The best that I could do was hope.

Passing Time

—◆—

I 'd returned to aid work as a nonsmoker, and to my amazement, everyone
else seemed to be smoking. European expats, national staff, even the refugees, it seemed, all smoked, and the enticing combination of the curling
smoke in the air and the easy, relaxed way of the smokers tempted me every
minute to have just one cigarette. I managed to avoid it, though there would be
moments when I wanted one desperately, and an evening at Catherine's, a bar
located just beyond the gates of Kakuma, guaranteed that.

One evening, Aimée and a Ugandan physician who'd joined our team
for a short stint invited me along to the local bar. It was the first I'd heard
of a bar here. Images of the American Club immediately popped into my
head, and I imagined comfortable chairs, cool wine, maybe even music. I
eagerly agreed, and we headed out just after sunset.

Surrounded by a chain-link fence with a tired-looking goat tied up at
the entryway, Catherine's seemed, at first glance, more junkyard than bar.
"This is it?" I asked, unable to keep the disappointment from my voice.

"*Oui*," Aimée replied. "A bit rustic, but fun." She exhaled a long plume of smoke, and I felt a sting of envy that she was smoking and I was not. Maybe the bar would offer an antidote, a remedy to make a cigarette less alluring.

We passed by the goat to enter, and my mouth dropped open. Garbage—plastic bags, water bottles, paper scraps—lay everywhere. The bar, brightened by a few Christmas lights strung about, held few patrons, though it was too dark to really say how many people were there. Rickety wooden chairs were scattered around a mud hut where we could order a Tusker beer or vodka, no wine. I ordered beer, and we three sat and sipped our drinks.

Before long, I was in need of the latrine and was pointed in the direction of a falling-down wooden outhouse, guarded by yet another goat, this one lying directly in my path. I made my way around him and into the latrine, which was unlit and pitch black when I pulled the door shut behind me. I did my business quickly and headed back out to join my companions.

I'm not much of a beer drinker, so although I went back to Catherine's, it was the camaraderie and uniqueness of the place that I craved. Nearly everyone there smoked. Watching as they flicked their ashes and stamped the tiny remnant of their cigarettes into the ground cured any longing I might have had. Still, it was the kind of place that grows on you, draws you back and swirls in your memory long after your last visit.

Occasionally, some of us—visitors to Kakuma and other expats, when they were around—would go to the camp's refugee restaurant for a change. The Ethiopian section held several restaurants, opened by budding entrepreneurs, and it was there that we headed. All of the restaurants served the same menu of *injera*, the Ethiopian flatbread; *wat*, a kind of stew; and *shiru*, a spicy chili dish. We used the bread to scoop the *shiru* and *wat* into our mouths. Those who wanted it could also get a bottle of warm beer.

One evening, we ventured into Kakuma village, the Turkana town that lay just beyond the camp, for dinner. There was only one eatery and the menu consisted only of fried potatoes and rice, nothing else. Ever. Still, it was a welcome change of pace and a means of stepping back, if only for a moment, from the work, from the sadness here.

The Children of Kakuma

———◆·———

I n the spring of 2001, not long after food rations supplied to refugees
were cut by the WFP, UNICEF sponsored a fairly extensive nutritional
survey that involved all of the children in the camp. The results,
showing lower-than-expected rates of acute, as well as chronic, malnutrition
(based on body weight to height ratios) seemed a contradiction to everything
we were seeing at Kakuma.

Despite the optimistic results of the nutritional survey, and the relatively
easy access to nutritional programs, the hospital was admitting more malnourished, dehydrated, and sickly babies. They were thin as a whisper; so
frail you could see their hearts beating through the paperlike skin on their
fragile little bodies. You could see, too, when those delicate pulses ceased,
as one after another slipped from this world gently and without a fight.
I'd been lulled into complacency by the presence of a nutritional program
and access to food for the refugees here. I'd believed that I'd see no more
starving babies, but I was wrong.

One of the babies was Sunday John—so named because he was born on a Sunday. Tiny, shriveled, malnourished, and about eight months old, he was born in South Sudan during the worst of the fighting there. It had taken his mother months to get across the border and into Kakuma, and only another day to have Sunday admitted to the pediatric ward for nutritional support. An intravenous line delivering hydration was taped to his tiny arm. A feeding tube snaked through his nose to his stomach, delivering the special nutrition he needed to recover and grow. He had large, soulful eyes that tracked my every move when I approached him. Fearful of another needle stick or exam, he let out a weak cry when I touched him. When I wrapped the tape measure around his arm to see how he was progressing, he moaned and tried to push me away. When his foot was pricked for a small sample of blood, he let out a weak cry and wrinkled his brow, watching me again until I whispered that we were done, then moved far enough away that he could be sure of that. He was afraid of everyone but his mother, who, when I was done, wrapped her arms around him and kissed his little cheek. I watched as the corners of his cracked lips lifted into a smile, and his eyes seemed to sparkle.

Weeks later, he was discharged to the little hut where he would live with his mother, and I knew that, at least for Sunday John, there was hope.

The children of Kakuma, who had no toys and few breaks from the monotony of their lives, were resilient and resourceful and filled with laughter at even the smallest chance for play. They fashioned toys from objects they scrounged from the piles of garbage that dotted the camp or simply found unclaimed in the road. From rocks and sticks they created trucks, and on larger sticks of wood they painted doll's faces. The ingeniousness of their strategy was admirable, but still, from my Western perspective, I wished I'd brought toys—balls and bubbles and books—but I was as empty-handed as the children here.

One day I noticed a cluster of children crowded around one small boy who held a shiny yellow marble in his outstretched hand. It glistened in the sun, seeming to throw off a brilliant light of its own. The children leaned closer, clearly wanting to hold it for themselves, to feel the glossy, cool smoothness in their own dirt-streaked little hands. They milled about, watching, waiting, and hoping for a chance to just touch it. That shiny yellow marble was the center of the universe for those children on that day. That simple glass ball held a special kind of magic in that desolate place until the young boy curled his hand over it and slipped it back into his pocket. The magic was gone and the children who'd gathered to watch groaned in unison, their little shoulders sagging as the boy who owned it stepped back into the road, kicking stones and dirt as he went. And as I watched, I wished for all those children a life filled with the magic of shiny yellow marbles.

I especially wished that for Agnes. She was ten years old when I first saw her in the pediatric ward of the hospital. She had been admitted with nephrotic syndrome (kidney failure), likely resulting from tuberculosis. Her body was swollen to twice its normal size; her heart always raced, and she took her breaths in small, shallow gasps. For Agnes, that effort to breathe required all of her strength and prevented all other movement, including the small bit of energy needed to smile. She could not even lie flat to sleep; her efforts to breathe meant that she had to sit, and even sleep, upright.

In this late stage of her disease, treatment was minimally effective; our best hope was to make her comfortable. But comfort was relative here. Agnes had to share her hospital bed with another patient—always, it seemed, a squealing baby.

Agnes's lone dress looked like an old sack that had been sewn together at the shoulders. It was the dull, lifeless gray of the ration sacks and likely had been just that not so long ago. She wore and even slept in it every day, and it added to her weary appearance. Her close-cropped, dull, and dusty hair further added to the impression that she was old, if not in years, then in suffering.

Her family had too many responsibilities to stay with her in the hospital, but her mother and toddler brother visited frequently. The only piece of clothing her tiny brother had was a ragged old sweater. He didn't even have pants. He strutted about wearing only the frayed sweater; it never deterred him from laughing and playing. He was lucky; at least he had some covering. Many children didn't even have that, and they ran about bare-skinned and without any protection or covering for their little bodies.

Even in camp, there were degrees of poverty, and Agnes and her family were destitute, with nothing but hope to call their own. For Agnes, even hope was elusive. Her childhood had been stolen; she had the sad, bloated, and burdened face of an old woman. Still, even through the long days and nights of sharing her bed with another patient (I always thought of it as her bed since she lived in the hospital), she never complained, though she never really spoke either. Words sapped her energy, and to speak with her, I had to learn to read her eyes, for it was there I could see a sparkle of joy or the unmistakable flat reflection of her melancholy.

One day, in one of many efforts to induce a small moment of joy, I let her listen to the sound of her own heartbeat with my stethoscope. For the first and only time that I knew her, Agnes looked straight at me and, her eyes shimmering, drew her lips into an unexpected and rare smile.

A few days later, on an especially warm morning with the sun beating down hard already, I stopped at the pediatric ward to see Agnes. I poked my head in, my eyes scanning the ward, but she was nowhere to be found, either in her bed, or elsewhere in the large tent. I headed outside to continue my search.

"Where is she?" I asked everyone I saw.

The only replies were shoulder shrugs or head shakes. No one had seen her, and no one seemed worried. My heart pounded as I raced along the tent's perimeter, and then, with blissful relief, spied her there. Someone had moved her outside to the rear of the tent for a bit of fresh air, and there she sat on a stiff wooden chair. Because of her chronic difficulty breathing, she sat perfectly upright, her back straight as a ruler, her dress spread out covering her knees—a princess of sorts overlooking her kingdom. I gave her an especially warm greeting that morning. She raised a brow, likely confused about my joy at seeing her, but it was absolute joy I felt. I stopped daily to see Agnes, to say hello, to share a smile, to tell her funny stories; she sometimes offered a thin smile, but she never spoke.

When I went to say good-bye to her to let her know I was going home, she barely acknowledged me, and it occurred to me that I was only one of many aid workers who'd passed briefly through her short life and then just disappeared. My chest tightened at the thought. I was deserting her just as everyone before me had. I leaned down to give her one final hug. I was going home. Agnes was already there.

I have tried in the last months, now years, to get word of Agnes, but sadly, there is no news. I suspect that her child's spirit, entombed in an old and battered body, simply gave up the struggle. Agnes was possessed of a rare courage and an almost angel-like serenity. She is surely an angel now, freed from her struggles and pain. She will always be an inspiration to me for her unfailing goodness in the face of so many unfair burdens.

The Lost Boys

————•◆•————

Best known among the Sudanese refugees were the Lost Boys of Sudan, a group of boys, mostly young men by 2001, who were separated from their families during the worst days of Sudan's civil war in the early 1990s. They escaped the murderous carnage in their villages by taking to the surrounding jungle. There were no adults among them, and the boys' ages at the time ranged from three to sixteen years. To survive, they learned to fend for themselves, and among a host of frightening experiences, they later recounted, they were forced to swim across a crocodile-infested river to the relative safety of the opposite bank. During the harrowing swim, it was said, many boys disappeared, never to emerge on the other side. Some probably drowned, and some were likely eaten by the crocodiles. The boys told their tales with little emotion, the trauma of their experiences still raw even years later.

Once on the other side, the ordeal continued. Without food, the boys foraged in the jungle; they were attacked by wild animals or died of hunger and dehydration and exposure and untreated disease. Finally, miraculously, many of the boys made it to the safety of Kakuma, a refuge of wonder after their experiences. Once they were registered by the UN, the boys were allowed to live in small groups sharing the mud huts; they had, after all, become family. They were enrolled in school, and most became eager students.

When they first arrived at Kakuma, I was told, many were unable to talk about the terror they'd survived and told their stories through crude drawings depicting their ordeals. By the time I arrived in Kakuma, many of them worked in the clinics as assistants, and they were eager to share their own stories. Francis, a six-foot-tall young man of about twenty, worked alongside me one day in the clinic, and, with a surprising lilt to his voice, he told me that he was one of the Lost Boys.

"I've heard the stories," I said during a break between patients. "It must have been just terrible."

He pulled up a chair and sat down, a fine sheen of sweat covering his brow. "Very bad," he said, picking his front teeth with a small wooden twig. "We traveled for days through very bad conditions." He slipped the twig into his shirt pocket and sat very still. "I am one of the lucky ones, you know." He paused and plucked a paper from the notebook he'd carried to the clinic. I'd assumed it was for taking notes, but when he opened the pages, I saw drawings—some colorful, some stark pencil sketches—all dramatic pictures of rivers and animals. He placed the loose paper on the desk in front of me, and my mouth fell open as I saw what he had drawn. It was a crude sketch of a young boy at the edge of a river—crocodiles in front of him, lions behind.

"Is this you?" I asked, pointing to the image of the boy.

He nodded. "We couldn't tell our stories when we first came, so we were given notebooks and colored pencils and asked to draw what happened. This is my story." He passed the notebook to me and I turned the pages slowly. The first pages were drawings of fire—bright orange flames eating at small brown huts. I lingered over the last—the one depicting small figures in the flames. "Your village? Your family?" I asked.

He shrugged and flipped the pages until he came to pictures of greenery—shrubs and tall grass and trees. "This was where we hid from the government troops who wanted to kill us. They'd burned our villages, killed our families, and we ran and ran, and hid in there, until it was safe to go on."

My own heart pounded listening to his story. "How did you know it was safe?"

"When the only sounds we heard were the animals—the lion's roar was the one we dreaded most—we knew that the lions would eat us before the crocodiles could get close enough. The lions attacked and ate some of my friends, and I could do nothing. I was helpless, so I ran and hid."

He spoke, not in the fearful way of someone reliving fresh memories but in the practiced, flat monotone of someone who's grown used to retelling the same story. It seemed to me that he'd released his sadness into his drawings so that he could manage to live again. "This one," he said, pointing to a rough sketch of a stick figure in the mouth of a lion, "was my friend, Joseph. He didn't make it."

"The lions?" I asked.

Francis didn't answer. He pushed the notebook away and closed it. "Things are better now. You know they are sending some of us to America?"

I shook my head. "To visit? To tell your stories?"

He sat forward. "No, no. We are going there to live." For the first time since he began to tell his story, he smiled, a wide, toothy grin that made him seem not so far from the little boy who'd escaped Sudan all those years ago. "Your country is taking us in. Understand? Some have left already. More are going this month."

I'd seen the planes, usually on Sundays, as they'd landed and idled just outside the camp—a line of young man standing nervously, clutching new backpacks, as they'd waited to board. I'd wondered if they were going to Nairobi for work or school. Hundreds of refugees had invariably gathered to watch, their heads all rising as the plane lifted into the sky. I hadn't known then that the young men flying away were the envy of everyone else in the camp, that just about every single camp dweller—Ethiopians, Somalis, Ugandans, Congolese—all longed to be the next to go. In Pakistan, the Afghan refugees I'd met had only wanted to go home, but here, the refugees, to a person, it seemed, wanted to join those boys on their flights to freedom.

"I hope to be in the next group." Francis explained that several times a month a list of sixty or so of the Lost Boys who were headed to the United States was posted on bulletin boards throughout the Sudanese section of the camp.

"You don't know until you see your name on the list that you're going? They don't just tell you?"

"There are too many of us. It is better that way. No arguments."

Days later, I saw a group of young Sudanese men gathered around one of the camp's bulletin boards. Some were gesturing excitedly, others were searching the list, still others—heads down, shoulders sagging—were turning away. I felt my own shoulders slump knowing that the last group likely hadn't seen their names on the cherished list.

IOM (International Office of Migration), the agency coordinating the Lost Boys' migration to the United States, had regular meetings in the recreation center with the young men who'd be leaving soon. Intended as an orientation to American life and traditions, the young men sat and watched as the tutors explained refrigerators, flush toilets, telephones, supermarkets, and more. The boys listened wide-eyed and open-mouthed, and I wondered if they'd remember any of this. Each would be assigned to a different city—Dallas, Phoenix, Chicago, Boston, and more.

They gathered around maps of the United States, studying the places they'd been assigned. "Will it be cold?" a young man named Gabriel asked. He was headed to Chicago and was nervous that the weather would be bad and that his English might not be good enough to get by. The IOM representative reassured Gabriel and the rest, but they shuffled their feet and seemed to pay little attention. "But, will it be cold?" he asked again.

"Yes," the tutor said, pulling an ice cube from the small cooler at his feet. He dropped the frozen ice into Gabriel's hand. We watched as he shivered, and suddenly the one hundred degree temperature, the dust and the dirt all faded away as the tutor described snow and ice and bitter winds. Gabriel's deep blue-black skin seemed to grow pale. "Will I get a coat?" he asked. The tutor nodded and moved on to a description of the next city—Phoenix—which, he explained, had the familiar warmth of Sudan.

The planes continued to take off, a few even landed carrying visitors, and we all watched as several news organizations, including a crew from *Sixty Minutes*, disembarked to chronicle the Lost Boys' journeys. I never did see Francis after our day at the clinic. I assumed he'd made the coveted list and left us all behind.

I met several of the boys a year or so later in Boston when they presented to the emergency room where I was working, with minor complaints. They were invariably exhausted from working long hours and adjusting to the pace of life in the United States. Samuel, twenty years old, was working the night shift in a supermarket earning minimum wage and hoping to attend a local high school during the daytime. He shared a small apartment with four other Lost Boys, and together, they were learning to use the stove and to shop and to navigate the confusing maze of Boston's streets. Although he'd planned to attend high school and then college, Samuel just couldn't muster the energy it all required.

"I must take two buses to work," he told me, "and if I forget the stop, I am lost and I must go back to the beginning and start my trip once again." The simplest tasks seemed to require the greatest concentration and energy. "Our stove has no flame, just coils that get hot and turn red and burn our food. And our neighbors don't talk to us. I thought, we all thought, it would be different here. I think maybe I'd like to go home."

"Sudan?" I asked.

"Yes. I'd like to see if any of my family is there. If I can find them and bring them here to be with me, it would be better."

I saw Samuel and some of the others intermittently in the ER and later in the clinic. They were all lonely, for although they had friends among the Lost Boys' community, those were forced friendships, and though they had much in common, like all of us, they had many differences. Some wanted to go to college. Some wanted only to go home. A few had discovered the solace that alcohol offered. Samuel was one of those. He lost his job and, later, his apartment. His roommates had moved on, one becoming a kind of minister and mentor to the boys like Samuel, who had such trouble fitting in.

I lost touch with Samuel and assumed he'd been able to find his way home. Then one day a public defender called me. Samuel had been arrested for public drunkenness and lewd behavior. He'd apparently urinated in the middle of a crowded street. The attorney asked if I would write a letter on Samuel's behalf, explaining that Samuel was a stranger in what surely seemed to him a strange land. I wrote the letter. The judge issued a continuance of the case without finding, which meant that as long as he stayed out of trouble, the charges would be dropped. Samuel was able to get a cell phone. Though he was living in a shelter, he managed to stay in touch—calling or coming to see me at the hospital. And then, he was gone.

Without a trace.

I asked some of the other boys if they'd seen him. No one had. They promised to keep an eye out, but it was as if he'd disappeared into thin air. It's been a few years now, and there's been no word. His cell number now belongs to someone else. There's no way to know how he is, or where he is, so I've decided to hope for the best—he's surely at home in the dust and heat of Sudan, happy at last to just fit in.

But the new reality of South Sudan is one of familiar misery. Civil war and famine have broken out again; young men are plucked away to fight for one side or another. For many, the choice is easy—fighting offers food, camaraderie, and something to do.[1]

These days, I rarely see the others. Many have learned to find their way here. Appliances, stores, even bus routes have become easier to navigate. Many are still working several jobs and attending school while they dream of finding success here; others dream only of returning to Sudan, but the war there holds them back. Several have graduated from the University of New Hampshire, a feat of enormous proportions for those boys who, not so long ago, were confused by the workings of a handheld can opener.

Interval

———•◆•———

When I returned to Boston, I had difficulty adjusting to my full-time job. It wasn't likely that I'd be granted another leave of absence anytime soon, yet I longed for the work I'd left behind—for the stark honesty and reality of refugees. I realized that when I was working with them, freed from the stresses of daily life—lines at the bank, rush-hour traffic, an endless list of overdue chores—I was able to be my best self, to be the person I was meant to be. I don't mean for that to sound self-serving. I think it's true for all in-the-field aid workers. It's what draws us back again and again—a healthy addiction to doing something that feels more important than the next bubble bath or glass of wine. It doesn't mean that I didn't crave those. I did. I just craved the work a little more.

I finally gave my notice at the law firm and returned to the hospital to work in the ER and clinics on a per diem basis, which meant that I could come and go as I pleased. I wouldn't have to ask anyone's permission to work with refugees again.

Afghanistan was still on my radar. I came home from Africa to find a full envelope of Irish ancestral documents waiting for me. I quickly gathered the other paperwork required, and in late July, I headed to the Irish consulate in Boston to apply for an Irish passport. I followed up with a phone call in early September and was assured that my passport would be mailed shortly. Elated, I called Bendu, the MSF recruiter in New York who'd first made the suggestion about a foreign passport. "I'll have my Irish passport soon," I told her. "Can I go to Afghanistan now?"

She paused, and I heard the rustling of papers and the tap of computer keys in the background. "I'll let you know," she said and hung up abruptly.

My heart sank. All that work. For nothing.

But on September 10, Bendu called and asked if I'd be willing to go to northern Afghanistan to work on a mobile clinic. "The assignment is for six months," she said. I hesitated. It would be my longest trip yet, and it wouldn't just stretch my savings, it would demolish them. Still, this was exactly the mission I'd been waiting for, and I said I'd go.

"Alright, then," she said cheerily. "We'll speak later this week."

The following morning, on September 11, 2001, the world changed forever as the Twin Towers and Pentagon were viciously attacked, killing not just innocent, helpless people but, as a villainous aside, American innocence and trust as well. I watched in horror that morning as the Twin Towers fell, my heart breaking at the sight. I was glued to my television, and like thousands of others, I called the volunteer number that flashed across my television screen. I wanted to help. I'd know what to do, and though I called several times, no one ever returned my call.

When the newscaster announced days later that all international aid workers were being evacuated from Afghanistan, I tried to call MSF, but all lines were busy. When I finally reached Bendu weeks later, she confirmed that MSF was, at least for a while, out of Afghanistan. Once the coalition's bombing campaign began there in early October, any aid work there began to seem an unlikely prospect. I was heartbroken. As the world's attention focused on that destitute corner of the world, the devastating truth of the Taliban's rule began to emerge; torture, murder, and unspeakable crimes against these people. It was worse than any of us had imagined.

When IRC asked if I'd go to Macedonia—the site of civil war, destruction, and population displacement earlier in the year—to coordinate their health programs, I accepted. It would be only a short assignment—two months at the most, and if things changed in Afghanistan, I'd be ready to go.

III

THE BALKANS

2001–2002

A European War

———◆———

J ust after Thanksgiving 2001, I headed to Macedonia, a country in southeastern Europe where refugees from Kosovo had sought safe haven during the brutal war in their own nation several years earlier. Many of those remained there still. Earlier in the year, fierce fighting had broken out in Macedonia between the ethnic Albanians and the Macedonian majority. The government of Macedonia had bombed a number of Albanian villages in an effort to stop the uprising. In August, a peace agreement had been tentatively brokered between the ethnic Albanians and the government of Macedonia, but fighting still continued in many areas and ethnic hatred still lay festering just beneath the surface.

Even before this crisis, Macedonia, though industrialized and developed, was a poor country with few resources. The national health system was not able to meet the basic needs of the country's residents, and there was no medical care at all in the "crisis zones"—those areas where fighting continued.

To meet the needs of the thousands of Kosovans still there in refugee camps and the many thousands of displaced Macedonians, IRC ran six health clinics, along with providing shelters and school reconstruction. Kosovo had seen the largest outpouring of refugees in Europe since WWII, and the vast majority of them were women and children. Macedonia, among the poorest regions in Europe, with 24 percent living below the poverty line in 2001, had a limited capacity to host the refugees. In 2001, UNICEF declared that the children of the Balkans region were among the most endangered children in Europe due to wars and sanctions.

Displaced Macedonians, mostly ethnic Albanians, were only then returning to their villages, hoping to rebuild their lives and homes. My responsibilities would involve overseeing the network of primary care clinics already providing care to refugees and internally displaced persons (IDPs), as well as undertaking needs assessments in order to expand the scope of our programs if necessary to meet the changing needs of the population.

A Comfortable Post

———•◦•———

I arrived in Skopje, the capital of Macedonia, during the coldest winter on record. I was ill prepared and had packed only a few sweaters and a light leather jacket for temperatures that were bitingly cold and three feet of snow blanketing the ground. Because there was no snow removal equipment, the snow remained, added to with each new snowfall.

Skopje lay nestled at the base of several mountains. From the air, the red-tiled roofs and the fresh snow of the countryside combined to create an exquisite and picturesque winter village scene. Lights twinkled everywhere, which meant electricity. I was assigned a "flat," which I shared with an American volunteer who, more often than not, spent the night with a friend, so the flat was really my own. We had electricity, heat, running water, a kitchen, all of the amenities of home. I lived within walking distance of the IRC office, so each morning I walked through the village roads to work. I came to know many of the shopkeepers and waved to them as I passed;

it was an exquisitely quaint European village. I would make instant coffee each morning, and on the way to work, I would stop and get a piece of fresh warm bread from the village bakery. This would be no third world hardship post. I was living well and I knew it. It's almost easier when I am away on mission to live in rugged deprivation. To live so well made me feel guilty.

The IRC expat team here was small: Jane, a British logistician (she managed our resources); Mitch, a British water and sanitation engineer; and Alan, another American, who ran the information and protection program for refugees and IDPs. And although there was no American Club here, there were plenty of bars and restaurants, and we made it a point to visit most of them.

But I was here to work, and that came first. I would run the health programs, which employed a staff of eighteen, including nurses, doctors, and an engineer, all of them Macedonian except for one lone Croatian nurse who was a refugee here, having fled the brutal war in her own nation. I was happy to note that every single woman here wore bright red lipstick. I knew that I would fit right in.

Roza and the Refugees of Kosovo

———◆———

As comfortable as the accommodations were in Skopje, the surrounding countryside told a different tale. A fresh dusting of snow softened, but couldn't quite erase, the gaping holes and skeletons of houses that dotted the landscape. Burned cars, tanks, shells, fragments of bombs, all littered the space in between. They were all slivers of the silent, haunting emptiness that surrounded the now abandoned villages. Traces of real life, of toys and worn shoes and pieces of broken furniture, littered the landscape, reminding us that not so long ago, these shadowy, near-empty places had been filled with families and life and laughing children.

Most areas remained without electricity and heat. To generate a bit of warmth in this cold and snowy climate, the people who remained, even tiny kids, set a match to piles of garbage on the side of the road and huddled around the fire, oblivious to the danger as they rubbed their hands together over the roaring flames.

On my first full day, I toured the camps and clinics where IRC worked. The Kosovo refugees lived in UN-sponsored camps that barely provided adequate shelter, especially in this bitter cold. In our clinics, the staff reported that upper respiratory infections (URIs) were the primary complaints. Luckily, those were easily treated with antibiotics. The freezing temperatures actually kept down the numbers of communicable and waterborne diseases such as diarrhea, so often found in the crowded camp environments. Just as in Sudan, food was provided by the UN World Food Programme (WFP), but here, a family member had to brace the winds and cold each day to collect rations from the designated site in the camp.

At Shuto-Orizari, one of the UN camps just outside of Skopje, over one thousand Kosovan refugees lived in ramshackle huts that were connected to one another in long rows, like old army barracks. Rickety slices of old wood served as doors. Each family had one or two rooms. Blankets covered the entrance to the living area, a poor attempt to block the cold winds that whistled though the shelters. Each entryway housed the kitchen area, really just an open fire over which a pot of water always stood boiling. The water would be used for food preparation and coffee, and what was left would be used for washing—people, clothes, and dishes—usually in that order. Sometimes clothes and underwear could be seen in the pot as they were swirled about with a long stick. Latrines and showers were housed outside in a separate area. To shower or just urinate, refugees had to brace the cold and snow. Not many showers were taken that winter.

The clinic in this camp was housed in a converted cargo container with just enough space to hold two desks and an old filing cabinet, which stored the drugs available for treatment. In this bitter cold, an electric heater filled the small space with warmth. The staff here, an IRC doctor and nurse, saw an average of eighty patients per day. Because of the bitterly cold air, patients waiting to be seen tried to crowd into the room to wait their turn. Those who couldn't squeeze in huddled outside.

One of the refugees I became friendly with was Roza, a 46-year-old woman whose stooped shoulders and deeply furrowed brow gave her the appearance of someone much older. Her ruddy skin hung loosely over the broad planes and hard angles of her face. Her eyes were a flat gray, the color of a sidewalk in winter. She wore a moth-eaten sweater over an old dress cinched at her thick waist—the last remnant of the rich life she'd once lived. Heavy stockings covered her legs and a woolen kerchief tied in back covered her head. Although she'd once lived a secure middle-class life in Kosovo, she now shared two small rooms with her husband, four sons and their wives, and three grandchildren. They slept on pads on the floor, curled into one another for heat. In these close quarters, they shared repeated respiratory infections, all of which were easily treated at our clinic, but with one or another always sniffling and coughing, it was a never-ending cycle of sickness.

Although Roza lived a life of crushing poverty, she was certain that this month or maybe the next, her dream of returning to her once comfortable existence would be realized. "Come in out of the cold," she beckoned me one icy winter day. Glad to be out of the biting winds, I accepted her offer, rubbing my hands together over her pot of boiling water.

In perfect English, she introduced herself and her family, and insisted that I stay for tea. Before I'd had a chance to answer, she ushered me to a floor pillow in the corner of the main room. As I settled myself in, she told me of her own childhood and her life, as if we'd known each other longer than the few minutes it had been. She'd led a charmed life, she said. She'd learned English at a private boarding school and had married at age nineteen. She smiled, a sudden sparkle lighting up her eyes; even her skin seemed to glow as she spoke.

"I was beautiful," she said proudly, tidying the spray of hair that spilled from under her scarf. "You might not see it now, but I was, and my husband—he was a handsome man. Oh, we were something to see." She reached for a framed photo of herself and her husband smiling shyly into the camera. She wore a fitted black dress, her husband a shiny suit, and they stood together in the fashion of photos at the time—sour expressions in place of smiles. "We were serious about our future even then." She nodded her head, remembering that moment and those days when anything seemed possible.

She and her husband had built a successful construction business and a happy, healthy family; her life was safe and sheltered and carefree. Then Kosovo's Serbs increased their almost decadelong campaign of brutal violence against the Albanian majority and ethnic tensions erupted into war in her native land. The NATO bombing campaign of 1999, designed to end the war, actually for a time allowed the Serbs to increase their atrocities under cover of NATO bombs. As members of another tortured ethnic group, the Roma, Roza and her family were forced to flee Kosovo or risk certain death at the hands of their own countrymen, some of them their own neighbors. They fled to Macedonia and were sheltered in Shuto-Orizari camp for what they thought would be a short stay. Weeks turned into months and months into years. When I met her, she and her family had been refugees for almost three years.

Although the UN had begun repatriation of Kosovan refugees in late 1999, many—Roza and her family among them—remained in Macedonia, terrified of what they had endured and witnessed, and rightly concerned that it could all happen again. "People we'd thought of as friends turned on us. Who can say that things have changed, that we will be safe?" She shook her head and answered her own question. "I won't go back. Not yet."

They remained in a state of limbo inside the camp, hoping to go home, but still anxious and fearful of the dangers that lurked there. They had learned that their house had been destroyed and their business was gone, stolen by people they'd once trusted. Despite the presence of an international peacekeeping force, the tensions and danger in Kosovo remained.

Not long after meeting Roza, I learned that the UN planned to close these camps and repatriate the remaining Kosovan refugees.

"What have you heard?" she asked me one day. I shared what little I knew and reassured her that as long as she remained here, we would provide health care and that we would advocate for the Kosovan refugees with the UN.

The UN, however, was firm: the camps must be closed; the refugees would be returned home.

Roza's smile disappeared when I delivered the latest news, and she clutched her kerchief's knot, now tied tightly under her chin. She loosened the tie, her fingers fumbling there for a moment. "They will force us out?" she asked, her voice cracking. As miserable as this place was, it had been a safe place to stay. I didn't know how to answer her question. It seemed unlikely, but I was in no position to make promises. She adjusted her scarf and bent back to her pot, intent on swirling the clothes in the soapy water. She was tired and fearful, and yet, despite her continued hardships, she remained a gracious hostess, for whenever I turned up on her doorstep, always without warning, since there was no phone or way to communicate with her, a feast of sweet tea, pastries, and candies, likely borrowed and begged from neighbors in the camp, would appear as though I had been expected.

"Come in, come in, you must have tea with us," she invariably said, as though I'd been a long-cherished friend. She never asked for anything aside from a promise of safety, something I could never guarantee.

The Albanians

———•———

efugees were not our only focus. IRC also provided services to the internally displaced persons (IDPs) of Macedonia. They were primarily ethnic Albanians who had been forced to flee their own villages almost a year earlier when ethnic tensions erupted into civil war. We provided health and other services to IDPs in former government clinics throughout the country. We used the government facilities to house our clinics so that we could avoid creating a parallel system, a system that might be perceived as favoring of the Albanians by the Macedonian majority and thus create further tension. In all of our clinics, for both refugees and IDPs, IRC staff included an Albanian and a Macedonian. This helped foster better understanding and allowed the community to see that they could all work together, at first in clinics and later, we hoped, to rebuild their nation. The clinics for IDPs were always busy, and though housed in better quarters, they, too, saw many patients with a variety of ailments.

The roads leading to the Albanian villages were stark reminders of the recent war. Homes, cars, anything that hadn't been destroyed by bombs were riddled with bullet holes. Although the gentle blanket of snow mitigated the scenery somewhat, the damage was still visible. The Albanians' villages and homes had been destroyed and bombed by the Macedonian majority. Just as with the Kosovan refugees, there was still a fear that to go home would somehow spark further tensions and more fighting.

It wasn't long before the roads cleared enough to allow us to move farther from the cities to get some rural assessments completed. The remote village roads, many built into mountainsides, were treacherous. Some ran almost straight up, but our driver somehow managed to coax the car up a snowy, ice-covered road in a distant town. The villagers stopped to watch as we maneuvered along the roads. They traveled in winter on horses and skis.

Our first stop was an authentic old-fashioned European village, untouched by time, still peaceful and quaint. No noise of cars (aside from ours) or radios here, just the hum of everyday conversation, the whinny of horses, the barking of a dog, the shrieks of children at play. Unfortunately, the picturesque surroundings meant poor access to medical care. There was only one doctor for several surrounding villages and he traveled by horseback. Still, the villagers were a hardy lot and got by on the twice-monthly clinic held here. They hoped for better access to medical care and knew that would come with the spring thaw as the roads cleared enough to allow rides into the city for hospital and specialty consults. A clinic would have been greatly appreciated here, but we all knew that our resources would be better utilized if directed elsewhere where the needs were greater.

I had coffee with the locals in the village center meeting place, a smoky, wood-stove-heated lodge where everyone gathered. We huddled on old lawn chairs around a plastic table and were served cups of oily, thick coffee. These were Albanian villages, and the villagers believed that their fight was far from over. In fact, they told me they were stockpiling weapons and preparing for increasing hostilities in the spring. "We will fight again."

They planned to avenge lives, loves, and homes that had been lost forever amidst the carnage of earlier conflict. Further, they hoped that IRC would provide assistance solely to their side should more fighting break out. I tried to explain that our mandate was to remain neutral and nonjudgmental so that we could simply deliver the best care possible to whoever was victimized or persecuted. "We cannot support you in those plans; we can't be part of that," I explained.

There was, even in this bitter cold, fighting going on in nearby villages, which prevented us from venturing further for assessments. Although the people in this area predicted and even prepared for more war, it never materialized, perhaps due to the presence of the NATO peacekeeping force stationed throughout this volatile country. Or perhaps the lure of peace was even more enticing than the prospect of bitter, long-drawn-out hostilities.

Any increase in aid for this area never materialized either. The UN and donors, those to whom we proposed programs in the hopes of gaining funding for the work, were growing weary of the Balkans. The needs here were no longer quite as critical as they had been or currently were in so many other parts of the world. Without donor interest and money to fund the programs, there simply are no programs. The UN and donors felt that there were greater needs around the world that required their urgent attention and funds.

The potential loss of UN and NGO money and jobs concerned the national staff. The infusion of international aid had so boosted the economy that they felt certain that Macedonia would face a fiscal crisis once that aid was removed. One staffer jokingly remarked that perhaps the Albanians should renew their fight to keep the world interest and money here. That was not a new concept; it is an issue that concerns the world aid and development community. The possibility of deception by beneficiaries, by warlords and others who may prolong conflict in order to reap the benefits of world attention, international money and aid is a concern for all NGOs and donors who want to see their money spent the way they intended, not siphoned off to warlords and dictators and their cronies. The debate, to maintain the financial and humanitarian support of refugees and displaced in spite of the risks, continues even now. The answers are few, the needs are enormous, and we are all watchful, for our intent is to provide comfort and to stop misery, never to prolong it. The oversight by donors and donor agencies has appropriately tightened over the years. The required reports and proposals are sometimes overwhelming, but they are vital in determining true needs and establishing guidelines and parameters within which to provide the necessary aid. It is a far cry from the incredible lack of oversight and accountability in the days of the Soviet invasion of Afghanistan. In those days, money was almost thrown at NGOs willing to help; accountability was not a great concern unless there were great gaps in the financial reports. Those changes have improved the delivery of aid; accountability makes us better at what we do.

The refugee camp in Shuto-Orizari, Roza's home for so many years, closed in 2003. Many of those residents were moved to Katlanavo, the barrackslike camp whose numbers had dwindled to six hundred refugees, a far cry from the one thousand plus in each camp when I left in late January 2002. Still others chose to live with family and friends in Macedonia or elsewhere. Afraid to return home, afraid to take the first step, they waited, with fewer resources, fewer options, and little help. None of the refugees I met there, including Roza and her family, expressed any interest in relocating to the United States or anywhere else. Like Asma from Afghanistan and Grace from South Sudan, they wanted only to go home. One or two staff members, however, did want to leave, and had already started their paperwork to emigrate. Much like the Lost Boys of Sudan, they waited anxiously for word.

In 2015, a fierce gun battle erupted between police and militants not far from the rural village where I'd been warned years before that the fighting wasn't over. In late 2017, the ringleader was sentenced to life in prison, the remaining twenty-six to lesser terms in prison.[1]

I recently met several Kosovans in Boston. They'd come to the United States several years before for the same reasons that kept Roza and her family in Macedonia—fear of reprisals and still more trouble at home. None of them knew Roza or her family, and I am left to wonder if she stayed behind in Macedonia or somehow made her way home to Kosovo.

Few programs remain in Macedonia today, and fewer still throughout the Balkans. There will always be need there. There will likely always be greater need somewhere else as well.

Waiting

———•◆•———

I returned home in midwinter, when the sky was somehow grayer, the traffic heavier, the roads slick with ice, the familiar miasma of winter's melancholy in the air. I watched the news with renewed interest, read everything I could about Afghanistan, and waited for the call that would surely come soon.

As the smoke of war in Afghanistan began to clear and aid workers filtered back to Afghanistan, the destruction wrought by the Taliban became increasingly clear. By early 2002, the people there had endured over three decades of war and torture. I learned that the infrastructure, especially the health system, had been unable to meet the needs of the population. It was estimated that one out of every five children born would not live to reach the age of five.[1] For women, the reality was equally dire, and it was estimated that one of every six women would die in childbirth or of pregnancy-related complications.[2] The conditions seemed as dire as they had in 1986.

I was desperate to help, and finally in April 2002, MSF called and asked me to join a mission in central Afghanistan. In early May, I left, an industrial-strength lipstick and Irish passport tucked into my bag. My first stop was New York to speak with the recruiter there, to sign a six-month contract and papers saying that neither I nor my heirs would sue MSF should I fall victim to murder, rape, kidnapping, robbery, dismemberment, disfigurement, or a host of other calamities.

I flew from New York to Dublin through London to get authentic visas and stamps in my Irish passport. As I raced through Heathrow Airport to make my Dublin connection, I stashed my American passport deep in my bag and fumbled to fish out my Irish one. By the time I made it to Dublin, my heart was racing and my cheeks were flushed, and although my Irish passport was legitimate, I was sure I would be stopped and questioned. I was speechless with relief when the authorities simply waved me through.

Once in Dublin, I met up with a friend who'd worked with UNICEF in the Balkans. With a long-ashed cigarette dangling from his lips, Seamus helped me get the necessary passport stamps and paperwork. I purchased a few small products—gum, candy, a notebook, all marked with Dublin price stickers—that I could carry to quietly prove my Irish background. I already possessed a convincing and authentic Irish brogue, perfected in childhood to imitate my immigrant Irish grandmother. I was ready.

After two days in Dublin, I flew on to Paris for a day of briefings. Although MSF New York was aware that I'm American, they had advised me to keep that information to myself. Even MSF Paris believed that I was Irish. When I arrived at the Paris office, an Australian man and I were ushered into the office of the Afghanistan specialist for briefings. The Frenchman in charge of the Afghanistan desk looked up from his work and said, "No Americans, right?" We shook our heads, and the desk officer said, "Good. Too dangerous."

I felt a momentary shiver run along my spine, but I shook it off. I was going. No matter what. And as long as everyone believed that I was Irish, things would be fine.

IV

AFGHANISTAN

2002

Bamiyan Village

———•◆•———

After a quick stop in Peshawar—a city still packed with aid workers, journalists, and the American Club—for new clothes and a burqa, I was on my way to Kabul with nary a chance to at least circle the club.

Kabul, the capital of Afghanistan, was a desolate, demolished, and desperate place, teeming with people, animals, all manner of vehicles and dust, all competing for space amidst the rubble. The dust seemed to be winning. Although music was playing there for the first time in years (it had been forbidden under the Taliban), the people in the streets were destitute and joyless; they had been stripped of everything but hope. Burqa-clad women, their faces covered, seemed almost to blend into the background, another haunting slice of the scenery. Most of the men hurried along, heads down, hands stuffed into pockets, while others—men, women, and children—stood quietly, some with their hands out, haunting, hungry eyes searching for money, food, anything to get through another day. I couldn't stay to help. I was headed to Bamiyan in central Afghanistan, where, it was said, the need was even more pressing.

I fell into bed in the MSF Kabul house, not much more than a series of bedrooms for aid workers on their way in and out of Afghanistan. I fell into a restless sleep, and by 5:00 A.M. I was awake, dressed, and ready to leave. After a quick cup of coffee, I climbed into a sparkling white Range Rover with the Afghan driver and the Australian man I'd met in Paris, and we headed out of the city, on our way. The ten-hour drive over rocky terrain was memorable for the signs of recent war—the rubble of destroyed houses and villages, minefields marked with red danger signs, the carcasses of stray dogs, and the lingering scent of death. In one particularly devastated village, people ran alongside our obviously foreign SUV with the bright red MSF logo on the side and yelled "Thank you" in clear English. It made me sad; we hadn't even done anything yet and they were grateful that we were there. Along the road, amidst all of the devastation, were bursts of sweet, colorful flowers growing, struggling through the scorched earth to be seen; wonderful reminders that beauty still existed here. I took a deep breath; there was no mistaking that I was in Afghanistan at last.

After nine hours on the road, I could no longer wait to use a latrine at the MSF compound. I noticed an old, bombed-out, falling-down mud farmhouse and asked the driver to pull over so that I could pee. I pulled my hijab tight, ran in, scouted about for land mines, and squatted in the dust, adjusting my wide pants, long dress, and sandal-clad feet, careful to keep the run-off away. It was an art that would take me months to master.

As we neared Bamiyan, the air here in the mountains, even in early May, was much colder than I'd expected or packed for; no sweaters or jackets in my bags. No matter the preparations and research, it seemed my clothes were always for another climate. It wouldn't be until early July that summer finally settled here in the mountains.

The MSF compound, located just outside the village center, was a series of mud buildings surrounded by a high mud wall and metal gate. The compound housed both offices and living quarters. The housing area consisted of an L-shaped mud building with separate bedrooms along a long outdoor corridor, a dining area, and a bathroom. The bathroom, about the size of a closet, consisted of a small water tank and a heating urn.

This had been a Taliban house not so long ago, and signs of them were everywhere. The walls in the living area were covered with simple drawings—apples, trees, an occasional flower, hinting at someone who was perhaps not quite so filled with hate as we all believed. The flowing Persian letters that seemed at first glance to be symbols of beauty spelled, an interpreter quickly explained, words of hate—for the local villagers, Americans, nonbelievers. And the walls held still more secrets; bullet holes marred the surface of walls both inside and out. No one knew, or would say, if people had died here, and it wouldn't have changed anything anyway. I was here to stay.

The team consisted of five others—a South African doctor, an Australian midwife, the logistics manager I'd arrived with, and the French coordinator and his wife, and every one of them had been told that I was Irish. I greeted them in my soft brogue, and when the coordinator asked for everyone's passport to keep in his safe, I shuffled through my bag and produced my Irish passport. I would keep my American one hidden, moving it every now and then. The advice from Bendu had been clear—keep your identity a secret. I planned to keep it that way.

A quick orientation revealed that in order to bathe, I would have to first start a fire under the urn, fill it with water from the larger water tank, and wait for the water to heat. Once the water was warm, I would pour the water into a bucket and take a "bucket" bath by squatting beside the bucket, wetting myself down, soaping up, and then rinsing off. Our water was supplied from a nearby village well and delivered by a weary old donkey that spent his day shuffling back and forth from the well with large buckets of water lashed to his sides. There was no electricity and the bathroom was windowless, so the only light was supplied by a kerosene lantern. The toilet was a mud latrine (literally a hole) in another closet-sized room, built onto the roof. We had to climb a set of mud stairs to get there. Again, no light, so a lantern or flashlight was always needed.

For meals, we would sit on the floor in the dining room and share the Afghan food, always sweet tea, rice, and bread, sometimes meat or fried eggs. Breakfast was instant coffee.

My own room was an austere mud room with a pad on the floor for sleeping. I tried to make it more comforting by decorating. I taped a world map labeled in Arabic on the wall and placed my own things around the room, but come night I was not alone.

As I lay on my sleeping pad that first night, I heard a loud chomping sound just above me. I froze, my heart pounding as a bead of sweat trickled along my neck. I took a deep breath, reached for my flashlight, and angled it toward the source of the sound. The room's ceiling was flimsy—straw and mud and a rare slice of rough wood. The straw that was visible was moving—just a little—but enough to show that something was eating away at my flimsy ceiling. The chomping was too loud for a mouse, too light for a dog, but what could be up there? I moved my sleeping pad out from under that patch of thin ceiling and watched warily, certain that whatever was up there would be crashing through any minute. But it didn't. Not that night and not any other after that. I was soon used to the noise and slept right through til morning. There's a lot to be said for exhaustion.

The People of Bamiyan

T he people of Bamiyan Province are Hazara, an ethnic minority in Afghanistan. Historically, they had been discriminated against and treated as lower-class citizens, but their fierce stance against the Taliban leadership from 1996 through 2001 earned them a grudging respect from their countrymen and a target on their backs from the Taliban.

The Hazara are indeed different from most other Afghans. Physically, they have an almost Oriental appearance, with broad, flat faces and deep-set, almond eyes, lined with slashes of black kohl. The women wore loose pants and large, colorfully embroidered dresses topped by exquisite, delicately sewn vests covered with tiny mirrors and sparkly beads. On their arms were sparkling jewel-encrusted bracelets, and on their dresses precious antique amulets. Though they covered their heads and sometimes even their faces with a veil, they rarely wore the full covering of the burqa. On their feet were the local, flimsy plastic sandals that I also wore. Unlike so many

Afghan women who preferred to fade into the background, the Hazara were outgoing and friendly, and eager to talk to foreign women. The men, too, though bearded and dressed in the traditional loose pants and large shirt of all Afghans, were much more open than men in other parts of the country. And though they'd always struggled here in Bamiyan, they remained optimistic and kind, generous and grateful, for whatever small help they were afforded.

Bamiyan, home to centuries of Buddha sculptures carved into the mountainside, had once been a tourist destination and a bustling, busy town, but in the spring of 2001 the Taliban had blown up the long-cherished statues. There was an international outcry for the statues' fate, but none for the people who'd been targeted, none for the massacre of large groups of villagers and destruction of homes, crops, and animals. Despite the ferocity of their acts, the Taliban were never able to crush the spirit of the Hazara population, who lined the streets and celebrated when the American soldiers arrived and the Taliban were sent running. When I arrived, Bamiyan was just emerging from years of misery, still struggling to get back on its feet.

The village center consisted of one long dirt road with simple mud or sometimes wooden structures lining either side. The mostly one-story buildings held everything you might need in a small village—a tailor, a music store, a butcher, a variety store where you could buy English tea, French soap, Chinese toilet paper, or an antique Persian carpet. In front of many small shops were wooden hitching posts to tie up your horse or donkey if you were lucky enough to have one. There was even a busy restaurant called Mama Najaf's (in Dari, *mama* means 'uncle'), which served only beef kebabs, bread, and rice and was popular with locals and foreigners, who sat side by side on the floor of the rustic eatery.

On the surface, the village seemed to be a peaceful spot, the scent of wood cooking fires in the air, the sound of children laughing, but the surrounding landscape told a different story. Littered with burned-out Russian tanks, Taliban trucks, abandoned shells of homes and thousands of land mines, Bamiyan was still a dangerous place. The work of the mine detection and clearance teams was painstakingly slow, and there were daily explosions of newly found ordnance. To mark roads that had been cleared, the mine teams placed small piles of white rocks. In areas that had yet to be cleared, rocks painted red ringed the spot. Most areas were dotted with red-colored rocks. A local prison held more than one hundred Taliban prisoners. It was amazing that the Hazara people had survived at all.

Thousands of the villagers whose homes had been destroyed were living in the caves surrounding the hollows where the Buddha statues once stood. They had crafted ladders from bits of old wood, and to get to the higher caves, they climbed up the ladders and maneuvered over the crevices, carrying food or laundry or buckets of water. They cooked in pots placed inside their little caves, fanning the smoke out through the small opening. A trace of soot lingered on most who lived there.

In early spring, the Afghan government announced that they planned to evict the cave dwellers, but these families had nowhere else to go. Their homes had been destroyed by the Taliban or had been collaterally damaged during the US bombing campaigns. This was their village and they were determined to stay. To rebuild would take time and money, resources they didn't have yet. To remain in the caves, they had to become invisible, which meant that anything that might attract attention, even cooking, was a danger. It was a primitive and demanding existence. There was so much time and effort spent on simple survival here that there was no time left for anything else.

MSF could offer only health care. We supported the village hospital and clinic and several outlying clinics in distant villages. We also ran mobile clinics, which meant that we hiked from the outlying clinics to more remote, less accessible areas to see those people who would otherwise have no access to medical care. The outlying and mobile clinics were my favorite places to work, places where the need was great and we were able to provide basic health care, even with limited resources. We carried only the absolutely necessary medicines, such as common antibiotics, skin preparations, antiworm and other stomach medicines. We not only provided medical care in these villages but we were also able to recognize potential outbreaks such as typhoid and provide early intervention to prevent large-scale epidemics.

When I first arrived, MSF was in the midst of dealing with a typhoid outbreak in several remote villages. It was quickly contained, and though we were on the lookout, there was no large-scale outbreak again, aside from scattered cases. By early July, there were few new reported cases of typhoid.

Early Days

———•◆•———

S hortly after I arrived in Bamiyan, I was walking along a dusty village
road when a US Army jeep passed by. I wanted to shout, to run after
them, but MSF had been clear: no fraternizing with the soldiers, the
"invaders" they called them. They very likely would have said the same if
the soldiers were French. Neutrality is at the very heart of their work, and
I, after all, was Irish. So, instead of shouting after them, I remained quiet,
went on my way, and hoped they'd find me.

I'd already quickly settled into a routine. Whether in mobile clinics
or hospital and OPD, I rose early and heated water for my cup of instant
Nescafé coffee. I washed up and dressed, and by 7:00 A.M., I was on the
road, either by foot through the irrigation fields to get to the hospital, or in
an MSF jeep going to the mobile clinics. For that, I had an interpreter and
a driver, both Afghans, with me.

The start of each day in clinic, whether mobile or hospital-based, meant
accepting copious greetings and handshakes from the staff and any men who

wanted to greet me. "*Salam-aleikum, chetore asti, khoob asti, jonna jurast?*" The greetings were endless. When men were clearly uncomfortable with my outstretched hand, I would put my right hand over my heart and nod my head, a way of showing respect without touching.

The women were friendlier, and one morning, as I scanned the waiting group for anyone who might be seriously ill, I felt a tap on my shoulder. I turned to see a burqa-clad woman holding up a lipstick tube. I smiled. "Lipstick in Afghanistan," I whispered, as though I'd just sighted a unicorn. The woman bobbed her head and passed me the tube. I shook my own head. "*Nay,*" I said. "It's yours." She lifted her burqa, revealing her face and a swipe of tangerine-colored lipstick across her smiling lips. "For you," she insisted, and it was then I remembered Asma, the woman in Thal with the chickpeas, and the unspoken rule that you must accept an offered gift. "*Tashakore,*" I said, tucking the tube into my pocket. She readjusted her burqa and sat to wait while I went to work seeing patients and supervising staff and wondering if, under every burqa, there were brightly colored lips, not so different from my own.

Though busy, I wondered about the soldiers—where they lived, where they went every morning, and would they ever come to the clinic—but I was too busy to linger over my musings or my new tube of lipstick. My memories of the Persian language had emerged shakily from the dust and recesses of my mind, and though I spoke enough Dari to get by, I usually had an interpreter at my side. Aasif was nineteen, and until recently, he'd lived with his family in Kabul. Life in Bamiyan was an adjustment for this city boy who was used to at least some electricity and amenities, neither of which was readily available in Bamiyan. He was always dressed impeccably, his clothes clean and his hair neatly combed. He missed his family tremendously, his mother, father, three brothers and two sisters, but he hoped that this job with MSF would lead to more opportunities, perhaps in Europe or the United States. Aasif was wise and mature beyond his years, probably due to the ever-present war and chaos in his country. He was shy and sweet and more comfortable with me than other Afghans his own age. His family had some money, and he had been encouraged to go to school; most Afghans don't have that luxury. When they are able to walk, they are able to help the family and work at something, whether gathering wood or cow dung from the fields, or tending sheep or assisting farmers. Children had no time for growing up—only for growing old, one backbreaking chore at a time.

But for Aasif, it had been different, and that difference set him apart from the other national staff. At first, he sat alone at meals, lived in a rooming house in the village center, and studied every chance he had, hoping to be admitted to college one day. His English was perfect. He spoke Dari and Pashto and was trying to learn French. "It will help me with MSF. Do you agree?" He wore a permanent smile, and he was never happier than when he was working alongside one of us. He arrived at the MSF compound each morning to accompany me to whichever clinic I was assigned that day. "Good morning," he said without fail, a smile always on his face.

I divided my time between the hospital and clinic in Bamiyan village and the outlying and mobile clinics. I worked, as the others did, independently and only rarely worked with another expat. My primary responsibilities were to supervise and train the national staff as needed. I spent the first few days at the hospital and clinic getting comfortable with the staff and protocols there. The hospital was small, with only eighteen beds. Admitting a patient meant admitting a part of the family; it was disruptive to their lives, to their struggles, and meant an interruption in field work and family life. Not even being hospitalized provided rest for the weary patients and families, because they were responsible for their own meals and basic care.

The International Committee of the Red Cross (ICRC) provided surgical services in a smaller building across the compound. The surgeon, Franz, was a retired Swiss physician, always available and never too busy; he had time for all of us—no questions, no consults off limits.

The MSF clinic on the hospital grounds was always busy. The staff saw and treated about 150 patients a day. When I arrived, the clinic area was chaotic; there were hundreds clamoring to be seen, and many were turned away. The loudest and those who were able to elbow others out of the way seemed always to be seen first. There was no triage system, no way of deciding who needed care or who should be seen first. Those who were turned away were understandably angry with MSF's way of doing things. MSF asked us for suggestions, and I proposed a nurse clinic, similar to others I'd worked in all over the world, where expat nurses saw patients, diagnosed and treated disease based on well-established protocols. MSF had their own handbook of well-used and respected clinical guidelines, perfect for a nurse clinic. The coordinator agreed to give it a try at both the hospital base and outlying clinics, and once we started, we were able to see most of the people who presented at our clinics. It was good for MSF and good for the Afghans.

In those first days, I saw and admitted several people with anaphylaxis (a severe and sometimes fatal allergic reaction) caused by a toxic weed that they were eating. Most who ate it wouldn't develop the terrible and potentially dangerous facial swelling that could halt their breathing, nor would they develop the necrotic sloughing off of skin or swollen extremities. And, because of that, many people in the countryside took the chance and ate those weeds, which grew in abundance, the only thing that mattered when people are starving. We saw only those who developed the allergic reaction and made it to the hospital. Those villagers, we could treat. For those who developed anaphylaxis and lived too far away to get help in time, the price for eating the weeds would surely be death. We would never learn the actual numbers of those so affected. When someone died in a distant village, they were buried there without the benefit of epidemiological studies. We tried to pass the word to avoid that particular weed, and we did start to see fewer and fewer of those patients. But for people who were starving, the temptation to feast on weeds, regardless of the risks, was irresistible.

One morning, as I arrived at the hospital clinic, the Afghan staff summoned me and announced that there were five Taliban prisoners waiting to be seen. At the time, there was a Taliban prison a short distance from the hospital, which housed about one hundred prisoners who had been captured several months earlier. I was told that these men were particularly vicious murderers, and because I was the only expat in clinic that day, it would be my decision if they were seen or not.

I walked up and stood toe to toe with them. I wore sunglasses and a splash of color on my lips. The prisoners wore sullen expressions that peeked through unkempt beards on gaunt faces. Their raggedy *shalwar kameez*, the traditional pants and shirt, hung on skeletal frames so embedded with grime that it might have been a second layer of clothes. Some men wore the traditional turbans, others had long, unkempt hair. I felt not an ounce of sympathy for any of them. Neither did they make me fearful. They were a ragged sorry lot, a far fall from the evil bastards they'd once been.

I moved closer, and they seemed to cower as I asked each of them, in Dari, what was wrong. *"Mariz? Che taklif dori?"* ('Sick? What's your problem?') Each had a minor complaint, a cold, scabies, not a really sick one among them. As an American, I hesitated before answering the question of whether or not we would see them in the clinic. My stomach clenched and I chewed on the corner of my lip. MSF is unwavering in its position on neutrality in all circumstances. I knew there'd be hell to pay from the coordinator if I sent them away, and he would surely wonder why this Irish nurse was so intent on punishing them further. So, I took a deep breath and spoke. *"Balay,"* I said in a whisper, and then louder when it was clear they hadn't heard me. They nodded and smiled happily and were effusive in their thanks. *"Tashakore,"* 'Thank you,' they said as they folded their hands and nodded their heads as if in earnest prayer.

Once I turned my back and walked away, I could hear their low murmurs—insults, I was sure, that a brazen woman would dare to look them in the eye. They would return frequently over the next months until the prison finally closed and they were all released back to their own far-off villages. I had long since tired of their whiny complaints and darting eyes, and I was glad to hear they finally were gone from Bamiyan.

In mid-June, just when the novelty of my Irishness was wearing off, at least for me, an American soldier appeared at the hospital-based clinic looking for health posters. He was wearing a New York Fire Department

(NYFD) baseball cap. The sight of the soldier in that cap filled me with a quiet sense of pride. Though I'd often seen the soldiers on the road or in the bazaar after that first sighting of them, I hadn't had a chance to speak with them, and I was almost desperate to tell someone that I was an American.

The soldier, tall, tanned, and smiling, stuck out his hand. "Matt," he said, introducing himself.

I took his hand, gripping it tightly. "Roberta," I said, smiling. "I'm an American, too," I whispered. It felt so good just to say it, like releasing a long-pent-up secret.

His eyes opened wide and he looked at me. "We didn't think there were any Americans here. You must know the risks. How have you managed it?"

I explained that I had an Irish passport for safety's sake, and I spoke in a brogue around my own team. He looked at me and smiled. "Wow," he said. "I was watching you speak to an old man in Dari, too." He shook his head. "I never would have guessed you're an American. I'm proud that you're here helping, but I have to report this. We need to keep you safe. I'll be back," he said, striding off with a wink and a wave, and without the posters he'd come for.

Days later, as Aasif and I were cutting through the village bazaar on our daily trek to the hospital compound, an army jeep pulled up and screeched to a halt. Matt and another soldier jumped out and walked back to me. Luckily, Aasif had just made a detour to visit a small shop, and I was waiting outside for him. I was aware that the soldiers and I had attracted the notice of some passersby. "We can't talk in the open," I whispered. "MSF has a strict rule about that." I looked around nervously, praying that no one on my small team was around. I was more worried about MSF finding out that I'd been seen with the soldiers than the possibility that any terrorists might be lurking about.

"We'll make this quick, then," Matt said. "We want you to come to the safe house tonight for dinner. We'll cook up something special for you."

The lure of good food and good company was strong, but I'd never be able to make it. "We aren't allowed out at night, and never alone," I sadly replied.

"Really? Can't you try?" the other soldier asked.

I wanted to go. "I guess I can try to sneak out," I said, not at all sure I could manage it. We set a time and place for a rendezvous, and I hiked back to the compound all the while thinking of how I would do this. The rendezvous (a bombed-out, decaying old shell that someone had once called home) was just around the corner from the MSF house. Just before four o'clock, I simply walked through the gate.

I'd been lucky. The team was smaller than usual—the coordinator and his wife had left for home, the physician was at meetings in Kabul, the midwife was sick, and the interim coordinator was up to his elbows in paperwork. No one would even notice that I was gone. I walked the short distance to our meeting place, slipped into a corner of the deserted building, and waited. Before long, I heard the unmistakable hum of a car engine, and when I peered out, I saw a US Army jeep approaching, Matt at the wheel.

He maneuvered close enough to the building that I could climb into the jeep without being noticed. I slumped down in my seat and was whisked off to the safe house, a short ride away. We pulled off the main road into a series of narrow alleys, then over a rickety bridge before pulling up to the house, a stone fortress ringed by barbed wire, booby traps, and gun and rocket turrets.

From the outside, the house appeared to be in total darkness, but when I stepped inside, the first thing I saw was an American flag hanging in the middle of the main room. There were lights, a television with the news on, someone cooking, and the sounds of American voices wafting through the air. Matt introduced me, and we sat to dinner—spaghetti, meatballs, warm bread, and Diet Coke. After a daily diet of beans, rice, bread, and, occasionally, goat, I couldn't get the food into my mouth fast enough. I never really had to do more than eat. The soldiers did the talking, and the first to speak was the Chief, a tall, thin man who used as few words as possible to say whatever it was he had to say, and today was no different.

"So," he said, his jaw tight, his eyes on me, "how have you been here for over a month without my intel picking you up?" His eyes swept the room, and I could almost feel the men sink a little in their seats.

"Well," I said through a warm crust of bread, "I'm here on an Irish passport, I speak in a brogue, and no one knows that I'm an American. I don't think it's a failure of your intel, I think it means I'm pretty good at this. Don't you?"

Easy laughter erupted. The tension faded, and the Chief nodded. "Now that we know you're here, I wanted everyone to get a good visual—a good look at you. If we ever have to extract you, we need to know who it is we're looking for."

All eyes turned toward me. A flush ran along my cheeks to my ears. I took a long sip of Diet Coke to wash down the last of the bread in my mouth. "Extract?" I asked.

"Rescue you," the Chief answered. Everyone nodded in unison. "You don't carry a weapon, do you?"

I shook my head.

"And you wander around this village and the countryside alone?"

"I'm not alone. I'm with clinic staff or an interpreter. Sometimes I walk alone here in Bamiyan, but I feel safe." And I did feel safe. Of that much, I was certain. The Taliban were under control (or so it seemed), the villagers were kind, and as a bonus, the soldiers were here. How could I not feel safe?

The Chief clearly saw things differently. He raised a skeptical brow and cleared his throat. "If you ever need us, leave a message with Basir at the music store in the center. Do you know the place?"

I did know the place, so I nodded agreement and finished my dinner. Once the dishes were cleared, the soldiers gave me a tour of their house. My jaw dropped as they showed me around. They had rigged up a real bathroom, built bunk beds into the rooms off the main hallway, and somehow hooked up a washer and dryer to an intermittent water supply. Damn, how I envied them.

When I glanced at my watch, my heart stopped. I'd been gone for three hours. I was more worried that someone might have noticed my absence at the house than I was about being targeted by terrorists. "I have to go," I announced. "I have to get back."

Matt and another soldier spirited me back to the vicinity of the MSF compound. I slipped soundlessly from the jeep, the soft hum of its engine the only sound as I made my way along the alleys and back inside the MSF compound. My stomach was full and my eyes were still blinking from the bright lights. I felt a little like Cinderella after the ball when I reached my room. I heated water and took a bucket bath and then read by flashlight. From the corner of my eye, I spied a scorpion stealthily making his way toward me. I froze, remembering the injuries they'd inflicted in Africa. And as the menacing insect neared, I brought my flashlight down hard on his shell. I scooped him up in a tissue and went outside to dispose of him.

Cinderella, no more.

The Children

—◆—

I didn't have much time to think of my dinner with the soldiers or my encounters with the Taliban. I had plenty to keep me busy at the clinics and even at home. My most frequent companions in Bamiyan were the children who lived in the nearby compounds. I spoke with them each morning on my way to work and spent time with them each evening. Some days we played with the magic bubbles I had brought from home. They loved the bubbles, the way the sunlight caught them and made them glisten, the way they were carried aloft by a whisper of a breeze until finally they burst. They taught me to use an *oo-lak*, a hand-fashioned slingshot made of carved wood and the rubber of old tires. To my delight, I got pretty good at it, and I taught the children to give me a high five when I made a particularly good shot. Then we'd all shriek in delight.

On those rare days when they did not have to work at collecting dung or scouring for scraps of wood for fuel, they would come to the hospital clinic to see me. They marched in, usually about six of them ranging in age from two to ten, and would ask for their friend Roberta, although they pronounced it Rabbitta. I would usher them into the triage tent and let them sit there for a bit, their chests puffing out with the privilege. They included Zara, a little girl of about four with sparkling gray eyes; brothers and constant companions—Hussein, about six, and Nasir, maybe nine or ten. The boys spent much of their time working in the fields or collecting dung, where they likely picked up their quick and mischievous natures. Noorem, a small girl who seemed always to be encased in an endless cloud of dust. Even at her young age, she always wore a veil. Zara rarely wore one.

Another child was Nasreen, a spirited seven-year-old girl with sad, deep eyes. The first time I saw her, she was busy beating an older boy. In any other place in the world, my instinct would be to intervene and give a lecture about violence, but here, in this repressed world, seeing a tiny girl take such control and be so sure of her own prowess filled me with hope for her and the women of Afghanistan. I know it sounds wrong, but in this land, I'd never thought that any girl would dare to do what Nasreen was doing and doing so well.

Finally, I did step in and separate them, but when I brushed the dust from Nasreen, I leaned in and whispered, "Well done." Later, I did tell her to learn other ways to assert herself, but it never quite sunk in. I saw her many times go after the boys who bothered her. And secretly, I always smiled to myself.

All of the children were dirty; to wash meant to go to the canal for water or to wash there in the icy water, not an easy or pleasant task for little kids. Their poor hands were cracked with the buildup of dirt. One evening, I snuck them all into the MSF compound; I peeked in first to make sure the coast was clear, and then we all scurried in. I brought them to our bathroom, heated some water, and scrubbed their hands and faces, slathering them with a rich cream to soften their skin. They all glistened and beamed and were quite taken with my scented soaps and creams. They smelled and rubbed their hands and faces for days until the clean, sweet-smelling softness was buried under new layers of dirt. The clothes they wore were most often their only clothes, so their mothers only washed them rarely, and I didn't see them as their outfits dried in the sun.

One day as I returned particularly tired and dirty from a long and arduous mobile clinic, the children raced to greet me and invited me to a potato party. I promised them that after I washed, I would meet them in the fields and join them. They looked skeptical, sure I wouldn't make it, but half an hour later, I heard their delighted squeals as they spotted me jumping over the canal to join them in the fields. The year's potato crop had been good and had just been harvested. Tiny potatoes had been left in the fields, those too small to take to market, so the children gathered them and celebrated their good fortune.

For a potato party, the children dug small holes in the ground and buried several potatoes there. Then they created mud tents over the holes into which they put kindling and set it ablaze.

One tiny boy just couldn't make his fire take off. "*Che taklif?*" ('What's the problem?') he screeched in frustration as he kicked in his mud tent. Minutes later, he was on the ground, rescuing his buried potatoes and trying again and again.

When the fires were really blazing, the children collapsed the mud tents and the potatoes baked while in the ground. After about ten minutes, they dug up the potatoes, peeled, and ate them. That was a potato party. It was very difficult to peel hot potatoes with bare hands and short fingernails. We squatted around the fires as the sun set, sharing hot potatoes and laughter. It was a night I will remember forever; tiny children baking potatoes that they had gathered. Even coated with mud, nothing will ever taste better.

Most of our patients were not as healthy or energetic as my little neighbors, and here, just as in Africa and Pakistan, malnutrition was a big problem. But MSF had a solution, just as IRC did in Africa—supplemental and therapeutic feeding programs for babies and small children. The sickest babies would be admitted to our hospital, while the others—those not in critical condition—could be treated on an outpatient basis, arriving weekly to collect their nutritional supplements, vitamins, antibiotics, and, often, re-hydration therapy.

Raziq was just two years old when his mother carried him into our clinic. He weighed just under ten pounds and suffered from severe malnutrition and diarrhea. He was all loose skin and brittle bones, with hair so sparse, he seemed more old man than little boy. His mother, a robust woman with a ready smile, stayed in the ward with him, sleeping on the floor, sometimes sharing his little cot. She'd left her house, her husband, and her other children in order to help her baby get well. Over the next weeks, we tried everything—antibiotics, IV hydration, tube feedings, oral supplements, and though he had a voracious appetite, he just couldn't gain weight. He cried and fussed constantly; nothing soothed him. His mother, anxious and frustrated at our inability to help her baby, began to pack him up one morning.

I approached her with Aasif at my side. "Don't go," I said. "Give us more time."

She shook her head. "I've been gone too long already. I have to get home." She piled a few of the nutritional supplements we'd given her onto her blanket and began to roll it up.

"One more day," I pleaded, not sure what I thought we could do in one day that we hadn't been able to get done in the last weeks, but something in my voice stopped her. She turned, a fresh line of perspiration tracking along her face. She swiped it away with the end of her hijab, blinking the last bits from her eyes. "*Balay*," 'Yes,' she said softly, plopping back down onto the baby's cot.

Our newest team member had just arrived. The South African physician was heading home and an Australian was taking his place. She'd be here shortly, I knew, to have a look at our facilities, and I hoped that a fresh pair of eyes might see something that we hadn't seen. It wasn't long before Lisa nervously swept into the hospital, her eyes darting from one room to the next. This would be her first humanitarian aid position, and though it had been years now for me, I remembered well the feeling of helplessness I'd felt in the face of such misery. I suspected she was feeling that now, and as her gaze rested on me and Raziq, who'd fallen asleep in my arms, I offered a smile. "Come and meet our mystery baby," I said.

"Who do we have here?" she asked as she moved close. I told her about Raziq's failure to thrive despite our efforts. She nodded and seemed to be mulling it over. "And you've treated him for TB?" she finally asked.

It was as if a light had suddenly gone off. Though TB was as common here as a cold was in the United States, we hadn't tried TB medicine. At her suggestion, we arranged for the medicines to be dispensed through UNICEF, and we sent him home days later with nutritional supplements and enough medicine to last three weeks. His mother had promised to bring him back so we could see how he was doing.

As the days, and then weeks, wore on, I convinced myself he'd likely be sicker if he returned at all. But three weeks later, Raziq appeared in our clinic, carried in by his smiling father. Although he had a way to go, he had gained weight, his face was filling out, the once slack skin on his hands was a little fuller, and, perhaps best of all, the gray of his skin was gone, replaced by a rosy glow. His mother was there, too, standing just behind her husband and hidden in the folds of her burqa. Still, she stuck her hand out and gripped mine tightly. "*Tashakore*," she said, her voice echoing from somewhere under the creases and pleats of the fabric that covered her so well.

Raziq came monthly after that visit, and each month, as we tracked his progress and watched him grow stronger and healthier, we marveled at the miracle of that one last opinion and the change it had wrought for this baby. He was laughing the last time I saw him as his father bounced him up and down. His mother's grateful keenings rang through the halls that last day as she wrapped him up and took him home.

Raziq was only one of hundreds of severely malnourished children that we cared for during my six months in Afghanistan. Many did well, but just as many died despite our best efforts. Often, the sickest among them, those most severely malnourished babies, were brought to us too late and then never returned for treatment. It was an added burden for families to have to come back frequently, and many never did. We tried to follow up on those babies, but in this land of nameless alleys, nameless streets, and long-forgotten villages, that was a near-impossible task. Occasionally we were able to find a family, but they were often just too busy trying to survive, regardless of the consequences for their children, to come back. They surely loved their children, but they had to worry about so much—food, shelter, just surviving—they simply couldn't spare the time or effort to get back to us. There are days, even now, when I can hear the sad and inconsolable cries of dying children, the saddest sound in the world.

But, children here, as in war zones around the world, were the first affected and the last to complain. They learn quickly to adjust and adapt, and they do it quietly and without protest. Their resilient spirits and infinite courage have always impressed me and touched me in ways I could never have imagined.

These tiny, bedraggled children were an amazing lot, and Hamid may have been the most memorable of all.

Hamid's Story

—◆—

Bamiyan's sky was cloudless, the afternoon quiet and still when I stepped from the clinic to the small courtyard, which had been teeming with patients earlier but was empty just then. Staff and villagers had scattered—some for lunch, others for midday prayers. I'd stayed behind to do an inventory of our small outpatient pharmacy located behind the clinic building. I'd jot down whatever we needed, most of which I could find in our pharmacy and supply room by the MSF office. I was headed there when I spotted him—a tiny boy with an old man's sour expression. He stood hunched over, propping himself up on adult-size crutches that had been sawed off midway through to make them easier for a child to use. But they had been made too small, and he leaned hard into the wood, his hands jammed onto the rough wooden tops. He heaved a noisy sigh when he spied me, then he turned, his head nodding to the woman who hurried to catch up. She reached us and pointed to the clinic. "*Basteh?*" she said in a rush, not bothering to share the long greeting.

"*Salaam-aleikum*, and *balay*, yes," I answered, relieved that I'd understood her question and eager to at least offer even a partial greeting. My Dari was still shaky, and though I could manage most everyday words and common medical complaints, I still relied on our interpreter for most of my conversations. But the clinic was closed and I'd just told her that much.

Her thin shoulders sagged, and her eyes welled up.

"*Che ast?*" 'What is it?' I asked.

She dropped her gaze to the young boy by her side and began to speak so swiftly that I could only catch the word for pain—*dard*. And when I leaned down and looked into his eyes—a dull, flat brown—he turned away. In that instant, I could see that his expression, which I'd assumed was simply disagreeable, was really one of great pain. The corners of his mouth drooped, his eyes drooped, his shoulders drooped. Everything about him was wilted and sad. "*Dard?*" I asked, tilting his chin so that we might look into each other's eyes. I wanted him to see that I would help. I offered a wide smile. He grunted in reply. Undaunted, I ran my hand along the crutches, old and rickety and filled with splinters and likely useless on these rocky roads. I sighed and stood up. Without an interpreter, the best I could offer right then was a pair of new crutches. Holding my hands up and bobbing my head, I asked his mother to wait. "I'll be right back," I said. "Don't move." I hurried to the small ICRC (International Committee of the Red Cross) surgical hospital, grabbed a small pair of smooth wooden crutches, perfect for a small boy, and strode back, feeling pretty pleased with myself. Even without an interpreter, I'd likely taken care of the reason for their visit. Or so I thought.

As I headed back, I saw that his mother, a woman likely not more than thirty, seemed as weary and tired as her boy did as she tucked a loose strand of hair under her hijab. She leaned down and brushed a bead of sweat from the boy's brow and whispered something into his ear. I watched as he balanced himself uncomfortably on his crutches. These crutches, I was sure, would make them both smile.

When I handed them to his mother she offered a faint smile and bent to replace the boy's old crutches with these new ones. He resisted, holding on tight to his familiar pair. His mother finally pulled each of the old ones away and settled the new pair under his arms. She tried to demonstrate where he should put his hands and she ran her hand along his back, perhaps to show him he could finally stand straight. But he would have none of that. He shook his head and pushed the fancy new crutches away. As they fell to the ground, he swayed. His mother caught him before he fell, and I reached for the old crutches and passed them back to him. He took them, his eyes filling with tears, his lips curling into a long frown.

"*Mazrat mekhwaham*," 'I'm sorry,' I said. "I thought this might be what you needed. I didn't mean to make it worse."

She held tight to the new crutches and scolded the boy in words so fierce, I knew she meant business. "*Tashakore*," 'Thank you,' she said through a tight smile.

"*Nay, nay*," I answered. "Do not thank me. *Parwan' ast*, no problem." It was hard not to admire his independent and determined spirit.

The woman mumbled something politely, tapped the boy on the shoulder, and turned to go. "Don't go yet. *Famidi?*" 'Understand?' I asked as my eyes searched frantically for anyone to help interpret for me. I held up my hands again in a stopping gesture. "A minute. *Lotfan*. Please."

She seemed to understand and they stood together, her hand resting on his shoulder, the other holding onto the new crutches. It only took a minute for me to spot one of the clinic guards, whose English was as rudimentary as my Dari, but maybe he could help, at least tell them to come back tomorrow morning.

"*Balay, balay*," he said, puffing out his chest a little as I told him I needed help. "My Dari *khoob n'ast*," I said. "*Famidi?*" Together, we approached the boy and his mother, and the guard began to speak to the woman and child. He turned once and pointed to me and then I caught a word here and there. "She is a nurse," he said, "come from far away to help." The woman nodded her understanding. The boy kicked at the dirt.

The guard turned back to me. "It's his leg," he explained, his words slow, his pronunciation awkward, the way I imagined I sounded to him. But all

I needed was to get at least some of the story. "It's bad, very bad," he said, reaching out to touch the boy's left leg. The boy winced and pulled back. It was then that I saw that indeed his left leg hung limply from his hip and only dragged on the ground when he shifted. His right leg and rickety crutches bore his full weight as he moved.

The crutches I'd offered would only be a Band-Aid. They offered no real help, no solution to his problem. No wonder he'd thrown the new pair to the ground. He needed X-rays and a surgical evaluation, something we couldn't offer in our small MSF clinic but something that Franz, the ICRC surgeon, could provide in their small hospital. He'd left for the day, but I knew he'd help.

"Tomorrow," I said to the guard. "Tell them to come back tomorrow." I tapped my finger on my watch. "Eight o'clock. Tell them to look for me. *Namay ast* Roberta. Make sure they understand."

He translated my words, the woman nodded, and they turned and began their trek home, wherever that was. I stood and watched, and for the first time realized that the boy was barefoot, his good foot hobbling slowly as his left leg dangled and his left foot dragged over the rocky ground. He leaned so heavily into his old crutches that even from where I stood, I could almost feel the pain of it.

I wished, not for the first time, that I was back home in the ER, where I could order an X-ray, page a surgeon, and offer instant help. Here, there was little I could do in this moment. My best hope was the ICRC surgeon, and as soon as I finished a cursory inventory of our pharmacy, jotting down what meds I'd need to bring the next day, I slipped my sunglasses back on, adjusted my own hijab, and hurried back toward my home—the MSF compound. At the last fork, I turned right instead of left, deciding to check in at the ICRC house to see if I could catch the surgeon.

Luckily, Franz was at home, getting ready to head back to the hospital for afternoon rounds. He listened intently as I spoke, a shock of white hair falling over his eyes. He laughed and pushed it back into place. "Time for a haircut, *oui*?" he asked before peppering me with questions about the boy and his condition. "I didn't really get a chance to look at him or his leg. He was in pain, his mother was anxious, I guess I was, too. I didn't even get their names, but I did ask them to come back tomorrow. Do you think you can help?"

"I think I'll have to if I want to keep you as my friend." He laughed and pulled me into a warm hug. We'd become fast friends, sharing stories, equipment, and medicine when needed, and I wished more than once that he worked full time with me. But even this—this ability to use him as my sounding board and my surgical consult—was better than not having him at all.

The next morning, I was outside at the clinic, where a pleasant chill, a remnant from the night, lingered in the air. I walked the length of patients waiting to be seen and eyed them all closely. We still didn't have an orderly triage system, so each morning, as patients lined up, I did a quick walking assessment, looking for those patients who couldn't, or shouldn't, wait—malnourished babies, anyone with a fever or the dehydration of acute illness. There were others, too—those who couldn't stand on their own or those who had trouble breathing. We saw the sickest of them first, but we kept our promise to everyone, and our clinic wouldn't close until every single person had been seen.

I hadn't forgotten the young boy from yesterday, and my eyes scanned the crowd for any sign of him and his mother. Finally, just as I was heading in to start my own clinic, I saw them. Standing just beyond the waiting crowd, they stood hesitantly, afraid, it seemed, to move forward through the throngs of people waiting. Anxious that they might just turn and disappear, I pushed my way through and reached them. "*Salaam-aleikum. Sob bakhir. Chetore asti?*" 'Hello. Good morning. How are you?' I asked.

"*Salaam,*" the woman replied, a faint smile on her lips. She nudged the boy forward, and I could see that he was leaning on the new crutches. A familiar frown told me that he still preferred his old ones. "Wait," I said, holding my hand up as I had yesterday. I turned and spied Aasif, our interpreter. I called out to him and he hurried to my side. I told him quickly what I knew, adding that Franz, the ICRC surgeon, had agreed to see the boy today.

"But I need more information," I said, slipping a pen and small notebook from my pocket. "I don't even have their names. I need that, and I need to know what happened to him. Was it an accident? A bomb, or maybe a land mine?" I asked, ticking off all the possibilities in my mind.

But Aasif was way ahead of me; he'd already started speaking, and I could see a trace of a smile cross the boy's lips. "Hamid," he whispered. "*Namay e man Hamid ast.*"

"Fara," the woman said, gripping my hand and squeezing hard.

Aasif rattled off a list of questions, pausing only briefly to fill me in. "She's his mother," he reported. "They came from out beyond Garganatu when they heard that there were foreigners working here in Bamiyan. They've claimed one of the caves as home for now. You know, the caves in the Bhudda hollows. Remember?"

I remembered. I passed by the pockmarked façade of the Bhudda hollows daily; the empty gaping spaces were a constant reminder of the misery the Taliban had wrought. But the tiny cave dwellings that had dotted the face of the mountain for decades remained, and people had claimed them as their own. It was the hardest of hardscrabble living. To get in or out of your home, you had to maneuver up the rocky mountain front, difficult for anyone with healthy legs. I couldn't even imagine how Hamid and his mother did it, and I was almost sorry that I'd asked them back today knowing now the energy it must take to get here.

"They will see the doctor now?" Aasif asked, breaking into my thoughts.

"Yes, but what did she say about his leg? Was it an accident? What happened?"

"He was born like that, with his leg just dangling. The village women said it would get better with time, but you can see for yourself, it's not good."

I wasn't sure if the surgeon could manage a congenital hip problem. He usually dealt with injuries from explosives or gunshots or falls. Still, it was worth a try. I went in search of Franz and found him just as he was finishing up on an old man's infected arm. "Ahh," he said when he saw me. "Good morning. Is our boy here?" I filled him in and he told me to bring the child inside. "We'll get a quick X-ray as long as the machine and the generator are working today, and then we'll see."

Aasif helped Hamid maneuver the three stairs to the ICRC hospital entrance, and I winced as he hobbled and struggled with each step. Once inside, I introduced them to Franz, who guided us along the short hallway to the X-ray room. "We'll have to get him up here," Franz said, patting the metal X-ray stretcher. I wanted to help and I turned and lifted Hamid, but before I could lay him on the table, he screamed in such pain, I placed him back down.

"It's his leg," Aasif said, hurrying to interpret Fara's words. "It hurts too much when it dangles from the air like that."

"Oh, God," I said. "Tell him I'm sorry."

Franz and Fara helped Hamid onto the table, Fara cradling the boy's bad leg, Franz laying him gently under the machinery. I watched helplessly, afraid to make things worse than I already had.

It wasn't long before we were all huddled under the radiology reading screen. Franz flipped on the light and we leaned in closer. The results were clear—Hamid's femur was not connected to his hip. There seemed to be a socket but no ball joint that would slide right in and hold everything in place. My heart sank. This problem was beyond the scope of the small hospital here.

"You see that?" Franz asked, tapping the screen.

I nodded. "What can we do though?"

"Kabul," he answered matter-of-factly. "Kabul. They can fix him there."

"Kabul? How? Where?"

"We have a hospital there. We have an orthopedic surgeon. He can do this. I'm certain. I'll try to reach him later, and we'll see. Okay?"

I shared the news with Aasif and watched as Fara and then Hamid grasped the meaning of Franz's words. Hamid's eyes opened wide, and a genuine smile draped his lips. His mother, tears in her eyes, clutched the doctor's hand. "*Tashakore*," 'Thank you,' she whispered, and I felt my own eyes well up.

The next day, Franz gave us the good news. The doctors in Kabul would see Hamid. There were no guarantees that they could help, but at least it was a start. All we had to do now was get him there, which sounded far easier than it actually was. In the rural countryside, there were no buses or trains. Even cars were scarce, but there were small vans that ferried people about for the right price. We just had to find one. That task fell to Aasif, who managed to arrange travel within the next two weeks. Now, we had to collect money for the trip. Hamid and his mother were alone. They had no one, no other family, no one to help. It would be up to us, to Franz, Aasif, and me to figure this out. Franz and I pooled our money, Aasif booked the seats, arranged for the driver to find a rooming house for Fara, and helped us buy socks and sandals and a new *shalwar kameez* for Hamid.

When the travel day finally arrived, I'm still not sure who was more excited—Fara or me. Hamid and his mother came to the clinic to say good-bye. He leaned easily into his new crutches as he stood waiting for the van to pick them up. It was a rare moment of joy for all of us. It was everything an aid worker dreams of—really making a difference. For Fara and Hamid, it would be the first time traveling to a big city. We gave Hamid cookies and his mother money for the trip, and once he was settled into his place in the van, he rewarded us with a shy smile. Though I didn't know it then, life would never be as sweet again as it was at that very moment.

Hamid and his mother were gone for three long months, and during that time, we had no word from them, no way to know how things were going. We couldn't even be sure if he was still alive. When he finally returned to Bamiyan in late September, my eyes passed over him in the clinic's courtyard. Nothing about him was familiar. No longer the sickly little boy who'd left us, he had grown taller and sturdier, or perhaps because he could now stand tall and straight, he only appeared bigger. It was Fara who caught my eye.

"*Salaam-aleikum*," I shouted, running to greet her, my eyes searching for any sign of Hamid until Fara pointed him out walking toward me, no crutches, no pain that I could see, a happy smile on his glowing face. I stopped cold, my eyes wide, my mouth agape, and then I pulled them both into a happy embrace.

To see him stand and walk without crutches was a moment of pure joy, but that moment of joy wouldn't last. Although none of us knew it then, Hamid was already very sick. Silently, bacteria were swimming through his bloodstream, attacking and destroying his organs, stealthier and more deadly than any bombs used by the Taliban. It took days for the signs of his sickness to emerge, and his mother likely just didn't see the gray tint that crept onto his skin, the utter fatigue in his walk and the listless sigh he heaved each morning. When she knew that something was wrong, she brought him back to the hospital, but by then, there was little that could be done.

I didn't know that Hamid was sick until several days after his admission when I stopped at the hospital on my way to the mobile clinics. Fara spied me through the window of Hamid's room and ran out to me. I was delighted to see her and thought she must be here with a friend.

"*Salaam-aleikum,*" I called out happily as I walked toward her. "*Chetore asti*?" 'How are you?'

But as I drew closer, I saw her tears and felt her panic. "Come, come," she cried as she pulled me into the hospital and into a small room, the shades drawn, the stench of sickness and rot heavy in the air. I gasped when I saw him lying there on the metal cot, his eyes closed as if in sleep, his skin the color of the faded rocks that lay in the sun too long. He was slick with sweat, his hair plastered to his forehead, but it was his breathing, raspy and rapid, that shook me to the core. My own wave of panic set in. I rushed to find the new Afghan doctor on duty to find out what was going on, but his English was poor and he hadn't known Hamid's history.

"He's septic," I shouted, as if by shouting he might understand me, but he only shook his head. I ran to the ICRC building to get Franz but he was gone, back to Switzerland for a break, they explained. He'd left while I'd been out on a mobile clinic. A staff member gave me a letter saying that he'd left, but I had no time for that just then. I shoved it into my pocket and went in search of Franz's replacement. Yuri, a young man with an easy smile, was the new surgeon. In a rush of words so fast I wasn't even sure I understood what I was saying, I told Yuri about Hamid and asked him to have a look. "He needs help," I begged.

He followed me back, and as Fara and I stood and watched, he examined Hamid and read his flimsy chart. We did not have a real lab. We couldn't do blood cultures or wound cultures or even white blood cell counts. We had to guess at infections and guess again at treatment. Yuri smoothed the sheet that covered Hamid's delicate frame and turned to me. "I'm sorry to say you're right," he said. "He's getting antibiotics, but they're not working. You can see for yourself. Even if we could get him back to Kabul, it would be too late. He's in kidney failure now. There's nothing I can do. I'm sorry."

How could this happen? I was so angry at this miserable place, this world, that would allow this little boy, who'd been so close to a happy childhood, so close he had touched it, to be so sick and so near death. And Fara, how could she possibly bear this? I took her hand and held it tight, biting back my own tears.

Hamid died in the still of a dark and lonely night, wrapped in his mother's arms. I learned of it the following day, but Fara and her boy were gone, and though I knew she lived in the caves surrounding the Bhudda hollows, I didn't know which one. I couldn't even find her to share my own sadness.

She came back to the clinic a few days later. She wanted to return the crutches I'd given him so that another child might use them. Even in her moment of greatest despair, she was a courageous and selfless lady. We hugged and cried and I told her how I had loved Hamid, too. I had taken pictures of both of them, and I promised to send them to Aasif so that she could have something tangible to remember him by. The story of Hamid, which should have been the sweetest success story imaginable, turned out to be the one that even now breaks my heart to share. But he is still remembered and still loved. I can see him even now on the day he returned to Bamiyan, his bright smile, his sturdy walk, his sparkly laughter.

I hope perhaps that you can see him, too.

Amir and the Distant Clinics

———◆———

Although there was misery here in Bamiyan Province, there was good news, too. We drove several days a week to distant villages to provide much-needed health care. In one of those clinics, in a village called Shaidan, a small boy of about ten pushed his way in and introduced himself. "*Salaam aleikum, chetore asti, khoob asti, jonna jurast?*" he greeted me. "I am Amir. I want to help," he declared, a sparkle in his eye. Though dressed in rags, barefoot, and likely hungry, he carried himself with the distinction and self-satisfaction that only a young boy can muster.

"What do you want to do?" I asked. He'd apparently been watching, and he pointed to the growing crowd. "I'll be your assistant, your *chowkidor*, a doorman."

"*Aacha*, okay," I said, still not sure exactly what he planned to do.

A heavy and tall wooden gate and mud wall surrounded this clinic, which consisted of a tent and small plaster building perched on a rocky ledge. The ledge was always crowded with people hoping to be seen. To help manage the crowds, I first triaged the group so that we might see the sickest first. Once that was done, we gave out numbers and tried to see people in some sort of order, women and children first, and then men. And that was where Amir took over. He kept track of the numbers called and happily shouted out the next number, granting entry to our patients only when it was their turn. He held out his hands and stamped his feet to keep people from crowding the door. Those waiting sometimes hurled angry insults his way, but he stood firm, guarding our door with an iron hand.

When I first met him, I wondered how he found the time to help us. UNICEF had opened a school in Shaidan, and Amir should have been there. "No, no," he muttered when I asked. "How can I go to school? There is too much to do. Besides, I know my numbers. That's all I need." He told me that he had to work as a shepherd to help support his family and that his father did not want him to go to school. That was the tradition here in the distant hills of Afghanistan: everyone had to contribute to the household. Amir was one of six living children; two others had already died. His family suffered from a chronic lack of food, money, and hope, but the little that Amir earned in the fields really did help his destitute family.

The Taliban had never encouraged education here and had actually forbidden it for girls. The Taliban knew what vicious dictators around the world know—an uneducated population, unable to read, unable to understand the world around them, is much easier to control. But with the Taliban on the run, UNICEF was fighting back, opening schools around the country and encouraging all children to attend. Those who did could be seen scurrying over the dusty roads, happily carrying their plastic UNICEF bags filled with notebooks and pencils and the seeds of dreams. I wanted all of that for Amir, who, though working long hours in the fields, appeared faithfully at the clinic when I was there.

I couldn't pay him. If word got out, there'd be trouble with the village elders, who'd want us to pay their own children. Instead, each week, I tried to bring him a small gift, something just for him. I asked the Afghan staff in Bamiyan to help me choose the gifts. At first, I asked them about toys. "Where can I buy toys?" I asked. "What do children here play with?"

The Afghans furrowed their brows and looked at one another. "Toys," I said again, louder this time, mimicking throwing a ball or driving a small truck. The Afghans laughed. "There are no toys here," they replied, and though they didn't say it, I could see it in their eyes—that, for a foreign woman, I was likely stupider than they thought. It turned out that children here, as in so many places around the world, created their own playthings out of objects that they found, much like the *oo-lak* that my neighbor children had made.

Although I couldn't give Amir toys, there was much that he needed. One week I got a sweater, then sandals, later a small world globe, and finally, a pen and paper, the last ones in hopes that he would someday go to school. No matter the gift, Amir was effusive in his thanks. "*Besiar tashakore*," he said, repeating it over and over. A friend from Maine sent me a box of toys after I had written about Amir and my fruitless quest to find playthings here. The box included small action figures and plastic soldiers. I was sure that Amir would need some kind of toy orientation before playing with them, but as soon as his grimy little fingers pried open the box, he quietly drew in his breath, grinned widely, whispered "*Tashakore*," and ran off before anyone could grab his treasures. He never returned to the clinic that day.

Amir and I often talked about his future; I told him that I hoped he would be president one day and to do that he had to go to school. "If you get an education, you can do anything," I said.

He always shook his head and giggled at my hopes for him; his own dreams for the future were much smaller and more practical—enough food in his belly and a place to sleep at night. I struggled to instill in him bigger dreams and hopes. For the future that Amir envisioned and that his father envisioned for him, school was an unnecessary distraction. Why learn to read, for after all there is nothing to read here, no books, no magazines, no newspapers, no reason to learn. To count one's sheep or goats at the end of a day in the fields, that was all that mattered to Amir and to millions like him around the world.

I pointed to a plane flying overhead one day. "You could fly that plane if you wanted," I said. His eyes followed that plane until it faded into the blue of the distant sky.

"How?" he asked, as though I'd offered the impossible, and in a way, I had. "School," I answered triumphantly, certain that he finally understood what I'd been saying all along. "You could even be president one day," I added. Amir rolled his eyes. I'd broken the magic of the moment with that last thought.

I didn't give up the struggle though, and when his father appeared at clinic to collect his son, as he sometimes did, I'd take him aside and ask him to reconsider school for Amir. He inevitably shook his head. "*Nay*," he replied firmly each time I asked.

"Well, just think about it," I pleaded, determined not to give up.

Amir missed clinic one day, and I assumed he'd been too busy in the fields, but at our next clinic, he arrived when we were just finishing up. "*Salaam-aleikum*," he cried, raising his hand in greeting. In his hand was a UNICEF school notebook. He opened the pages and pointed to the Persian script, which he was learning to read and write. He was the first in his family to attend school, and to wonder if someday he might fly that plane, or maybe even be president. And, busy as he was, with school and work in the fields, he still did his best to get to my clinic, to manage the door and the patient flow. I felt as proud of him as if he'd been my own child.

When I left Afghanistan, we had a tearful good-bye, and he promised me that he would stay in school and study. I think about him often, and I hope that he has been able to do just that. For Amir, the reality is that he is probably back at work in the fields, tending sheep and helping to support his family.

Another of our regular outlying clinics was held weekly in a village called Garganatu, a three-hour drive, compared to Shaidan's one hour. The roads were dustier, rockier, and more angular, curving through villages larger and smaller, but Garganatu was centrally located to several other villages, so it was there we set up our clinics in a crumbling but still serviceable one-room storehouse without windows and just one door-less entry that didn't allow in much light. One Afghan physician and I usually made the trip, sometimes with another expat, though most often it was just the two of us.

The villagers trekked for miles and waited for hours to be seen, and when they saw the dust of our jeep coming through the village, they ran to crowd the doorway. They stood outside waiting noisily, each one more aggressive than the last to prove that he or she was sicker and should be seen right away. They knew already that we could not see all comers, since the ride back was long and we'd have to leave enough time to be sure we would be off the roads before dark. This meant that many would go home disappointed, which made them all the more anxious to be seen.

Compounding the problem was the high number of malnourished babies here in Garganatu. A large part of the weekly clinic was follow-up and distribution of nutritional supplements to the babies and mothers. There were several acutely malnourished babies in this village whom we had wanted to bring to Bamiyan for admission to the hospital. Without intensive monitoring, IV hydration, antibiotics, and supplemental feeding, it seemed certain that some of these babies would die. The hospital at least offered a chance for the sickest of these babies. Very few villagers agreed to come to Bamiyan; it was just too far away and they were afraid—of the distance, the hospital, our Western ways, and the strangeness of handing their babies to people they didn't know for treatment they didn't understand. All it took was one whispered rumor of a baby who had died in Bamiyan, and the villagers were steadfast in their refusal. Despite my promises and stories of success, they refused to leave their homes or give me their babies for care. I understood their reluctance, and though I never did learn the art of convincing them to do what I thought best, they did what they believed best. It wasn't that they didn't love their babies, for they surely did, but the fear of leaving their villages, their families, and their responsibilities was a more frightening prospect.

Aside from the malnourished babies, these villages were inhabited by many elderly, who came with the usual elderly complaints of body aches and fatigue. I guess if anyone in the world is entitled to those complaints, it is these elders, who've lived through so much. Still, for all their complaints of frailty, I admired the way they pushed and shoved and demanded to be seen, and seen early and often. Many came every week, and they hated to wait. They were a feisty and engaging crew, and we tried to see them all. I still made it a point to see the children first, then the women, and, last, the men, unless clearly someone was sick enough to be taken out of turn.

We had to work quickly, and there was never enough time to just sit and get to know these people and hear their stories. It inevitably seemed that we ran out of time before we ran out of patients. Those we hadn't been able to see were promised that the next week, or maybe the week after, they'd be among the first to be seen, but promises are flimsy in Afghanistan, and more than one villager cast an angry glance our way.

We were holding a biweekly clinic now in the village of Acrobad, not quite as far as Garganatu but still another long drive from Bamiyan along winding, unpaved roads. In the village, we were given an old, dilapidated two-room house to set up. We used the first room as a waiting room for the women and children. That allowed the women time to socialize, lift their veils and share a laugh, a rare opportunity in their busy lives. Village women didn't just raise the children, cook the food, and tend the animals; they worked the fields, gathered firewood, and literally kept the home fires burning.

Acrobad's children were always covered in dirt and a fine layer of chalky dust that settled onto the dirt. It covered their skin and gave them a ghostlike appearance. I could never figure out where the white dust came from, and no else knew either, though one man thought it might be from the village's grain thresher. These children appeared at the clinic each time we were there, just to watch us. They hung at my elbow, stared at the patients, rested their chins on their hands, and observed intently as I examined patients. Since none of the patients complained, I let them stay. They were not just a welcome diversion for me; they were also a great help. They would laugh out loud at some of my Dari pronunciations and eagerly correct my mistakes.

"*Tashakore, tashakore.*" One small boy almost rolled on the floor mimicking the faults in my accent. He held his belly and shook his head. "*Khoob n'ast,*" he declared loudly. "*Tashakore,*" he'd shout, encouraging me to try again, and though I always did try again, my Dari never quite met their standards. But they never gave up. As long as I showed up, they did, too, rolling their eyes and poking one another at my pronunciation of their language.

Despite the lack of regular health care, the villagers were really a hearty bunch. Aside from the chronic malnutrition, which affected most to one degree or another, very few villagers were really sick. The complaints were nothing out of the ordinary—a cough, diarrhea, skin rashes—but here the women seemed bolder, more outspoken. They didn't hesitate to ask about women's issues—fertility problems and possible solutions. They smiled and giggled when they asked, and though we couldn't help with their fertility matters, they had some satisfaction in just asking.

As in all of the clinics that we ran, people invariably asked for soap, the little bars of magic which seemed to make their skin shine and glow if only for a day. We always brought plenty. It was such a small gesture, but by improving hygiene, the little bars of soap could literally save lives.

One woman came to our clinic, as so many did wherever I was, without any medical complaint; she only wanted some soap. Her name was Rasa-Begum, and though she guessed her age at about thirty-five years, her rheumy eyes and deeply lined face made her seem twenty years older. She was as thin and washed out as the clothes she wore. As with so many others, Rasa did not even have a place to call home. Acrobad was just a stop on the way to somewhere better, but that someplace was still out of reach.

In a slow, halting voice, with Aasif interpreting, she sat down and told me her story. "The Taliban have always hated the Hazara," she said, folding her hands in her lap. "You must have heard the way they tormented us—the killings, the torture, the fires—they were the face of evil, but we fought back. All of us. We ignored their new laws; we laughed when we could, and allowed our children to play. And they took notice, and the whispers spread. They'd arrived in Bamiyan, it was said, and they meant to crush us and bend us to their will." She paused, her eyes drifting beyond me, perhaps remembering.

"*Aacha*," 'It's okay,' I said, trying to soothe her. It wasn't okay at all, but it had become my go-to phrase, the word I used to let people know I would listen and try to help. But I couldn't help everyone, and Rasa seemed to sense that. Still, she continued.

"We lived out there," she said, pointing to someplace just beyond Acrobad, a smile creeping slowly onto her face. "Begum, my second name, means 'a lady of status,' and I was. My husband had a small shop where he sold tea, flour, biscuits, even Coca-Cola. We were happy, but the Taliban didn't want anyone in this country to be happy, and so they came." She stopped and spun the plastic bangles on her wrist.

I forced myself to be quiet. Though I wanted to say something comforting, I knew this was her story and she had to tell it her way.

"It was cold last winter. The coldest winter I can remember," she said, a sudden shiver rising to her shoulders.

"It's true," Aasif added. "In January and February, the temperature was below zero out here. Well below."

Rasa nodded. "And that's when they came, when they knew there'd be no escape for us because of the snow and the cold. We could only watch as they slaughtered our animals, and when they were done—they began to round up the men, and that night, as the snow flew and the cold clung to everything, we left. I think that everyone left. We wore our coats and just ran. We carried nothing, afraid of being slowed down."

"Not even matches?" I asked, thinking that a fire would have kept them warm.

Rasa shook her head. "Why?" she asked, her eyes crinkling. "A fire, no matter how small, would have given us away, and we thought the Taliban would just leave, and we would be back in our homes within days. We ran into the nearby mountains and huddled together, the cold deeper than we'd imagined. The mountains offered no protection from the snow and the freeze in the air. And, I suppose I might have thought then that maybe a small fire would have worked, but the Taliban thought the same, and within hours, our village was filled with flames. They'd set fire to our homes and our fields, and all we could do was watch, and maybe pray that the heat would reach us. It never did, and my husband and I and our two girls curled together to sleep."

"'Tomorrow,' my husband said. 'Tomorrow, we'll decide what to do.'"

"Where was everyone else?" I asked.

She shrugged. "In the mountains, we scattered. It was safer to be apart, or so we thought." A lone tear tracked along her cheek. "The next morning, I woke to a quiet I'd never known. I pushed myself up and saw that all that remained in our village was rubble. Smoke still rose, but there was no sound, there was nothing left. I turned to my husband and called his name, but he was as still as the air, and when I moved closer to his face, I saw the icicles frozen there on his beard and even his eyelashes, his skin was already blue. I clamped my hand over my mouth. I couldn't scream. I couldn't attract attention. I woke my girls and we slipped back to the village, scrounging for whatever was left."

I leaned toward her. It was late July. I asked how they'd survived, and if she'd been to Bamiyan to register with the UN office there so that she could get some assistance.

"*Nay*," she said wearily. "We have no way to get there. We're staying here until we can find a way to Bamiyan."

I looked at Aasif and knew he was thinking exactly what I was thinking. Our jeep was always packed with staff and supplies when we went to Acrobad, but if she could get to Shaidan, we could give her small family a lift from there. Aasif asked her about our hastily devised plan.

"*Inshallah*," 'God willing,' she said quietly. By August, Rasa and her children had made it to Bamiyan, where I saw her later. They were living in a tent and had acquired some small treasures—cooking equipment, clothes, and a washing bucket. Though her life was still a hardscrabble one, when she smiled, the color and life were back in her eyes.

These remote and distant villages, which were fast becoming accustomed to our clinics and our medicines, would be inaccessible in the winter months. Snow, ice, and freezing temperatures would make these roads impassable by January, but worry about that would have to wait. Our immediate concern, at the end of a long day in clinic, was to race the deepening shadows of dusk and make it home before darkness fell, before mines placed hastily in the road would become invisible to our drivers, before the bandits would appear from the shadows to rob or rape or kill us.

I never for a minute thought that anything bad would happen to me, to any of us there, but isn't that the lament of every single person who's run into just that kind of trouble? Still, for me, ignorance and that kind of deathly self-confidence were my own kind of bliss.

The Tragedy of Land Mines

O ne morning in late July, while working at the hospital-based clinic, I received a radio call that a land mine had exploded under a bus and there were many severely injured. I had recently developed an ER disaster plan with Franz, and we began the process of implementing it, a process that felt both familiar and comfortable to me. If there was anything that I could manage, it was exactly this type of incident.

We cleared all of the patients out of the clinic area, discharged hospital patients who could safely go home, and started setting up equipment and assigning roles to Afghan staff. We planned to use the MSF health education tent as an initial triage area, and we cleared that area, too, and set up necessary equipment. We set up our ER as a minor treatment room for suturing and wound care and expected about twenty-five badly injured victims, based on the initial radio call.

We heard conflicting reports—the severely injured would be arriving by helicopter and I needed to find a helicopter landing site. If a helicopter was flying the victims, I assumed my soldier friends would be managing the transport. I didn't know anyone else who had access to helicopters in the region. Franz and I hurriedly chose a suitable landing site in a dried-up irrigation field across from the hospital. Then we sat and waited, and in this land without phones, computers, or easy communication, we were at the mercy of the terrible road conditions and unreliable communication.

Finally, at 2:00 P.M., some four and a half hours after the initial reports of an explosion, the first patients arrived in the back of a car. There were no life-threatening injuries, but there were patients to triage, wounds to clean and sew, and tears to dry. Hours later, the last of the injured arrived. I went to the back of the car and evaluated people as they came out. A boy of about ten got out, cradling a tiny, frightened boy in his arms. The bigger boy was uninjured, but the smaller boy was covered in soot from the explosion, so I took them into the tent for a better look. The poor little thing was terrified, but luckily, once we got a closer look, he, too, was without injury. I got him dressed and, assuming their parents were somewhere in the tent, I asked the older boy where they were. He looked up at me with large, trusting eyes. "They are coming in the next car."

My heart stopped. The only car en route to us now was the one that we had sent to collect the eleven dead. To be sure, I checked the patient roster for their parents' names; they weren't there. My stomach churned, my eyes filled up, and I shepherded the boys to a room in OPD. I plied them with cookies and juice we'd purchased from the bazaar as I tried to figure out what to do. I had trouble looking at their exquisitely trusting faces, knowing what I knew. Finally, an uncle who had heard about the accident showed up and I took him outside to share the information we had. The uncle remained stoic and only nodded at the news. He went in, gathered the boys into his arms, and took them away, their pockets stuffed with cookies, their mouths draped with crumbs.

Their bus, I learned, had been returning its passengers from Bandi-Amir, a vacation spot here in Bamiyan. Bandi-Amir held snowcapped mountains, a glassy-surfaced lake, lush landscape, and some of the most beautiful views in all of Afghanistan. The passengers on the doomed bus were families from one small village who had spent two days and one night there, a trip they had long planned to escape the devastation that marked their lives. They had slept under the stars, fished for their dinner, frolicked in the cool waters. For two magical days, they'd left their sadness behind. The ride home was filled with laughter, traditional songs, and gaiety. For those last moments, they had no cares, no burdens, just the joy of being together.

And then, in the midst of songs and laughter, the bliss was over as the bus rolled over an antitank mine dug into the road. It can tear apart a tank, but it can obliterate a bus. In a millisecond, the bus was blown in half and passengers were trapped underneath the debris, screaming in pain, many dying as helpless family members looked on.

One passenger was chosen to go for help, and after a long trek along the hazardous road, he was able to get word to a village, which passed on the information to us and sent people back to help. But it was too late for the poor souls who lay bleeding and crushed under the twisted metal. That mine tore apart not just a bus that day but the lives and hopes of its passengers, including the small boys and their family. Their parents had three sons, the oldest a teenager who was newly married and not able to make the pleasure trip to Bandi-Amir. The excursion had been a treat for the two youngest, and they had possibly the best two days of their young lives; they had unknowingly created memories that would have to last a lifetime.

I'd always felt safe here, despite the soldiers' warnings and even the bus explosion. I'd long since discarded that wariness which keeps you on edge and keeps you safe. And it is then—when you let your guard down—that anything can happen. I was well aware that the roads to Garganatu, Shaidan, and Acrobad were littered with land mines and unexploded cluster bombs. The Afghan drivers made light of stepping on the gas as they navigated perilously close to the still dangerous remnants of war. The too-close calls and risk to all our lives made me angry as hell, but it never deterred them, and there was little I could do aside from passing the information and locations of the unexploded ordnance (UXOs) along to the soldiers so that they could clear them out.

There were many dangers here, not just from the UXOs but from either terrorists or bandits, or just criminals, who were now targeting aid workers. It was common knowledge that we carried no weapons, that we were "soft" targets. To attack an aid vehicle meant acquiring radios and money and sometimes even the vehicle, and all of it without a fight. It was hard to say who the perpetrators were, Taliban maybe, who wanted all foreign influence out of their country, or maybe bandits who just wanted easy money, or perhaps even Al-Qaeda regrouping and attacking as a way of creating chaos and fear and letting the villagers, the soldiers, and the world know they were back.

Either way, as the war seemed to wind down, the attacks seemed to pick up. After an MSF vehicle departed Bamiyan heading to another aid program to our north, that car was ambushed and robbed, a gun held to the head of a staff member. He left Afghanistan shortly after that incident. The others in the car were visitors from Paris, and they, too, left soon thereafter. Another time, an MSF car that was carrying money for staff payroll was robbed as it left Kabul; luckily the Afghan driver survived the gunshot wound he suffered. The dangers to aid workers grew each day, prompting MSF to issue a curfew and tell us to tighten security. In Bamiyan, we were already not allowed out at all after dark, no exceptions.

Another NGO's vehicle was ambushed at night; the men were beaten, robbed, and tied. The lone female, an American, was dragged away and brutally beaten and raped by several men. She survived, barely. An IRC car was ambushed, shot at, and robbed just outside of Mazar-I-Sharif, a city northwest of Bamiyan. All of these worrying incidents happened within days and weeks of each other. We had little access to outside news and events—the news trickled in slowly, often from the UN office or the ICRC staff. We had only one satellite phone, and it was often down. We communicated via radio, which was often unreliable. The MSF office in Kabul checked in once, sometimes twice a day, but when they couldn't reach us, they never panicked, they just tried again later.

Despite the MSF curfew, we were allowed to go off alone during the day. The reality was that daylight could be just as treacherous as the dark of night. Most villagers either carried weapons openly or had quick and easy access to them. It was how they had always protected themselves, and it was a mainstay of their tradition and culture. For us, it sometimes made it all the more difficult to tell the good guys from the bad.

In August, the soldiers told me that there was an upsurge in violence just north of us in Qumard, an area that had earlier harbored Taliban elements. Fighting broke out there between Taliban insurgents and locals who wanted them out. A school was burned there, reportedly by the Taliban, to remind the citizens that education, at least according to them, posed evil ideas and thoughts and was a threat to Islam. Unrest was simmering and gathering strength just beneath the surface throughout the countryside.

Even though there were weapons and likely terrorists still lurking about, I never really felt unsafe here. I rationalized the incidents and assaults on aid workers and told myself that if the victims had only traveled before dark and stayed on main roads, the clashes might not have happened. At least not to me. But isn't that how we all react to crime? *Not me. Not ever.* It wasn't that I felt immune or somehow smarter than the others who'd met a tragic fate, but I had the advantage of having come to know so many villagers throughout this region, and I felt sure that I would be protected if problems developed. I also knew that the soldiers were silently watching out for me, and as long as they were around, I would be safe.

The women of Afghanistan were not as lucky.

The Women of Bamiyan

———•◆•———

I n late summer, numbers indicated that maternal deaths were increasing
in the distant villages. Afghanistan already had one of the highest
maternal mortality rates in the world, mostly due to the lack of emergency obstetrical care. In addition, pregnant women, already in vulnerable
and tenuous condition from chronic anemia and malnutrition, just never
came to the hospital when problems developed during pregnancy or labor
and delivery. They delayed and waited so long that by the time they finally
arrived at the hospital, there was often little we could do. We had no blood
typing or transfusion capability, so women simply bled to death. The ICRC
surgical team could take women to the OR to repair tears suffered during
childbirth, remove placentas, or do D&Cs or hysterectomies, but when a
woman presented with an already life-threatening condition, our inability to
administer blood transfusions always made it a race against time and a race
against the odds. The odds were too often stacked against us. Something as

simple as a blood transfusion would have saved their lives. It was just one of the many contributing factors to Afghanistan's outrageously disproportionate maternal mortality rate.

For village women who had heard of the maternal deaths, it further convinced them to delay seeking medical care until the last possible moment. Many believed that the hospital was the source of the problem. This rationale just kept the cycle of death continuing. It was difficult to convince them that they had a better chance of survival if they would only come to us early.

One young mother, Laila, was still a girl, just sixteen years old, when she arrived in the back of a car accompanied by her mother and sisters. It was her second pregnancy; the first had ended at seven months when she'd delivered a stillborn baby girl. In this pregnancy, Laila was likely even more malnourished, more anemic, and less likely to survive complications. When she'd developed heavy bleeding and sharp abdominal pains during her eighth month of pregnancy, the village birth attendant knew that Laila needed medical help. Her husband, however, didn't agree, and it took a full day to convince him that she could die without it. On the second day, he gave in to her family's pleading and gave his consent. They pooled their money and hired a car. Only her female relatives accompanied her to the hospital in Bamiyan.

Laila arrived lying in the back of the car, her skin ghostly pale and covered with a glistening layer of sweat. She watched as we moved her, a look of sheer terror in her large, pleading eyes. Finally, with the aid of a translator, we tried to let her and her family know that she would need an emergency Cesarean section and possibly further surgery to save her own and her baby's life. In this country, neither she nor her female relatives could give consent for surgery; that could only come from her husband.

We sent word to her husband that Laila needed emergency surgery, and as the hours ticked down, we waited. It would take almost a day for him to get the message and longer still for a reply. At the hospital, we hovered over Laila, gave her IV fluids and medicine to help slow the tragedy that was unfolding in her uterus. It was all in vain. By the time her husband arrived, almost two days later, the light had gone from her eyes and the fetal heartbeat was barely audible. Both this fragile young mother and her baby were dying. In a last desperate attempt—and, I suppose, because we weren't ready to give up—the ICRC surgeon took Laila to the OR, but she and her baby, a son, died shortly after he was born. We struggled to save both but could not save either.

Another young and frail woman delivered a baby at home and began to bleed heavily; rags and pressure used by the village birth attendant didn't slow the loss of blood. Finally, a day after the birth, she was brought to us. Her skin was a dull gray, she was unresponsive, she was dying. But as dire as the situation seemed, we were desperate to help. I think that we all believed in miracles; sometimes, when you are in a place as cruel and unforgiving as Afghanistan, you have to believe.

We had all learned to estimate blood count by checking the eyes and mucous membranes of patients, and it was clear that this woman's blood count was critically low. On his exam, Franz found a tear in her cervix that was the likely source of the blood loss.

"Well," he said as though searching for the answer. "I might be able to save her." But his words were without conviction. Her husband had brought her to us, and he quickly gave his consent. Franz took her to the OR for repair, but there were numerous bleeding sites, so he was forced to do a hysterectomy.

This young woman, whose name I never learned, died shortly after surgery. The news brought her sad, hunched-over husband to his knees in fits of endless, wracking sobs. Her baby had survived and was at home, cared for by his mother and sisters. A simple blood transfusion would have saved this young woman, but it was beyond our capabilities.

Women had always suffered in this nation. They were the last to be fed, the last to be clothed, the last to be educated, the last to be heard, and yet it was the women who held the fabric of this society together; women like Fara, who struggled to save her son, Rasa who'd escaped the ravages in Acrobad, and all of the women here who kept the traditions, worked the fields, had the babies, cooked what little food was available, and gave hope to the children.

The women I met in Afghanistan were genuinely kind and gentle beings who worked from dawn to dusk—backbreaking work in the fields early in the day, and then on to the chores in their tiny mud houses until late into the night. But even with that, there were still celebrations and moments of joy. Healthy babies were born, malnourished children recovered, and hope was restored.

In September, we were invited to the wedding of one of our interpreter's brothers in a compound not far from our own. We had a new coordinator, who'd decided to lift our curfew for the night so that we could attend. The wedding was held in the groom's home, where the new bride would come to live. The home was large by Afghan standards—several rooms in one mud house. The preparations had been elaborate. There was enough food here to feed most of the village, and most seemed to have been invited.

In this repressed society, men and women, including the bride and groom, celebrated separately, each in a different room, with same-sex family members and guests. Women were guided into the bride's room, which was jam-packed with women and girls. Safely tucked away here, far from the prying eyes of men, the women blossomed; they were without veils, they wore brightly colored makeup, and they were laughing and dancing to the sounds of traditional Afghan music played on an old tape player. The joy was contagious; I had never seen Afghan women so carefree. For many, this was a short respite in a life of chores, and they enjoyed every minute.

The food was plentiful—specially prepared rice sprinkled with raisins and carrots, a tray of roasted goat meat, little cakes, warm bread, yogurt, melons, mulberries, more food than I'd seen in months. But there was no wine, no champagne toast. We settled for tea with enough sugar to put you to sleep.

Almost hidden in the crowd were the bride and her attendant, sitting against lush cushions and accepting congratulations and compliments on the bride's beauty. She wore a simple but elegant gauzy white gown. Her head scarf, made of delicate lace, was draped loosely over her head. Her hair hung free, long, thick curls reaching to her waist; her eyes were rimmed with heavy black kohl, and her lips were painted a deep ruby red. Against the powdered white of her skin, the effect was striking.

Who could say what her future held? That night, it didn't matter. For the remainder of the celebration, the women and men remained apart, each group celebrating without restriction. It was well into the night when we were summoned home, but the celebration continued into the next day, and I fell asleep with the echoes of their joy ringing in the air.

The next day, as I sat with Aasif and Abdul, a driver who lived here in the village, I lamented the life the bride likely faced. Aasif's jaw fell. The long crease in Abdul's forehead deepened as he ran his fingers along his beard.

"What?" I asked. "Are you both living on another planet? You've seen what I've seen. Women here are barely noticed aside from their babies and their chores. What's with the surprised looks?"

Aasif raised a brow and turned to Abdul, who dropped his hand from his beard and nodded. "Women are honored here. We care for our mothers, ours sisters, our children. It's not true that women are treated badly. You've surely heard the legend of the lady rebel?" he asked.

I shook my head.

"Ahh," he said, sinking low into his chair. "There is a lady rebel here in Afghanistan. When the Taliban first came to power, she saw their evil and watched their murderous ways, her heart breaking with every new story of torture and misery. And though she should have been afraid for herself, she was more afraid for her people. And one day, she left her family, her village, everything she knew, and she took up arms against the Taliban."

I leaned forward. "*Sai'est?*" 'This is true?' I asked, feeling a bit of my healthy American skepticism.

"Of course, it is true," Aasif said, a bit of irritation in his own voice. "Just listen."

Appropriately chastened, I settled into my own chair while Abdul continued.

"She is a warrior for goodness, they say. She wears men's clothes, and her hair, plaited and running halfway down her back, is uncovered. She carries an old Kalashnikov rifle in her saddle and a pistol in her hands as she rides bareback across the mountaintops."

"Is she alone?" I asked, now intrigued by the image of this lady rebel.

"No, no. She commands a group of men now, rebels who follow her lead, but she is in charge. They take their orders from her."

"Have you seen her? Do you know her?"

Abdul sighed. "I'm sure I've seen her," he said, leaning back and pointing to the nearby mountain range. "I think most people have, but I don't know her, though I am certain that she is one of us—a Hazara, for only a Hazara woman has that kind of courage. She remains hidden, and may be living here in Bamiyan. When danger strikes one village or another, she mounts her horse, gathers her men, and sets off. Understand?" He turned to Aasif. "What about you?"

Aasif shook his head. "She's never been to Kabul, I think. But she is here somewhere in the countryside, and yes, I think too that she must be a Hazara. *Inshallah*, I will see her someday soon as well."

"What exactly does she do?"

"Anything that needs to be done," Abdul answered. "Her deeds are legendary; her reputation for courage boundless, but she is most well known for killing the Taliban and rescuing villagers. It's been said that she's responsible for killing more of the Taliban than any man here."

"Where is she now?" I asked. "Surely, she can come out of hiding now that the American soldiers have crushed the Taliban?"

"The Taliban are quiet, but not crushed," Abdul said firmly. "They are still here, some in villages to the north, others in the south. She will stay a mystery until they are done."

As I listened to the stories of this remarkable woman warrior, I began to believe, too, and even now, I can almost see her as she flies on horseback across the top of a distant mountain range, her plaited hair flying out, a bandolier strung across her chest, as she saves her countrymen and women from one calamity or another.

Last Days

———•◆•———

I n mid-September, I finally took my much-needed break and went to
Thailand for a week. Before I left Bamiyan, I spent several days clearing
out any evidence that I was an American. It was likely that visiting
MSF staff would use my room while I was gone, and I felt it necessary to get
rid of American newspaper clippings and magazines that friends and family
had sent me. Each night, I used the papers as kindling for my bath water.
I had saved the newspapers and magazines to bring me closer to home, but
I knew that it would be better if they were not found.

In Thailand, I connected with Mike, the head of Freedom Medicine's
construction projects, who was retired and living in Bangkok. He'd arranged
a hotel for me, and, after two days of travel, I arrived tired and dirty, my
feet encrusted with months of grime. Instead of jumping into a real bed,
I jumped into a warm and inviting bubble bath in my hotel room and
scrubbed myself clean. I met Mike for breakfast, but all I was interested in
was a cup of hot, black, brewed coffee. I returned to the hotel, slept for a

while, and slipped back into the bath for another long soak before meeting Mike for dinner and then drinks at Cheap Charlie's—a famously rustic and eclectic expat bar, which has since closed.

Although I was happy to be in civilization, Bangkok was an assault on my senses. There were too many people, too many lights, too many cars, too many shops, too much food to choose from, and too much noise. I felt overwhelmed by it all. We visited the Buddha temples, went on a tour of the city, and shopped for bargains at roadside stalls and shops, and in the time left over, I sat riveted to the BBC news on television.

On my last night in Thailand, I stopped alone at an outdoor café and drank chilled wine as I watched the people, the stars, the civility of life here, knowing that not so far away, life was so different for so many, an endless struggle just to survive. It was difficult to reconcile that there was so much in so many places and so little in so many others, and after seven days in the chaos of a busy tourist city, I was glad to head back to Bamiyan.

The trip back would take another two to three days, and, depending on weather and road conditions, I wouldn't arrive until early October. My assignment with MSF would be finishing up in just weeks, but there was still so much to do for the people who'd become my family, my friends.

In early October, shortly after my return, I was told that MSF France had determined that we should close our outlying and mobile clinics. The very people so in need of our care would now lose it. MSF France felt that any emergency in Bamiyan was over, and they planned to redirect their resources.

MSF would inform the village councils that they would be ending their visits. The people here were used to disappointment; this was another in a long, endless line of defeats for the people here. Working the last of the mobile and outlying clinics was bittersweet; I knew that we had made an impact here, but I had fully expected the mobile clinics to continue to rove the countryside and provide health care in these distant, often forgotten mountainous regions. Shaidan, however, now had a permanent clinic, staffed by an Afghan physician and nurse who would also live there in the clinic building. Amir, though, would lose his job of *chowkidor*, and I hoped that would give him more time for his studies.

I didn't really have the luxury of sitting and lamenting all that would soon be lost here; there was still a lot of work to finish up. At all of the clinics, we had initiated "ORS Corners," where dehydrated babies and children could be rehydrated and observed for a day before being discharged home. So many deaths in babies result not so much from the primary disease, such as diarrhea, but from the often deadly consequences of severe dehydration. Around the world, we can save so many if we can only rehydrate them, a simple procedure. Taking the time to ensure rehydration also allowed us the necessary time to teach parents how to recognize and treat dehydration. Although we used and gave out packets of ORS (oral rehydration salts), it was easy enough to make at home using sugar, salt, and boiled water, and it was important that these people knew how to do that. We spent a lot of time teaching people how to make and use ORS. It may well have been our best and most lasting contribution here.

Though it had never really been consistent, the MSF expat team was in flux once again. People came and went with regularity, and we remained acquaintances, coworkers, but never really friends. We lived disparate lives in Bamiyan. I spent my free time with the villagers I'd come to know, or with the soldiers, or the Afghan staff. I spent more time at the ICRC staff house than I did at my own. I wanted to wring every bit of living here out of my experience in Bamiyan. I wanted to ride a donkey, eat with my fingers, work on my Dari skills, wash my clothes in the stream, eat dinner with the soldiers, and, when I was done, I wanted it to have mattered that I'd been here.

I had settled into this village as though I was one of them. I'd grown to love these stalwart people, these laughing children, the snowcapped mountains, the dusty roads, my secret meetings with the soldiers, and even, unbelievably, my mud room. I'd become a part of this place, even more so after a woman in Shaidan gave me a beautifully embossed antique cuff bracelet as a thank-you gift. I told her I'd wear it forever and remember her kindness every day. And I have.

I arranged a good-bye party at Mama Najaf's. The remaining MSF staff, including all of the Afghans—interpreters, drivers, physicians, nurses—attended, along with my friends from ICRC. We gathered for a dinner of kebabs and bread and Coca-Cola, a rare opportunity for most of the national staff. We danced and sang and reminisced, and when it was time to go, the Afghan staff presented me with beautiful gifts, which they could ill afford and which will always be treasures to me. But the greatest treasure I received was the one of friendship with the people of Bamiyan.

Saying good-bye to the soldiers was difficult as well. Although Matt, Joe, and the Chief left Afghanistan shortly before I did, others would be here longer, still missing home and family, reliable hot showers, and cold beer. They told me that the United States was making plans to invade Iraq. My stomach churned at the news. "Have we been attacked?" I asked, my voice cracking.

"No," the Chief said, "but we're going in anyway." He shrugged. "We do what they tell us."

I spent my final days in Afghanistan wondering about an Iraq invasion. What would happen here, where the peace was tenuous, the Taliban still lurking in the mountains, their very presence still striking fear deep in the heart of this country? But who could I ask? My questions wouldn't be answered here by a French team, and at this late stage, I didn't want to invite any ire or doubts about who I really was. So, I spoke in my soft brogue and counted the hours until I could be myself once again.

I was to fly out of Bamiyan on a UN flight to Kabul, a rare opportunity to see my beloved Bamiyan from the air. As I picked up my suitcase to make the short trek to the landing strip, the neighborhood children watched in dismay, frowns draping their grimy faces. A mother I'd only waved to came out as well and took me aside. "Can you take my boys?" she asked, pointing to the brothers who were part of the magical band of children I'd come to love. "*Lotfan*, please," she said softly just as Grace had asked in Africa only the year before. I could only shake my head. "I'm sorry," I said. "I can't." But my brain suddenly filled with the possibility of bringing them all home. It wasn't realistic. I knew that. Afghanistan doesn't allow foreign adoptions of children whose parents are alive, but it was always there for me—the unspoken wish to be with them again.

The children hadn't heard the mother's plea, and they followed me happily to the airstrip. As the little plane circled and then came in for a bumpy landing, the children began to cry. "Don't go," one shouted, while another threw her arms around my legs. I bent to them and held them all in one long hug that would have to last a lifetime. I boarded the plane, my face pressed to the small window, and I waved as the plane took flight and rose higher and higher until they were lost from my view, but never from my memory.

Several months after I'd left Bamiyan, Aasif and some of the other Afghan staff managed to save and pool enough money to rent time on a village satellite phone to call me. On their first tries, they reached only my answering machine, which recorded the great consternation in their voices as they tried to understand why no one was speaking, and why they only heard beeps. "Hello, Rabitta, it us calling from Bamiyan. How are you?" And then there was silence until Aasif piped in. "Rabitta, Rabitta, are you there? Hello, Rabitta, hello, hello . . ." These days, modern technology has allowed us to keep in touch in other ways. Aasif is back in Kabul, married now and with children of his own, and we are friends on Facebook.

I've kept in touch, too, with the soldiers who provided me a respite from my Irish brogue and sometimes just kept me going with laughter, food, and soap.

In June 2004, five MSF staffers were ambushed and shot to death in cold blood as they returned to their compound from a mobile clinic in Bagdhis Province, northwest of Bamiyan. That tragedy brought to thirty the total number of aid workers killed in Afghanistan since January 2004. It was an extraordinarily high number. In July of that same year, MSF announced that they were closing all of their programs and leaving Afghanistan.[1]

Abdul had been right—the Taliban were back and they were more evil than ever, targeting the very people who were there to help. The stark reality was that the danger inherent in aid work had increased. It was no longer simple rocks, it was bullets and beheadings, and there was no safety net. No one, it seemed, could rescue the rescuers, and that simple fact made my heart ache. None of us would ever be really safe again, but if we ceased all aid work, then the Taliban would win, and that somehow seemed a worse fate. Many NGOs pulled their international staff back to Kabul, where they would be less vulnerable. But the threat remains, and, sadly, many aid workers—myself among them—have chosen to stay away until there is at least some semblance of safety. And with ISIS and Al-Qaeda joining the Taliban, that time may be far off.

Late in 2004, the Agha Khan Health Services, an NGO that supports health and development in some of the world's most hardscrabble spots, stepped in to fund and upgrade the services provided at Bamiyan hospital. In 2017, they opened the new Bamiyan Hospital, a wonder of modern technology in the midst of such desolation. Today, they provide state-of-the-art outpatient and inpatient services, emergency care, radiology and lab capability, major surgery, and—so vital for the women here—expanded obstetric services, including blood transfusions.[2] It is the best thing that could have happened there, and someday I hope to see it all for myself.

Although tragedy and danger still linger in Afghanistan, triumph does as well. The long drought has finally ended, farmers are harvesting crops again, and though there is a long way to go, there are an estimated three million children now attending some form of school. The literacy rate for girls is only 32 percent, compared to almost 62 percent for boys, but there is better access to health care for everyone, including women, throughout the country.[3]

And the children I came to love so are still with me, their precious images running through my mind—Hamid with a sturdy walk and a steady smile, Amir clutching his UNICEF notebook, Zara, Hussein, Noorem, and the other children from the village, and little Nasreen—always ready to pick a fight with any boy who dared her, and who reminded me of the inspiring tale of the lady warrior. Perhaps the lady warrior does exist after all. It is certainly her legend that continues to inspire the people of Bamiyan and beyond, because despite its persistent miseries, Afghanistan is a place where even in its darkest hours, hope lives, and, for me, that hope is never more evident than in the legend of the lady rebel.

The Time Between

F rom Kabul, I flew to Dubai, a luxurious city of skyscrapers, lim-
ousines, and exclusive hotels. I was met by an MSF volunteer, who
drove me to a hotel somewhere in the crush of gleaming buildings,
posh malls, and people, the women in long black abayas and veils, only their
eyes peeking out, the men in fancy suits and shoes so shiny they seemed
to catch the sun. If Bangkok had overwhelmed me, then Dubai just might
send me over the edge. Two days before, I'd been listening to the chewing
of my mystery ceiling roommate, swatting at enormous flies, heating water
for a bucket bath and washing my own clothes by hand, and yet, in the
blink of an eye, I was in the midst of more luxury and extravagance than
I'd ever seen anywhere.

The hotel was likely average by Dubai standards, sumptuous by my own. Still dressed in traditional Afghan clothes, I'd planned a long soak in a warm bath, but I'd spied a bar on the way in, dark and smoky and mysterious, the hum of conversation and clink of glasses streaming through the entryway. The hell with my bath; I wanted to ditch my brogue and have a glass of wine. Trouble was, I had no money. In my room, I fished in my pockets and my backpack and came up with a few Afghan rupees, one euro, and two American dollars. Undaunted, I combed my hair, reapplied my lipstick, draped my head scarf over my shoulder, and headed down to the bar, wondering if I could afford a glass of wine and a moment of luxury on my paltry pocket money.

I took a seat at the bar and looked around. I was the only woman in a sea of men, and I knew immediately that my grimy skin, limp hair, and Afghan clothes wouldn't matter. I was right. Within minutes, two men offered to buy me a drink. "White wine," I agreed, nibbling on the free appetizers—not the rich cheeses and breads I might have expected in Dubai but peanuts and potato chips in little bowls scattered along the mahogany bar. But beggars can't be choosers. I'd fill up on peanuts and wine and head to bed soon. I had an early flight to Paris.

Don, a balding, big-bellied man in a plaid shirt, signaled the bartender for my first glass of wine and settled in to tell me his own story—something about oil fields and a home in England, but I was barely listening. I was watching the overhead television, looking for news of Iraq, but there was nothing. Edouard, a Frenchmen (wouldn't you just know?) nodded his head, and a second glass of wine appeared. He was more interested in hearing about me than sharing his own particulars, but I was wary and gently deflected his questions. After a second glass of wine and a sip or two of the third, Edouard invited me to his room. I wasn't surprised that he'd ask. Don frowned at being edged out, but he needn't have worried. "No thanks," I said, sliding from my stool. "I have an early flight." A deep crease appeared in Edouard's forehead. He cleared his throat. "So, you know, I thought . . ." he began, his smile fading, his accent thicker than it had been only a moment earlier.

"Thank you again," I said, waving him off as I slipped quickly from the bar and back to my room. The next morning, I rose late, just barely making my flight to Paris, where I was interviewed at the MSF office to see how the mission had gone. MSF had booked me into a rooming house, and I made my way from the office into the Paris subway and then through the winding streets to my place, a single room in a third-floor walk-up with a shared bathroom and no television. There was still no news of Iraq, no talk in the MSF office, no headlines in the newspaper kiosks on the streets of Paris. I was beginning to think it was only a rumor.

Less than two days later, I was almost giddy as I boarded my flight for home, and there, I learned it was true. The United States was planning to invade Iraq.

V

IRAQ

2003

Preparations for War

———◆———

In January 2003, I was asked to be a member of the IRC emergency
team that would respond to Iraq. We would be on call and deployed
into Iraq once the inevitable invasion was winding down. I had been
home from Afghanistan for just two months when I joined the team.

Although IRC expected that we would be leaving within days or weeks
at the most, political posturing and the search for international support
delayed the inevitable war and we waited. It haunted me that while we
waited for the conflict to begin, so, too, did the women and children of
Iraq. It was hard to imagine how frightening that must have been—where
would we attack and how, and would it happen that day or the next, or
the day after that? Impossible to imagine ourselves in their shoes, but we
tried to keep that in mind as we made our own preparations.

In those early days, it was widely assumed that the greatest danger
we would all face would be from chemical and biological weapons. In

preparation for that possibility, an IRC physician and I were sent to a three-day intensive training seminar in Washington, D.C., where we learned to recognize, deal with, and manage casualties from those potential scenarios. As emergency team members and supplies waited around the world to be activated, we also researched the country we were about to enter. This assignment would be my first to be *first in*, first to assess, design, and implement the programs. In the past, I'd slid into already established roles and spent my time taking care of refugees. Iraq would be a whole different ball game.

Prior to the Gulf War and international sanctions imposed in 1991, Iraq had enjoyed a modern health care system with large, well-staffed, well-equipped hospitals complete with modern technology, where health care services were readily available to most of the population. They'd had a modern infrastructure, including an extensive network of water purification and sewage treatment systems delivering clean, safe water countrywide.[1] But the 1991 Gulf War and subsequent sanctions resulted in a complete breakdown of those systems. We would be faced with an already frailer population. In many areas, people were without access to clean water, health facilities, schools, electricity, and more. Raw sewage, at the rate of half a million tons a day, was being pumped into the country's main water source, the Tigris River, creating an environment that fostered the spread of disease, since so many people used this as a source of drinking water. We assumed that the public health needs would be enormous, but, we were prepared. IRC had equipment and WHO emergency kits containing enough medicines to help us provide health care to ten thousand people for three months. The supplies were positioned around the world, ready to be shipped to Kuwait and on into Iraq once the team was working inside Iraq. We'd prepared for every possible scenario.

At least we hoped we had.

Deployment

———◆———

F inally, in late March 2003, within days of the US invasion and with industrial-strength lipstick and Irish passport in hand, I was deployed to Iraq by way of Kuwait, which had become the staging area for the US and Coalition forces and aid groups. Direct flights—in fact, most flights—to Kuwait had been cancelled due to the threat of bombings. I flew first to London and from there to Dubai, where the flight information screen described my final flight to Kuwait as "Cancelled." When I approached the airline desk to ask about it, I was asked for my ticket and passport, and then I was quietly informed the flight would actually be departing on time. The "Cancelled" notice was a ruse to trick would-be terrorists into thinking the flight was off. I spent the last hour there wandering around until I found an Irish pub. There wasn't time enough for that just then, but I filed it away for my return flight. Final boarding was announced at the very last minute, and I raced to make my connection.

Kuwait City is a modern desert city with paved streets and lush green lawns, the last made possible by the desalination of ocean water and its distribution throughout this wealthy desert land. The streets were populated with luxury cars, and the homes in the city center were more palace than house, each more ostentatious than the next. The workers here were not Kuwaiti; they were imported from dirt-poor countries like the Philippines, Bangladesh, India, and Pakistan.

This IRC team had gathered from around the world. Adam, the field coordinator, was from Australia; he had a chiseled, tanned face, an easy wit, a soft, honeyed accent, and he was relentless in his expectations of all of us. Phil was a member of the headquarters staff in New York but had been deployed to Iraq as a member of the initial team to provide communications expertise and leadership for this vital project. Phil, tall and distinguished looking, had a dry, sarcastic humor. The team consisted of me for health and Jason, another American, who lived in Bulgaria, for water and sanitation services. Considering that we had come together as perfect strangers, we became a perfect team, the best of friends in the worst of times. Although others would come and go, this was the core team with whom I would work.

Adam was responsible for logistics—getting our equipment ready to go once we were settled. Jason would do the water and sanitation assessments. Without the electricity that powered the water pumps, clean water was already an issue. I would be responsible for health assessments, proposal and grant development, and program start-up. I'd always been involved in providing care in well-developed programs with systems for medicines, equipment, and staff already in place. This time, I would be the person responsible for doing the assessment, writing the proposals, and designing the programs. We'd already done the research. We just needed to get into Iraq to see the situation firsthand.

We lived in an apartment/hotel in Kuwait City. Many other aid groups were living here as well, all of us waiting for the signal that we could move into Iraq. The hotel was an impromptu meeting place, where we could collaborate on programs and goals. The IRC team members were all housed on the same floor, and we kept our doors open so that we could yell to one another across the hall. We had kitchen facilities, television, electricity, and though there was a small restaurant on the first floor, none of us could afford to eat there every day. I wasn't a cook, so I bought eggs, peanut butter, bread and fruit, and wished for a glass of wine to wash it down. But this was another Muslim post—no wine, no beer, no whiskey, though there were always rumors that the French, or maybe the British, or was it the Swedes? had access to alcohol. It's true that the things you can't have are the things you always crave, including not just wine but freedom. I was required to stay covered again, all of this in the dreadful, sweltering heat of an Arab desert. I had brought clothes for a cooler climate; I seemed destined to never get it right.

Every morning we attended a briefing at the HACC (Humanitarian Assistance Coordination Center). The HACC was an effort by the Coalition forces and Kuwaiti government to keep the NGOs informed about the situation in Iraq and to allow us to keep them informed about our plans. The briefings were run by the British Army with input from US forces. These daily meetings were held in one of many large classrooms in a Kuwait City school that the Kuwaiti government had taken over for the war. When I first arrived in Kuwait, there was plenty of space in the meeting room and more than enough seats for the attendees, but within days, the room was crowded and we were all squeezed in.

Each morning, I slid into my seat and took copious notes, including in-depth security data that told us where the fierce fighting still raged, along with detailed information on land mines—where they were and what areas we should avoid (the whole country, I supposed, if we really wanted to be safe). Maps with meticulous coordinates of suspected land mine sites were just too detailed to make sense of, so we planned to do what we do around the world—stay on established roads, stay away from the shoulder of the road, avoid shortcuts and untraveled roads, and, finally, always look first. We all knew that countless victims followed all the rules until they stepped right onto a land mine. There are sometimes telltale signs—the shiny edge of a buried mine, disturbed ruts of earth, rocks arranged just so—but in the end there may be no signs at all. Luck is often the best we can hope for, and that extends to missile attacks as well.

Our daily briefings were sometimes interrupted by the screech of air-raid sirens signaling a missile attack. Everyone scurried to don their protective gear and gas masks. Ours hadn't arrived yet, and we moved quickly as we were herded into a "safe room" and waited for the all clear. Within days, the siren seemed more of a nuisance than a need to move quickly. Some missiles landed, most did not, and none landed near us. Just as some of us began to ignore the siren's wail, the attacks stopped. The invasion was well underway, and the Iraqi forces likely had more on their minds than vexing those of us hunkered down in Kuwait. And there were plenty of us to vex.

NGOs and humanitarian aid groups from around the world, some as small as the US Salvation Army and a Danish church group, along with all of the larger groups—IRC, MSF, GOAL, Mercy Corps, IMC—had shown up in Kuwait. The US government bureaucrats were here in the fullest force imaginable. The USAID DART teams (United States Agency for International Development Disaster Assistance Response Team), along with the newly appointed administrators of ORHA (the US Department of Defense Office of Reconstruction and Humanitarian Assistance) were so well represented, they could have filled the room by themselves. The USAID DART teams were here to assess the Iraq situation for themselves. As the branch of the US State Department that provided grants and money to the NGOs for their emergency interventions here, they were keenly interested in everything that was happening and in everything that we were doing. They came in full force to the meetings. Adorned in their DART bulletproof vests with gas masks and chemical suits at the ready, they stood out.

The ORHA representatives were presidential appointees and would administer the various sectors of the Iraqi government and run the country once the war was over. These, mostly men, were stationed in Kuwait along with all of the NGOs waiting to move into Iraq. Jay Garner, a retired general, was to head ORHA until a new Iraqi government was in place. He had been handpicked by Secretary of Defense Rumsfeld, in large part due to his leadership of Operation Provide Comfort, the US military humanitarian mission in Kurdistan after the 1991 Gulf War.

The ORHA officials that I encountered in Kuwait were surely capable and seemed to have the best expertise for the specific responsibilities they would manage. The physician who would be the interim director of health in Iraq was a well-respected, accomplished, and outspoken doctor with years of international experience under his belt. He, too, had been involved in Operation Provide Comfort. He was a forceful, highly regarded physician who could assess a crisis efficiently and determine quickly what interventions would be needed. His was an appointment that gave all of us faith that this situation would be well managed.

USAID and ORHA representatives were booked into the Kuwait Hilton, an ostentatious, overpriced icon of excess in this country of excess. I went there occasionally for meetings and was horrified that our tax dollars were being spent there. After one meeting, a USAID team member asked if I had brought a bathing suit so that I could swim.

I rolled my eyes. "Nah, I never pack swimsuits when I travel to active war zones," I replied dryly.

"Oh," she said, somewhat surprised, "you should."

I take my war zones seriously, I thought, but I didn't have the courage to say it out loud. (Well, I do take my lipstick, but that's another story.)

Waiting

·—•—·

With everyone who was here, the UN was conspicuous by their very absence. Although their umbrella organizations—UNICEF, WFP, and WHO—were here and working hard, the UN had stayed away. For all of the disagreement that we may have with the UN, it is they who take the lead in humanitarian crises around the globe. It is the UN that helps to define and focus the collaborative efforts of the NGOs in the field. The verbal skirmish between the UN and US government leaders regarding the invasion had left the UN feeling bruised and battered. Still, we knew that we needed them here and were relieved when, in April, they finally moved in and began directing our relief efforts.

Besides the daily military briefing, we collaborated with USAID, UNICEF, WHO, and the multitude of other NGOs on revisions to the WHO Rapid Health Assessment Form, a form that would guide us through assessments. Although called "rapid," the form was actually eleven pages long, and the information it requested was vital to our work—age and sex data, birth rate, death rate, immunization rate, frequency of disease, available medical providers, available medicines, accessibility to shelter, food and water, sanitation facilities, and health care. Because we were in the early days of the invasion, we also planned to look at other issues, structural damage among them. Were homes habitable? Were hospitals and clinics damaged or safe? What about the condition of schools, the water supply?

We were prepared. Our WHO emergency kits had arrived in Kuwait, and Adam was working with Customs to get them released to us. We were anxious to get into Iraq, and a few, tired of waiting for the go-ahead from the coalition, ventured in while the war still raged. An ICRC worker from Canada was caught in cross fire in Baghdad and was killed. An MSF French field coordinator I had worked with in Afghanistan was taken hostage and held outside Baghdad for ten harrowing days until he was found safe.

Three members of an Irish aid group decided to rent a car and go inside to see for themselves just what was happening. Unfortunately, the Irish had a terrible sense of direction and no compass. (GPS in 2003 only provided coordinates, not directions.) They took one wrong turn and wound up in Basrah in southern Iraq just as the fighting there intensified. Assumed by the Iraqi forces to be spies, they were taken in for questioning and held overnight in the crumbling Basrah Sheraton, which was without electricity, food, and running water. Informed that they would be sent to Baghdad at first light, the three spent a restless night, the sounds of war just outside their hotel, the sky illuminated by the tracers' and rockets' glare.

The luck of the Irish prevailed, however, and by the next morning, the Brits had captured the city, the Iraqis had fled, and the Irish fellows prepared to get back to Kuwait. When they approached the hotel's exit, they were met by a staffer, who handed them bills for their rooms. The trio took the bills, promised to send money, climbed back into their rented car, and sped back to Kuwait with stories that would keep us doubled over with laughter for days.

Within days, we were finally given permission to enter Iraq. My team would head to Nasiriyah to do our assessments. We did not yet have our expected all-terrain SUVs, so we rented a red Ford mustang for our first trip into Iraq. Aid workers usually traveled in shiny white SUVs; a Mustang, we thought, would give us cover and easy accessibility to areas that might harbor trouble. Four of us were going in: Phil, Jason, Salim—a Tanzanian who would help with supplies—and I. We had no idea whether or not we'd find sleeping accommodations, so we brought camping gear and our own food.

We packed crackers, peanut butter, cheese, fruit, instant coffee, sardines, and a few chocolate bars. We crammed the food into the trunk, camping and personal gear into the back seats, and then we squeezed in. It was definitely a squeeze. The old car had a tape player but no air-conditioning. Still, we headed into Iraq thinking we were pretty damn well prepared and pretty damn cool. But that feeling soon dissipated in the sweltering heat of the Iraqi desert, and, since we were alone in just the one car, we created a mini-convoy by following another NGO, Mercy Corps, into Iraq. We would split up once we arrived in Nasiriyah; they were headed further north.

The road into Iraq, the scene of fierce battles just days earlier, was littered with the fresh remnants of war. Burned-out shells of Iraqi tanks and vehicles littered the scarred roads; along the sides of the roads were fragments of bombs and other pieces of scorched and blackened debris. In the distant desert, we could see smashed and falling-down power grids. There was no doubt that we were in an active war zone. These modern battle scenes were traversed by camel caravans, which gave it all an odd, otherworldly feel.

For the entire seven-plus-hour drive, we were enveloped in a sand and wind storm. At every checkpoint along the route, we had to get out of the car and stand in the swirling sand while a variety of soldiers—Kuwaitis, Brits, sometimes an American—looked at our travel papers and decided if we would be allowed to travel further. The sand seeped into the car through the cracked open windows, and by the time we reached our destination, we were covered in the fine sand; even my nostrils and ears were gritty. We arrived in Nasiriyah tired and dirty, but finally, we were in Iraq.

Our first stop was the US military CMOC (Civil-Military Operations Center) to let them know we were here and to get a fresh security briefing and general information about the area. "There's no running water here," the soldier cautioned. "Have you brought enough?"

Shit! Shit! Shit! We hadn't even thought of bringing water. I shook my head and admitted that, as cool as we thought we were, water had never made our list of things to pack. We had a damn water engineer with us. How the hell could we have forgotten that? The officer didn't blink. Smiling, and likely chuckling to himself, he gave us two cases of water and invited us to stop by if we needed more.

After a few miles more, we reached Nasiriyah, the city where American soldiers had been ambushed, with some killed and others captured in the first days of the war. The US tanks, damaged and useless now, lay in pieces at the side of the road, a silent tribute and reminder to all who passed by of the terrible events and incredible bravery that had taken place here. The town itself had suffered heavy bombardment, although the targeting appeared to have been amazingly precise, for although there was some collateral blast damage, many buildings remained untouched.

We headed to the city center and stopped at a crumbling hotel that was somehow still standing despite the obvious damage of blown-in windows and walls. Several men were outside sweeping up broken glass. They stopped to watch us. "Any rooms to rent in town?" Phil asked. The men looked at one another and then at us. It was clear that they needed our money and we needed a place to stay. "Right here," one shouted in clear English as they ushered us in with warnings to avoid the shards of glass that littered not just the street but the hotel lobby as well. We made our way around bits of broken furniture piled high in front of the windows. "To keep looters away," one of the men said proudly as they showed us to rooms that hadn't been damaged too badly. There was no water, no electricity, but in the early dusk, the place had its own special ambience.

I was the only woman, so I had a room to myself. I had a smashed balcony door and shattered windows with glass scattered on the floor, allowing me a permanent and pleasant breeze, which deposited more dust and grime on the once-white sheets that covered my bed. The room next to mine had taken the brunt of the attack. The walls were blown in; debris remained strewn all over the room, the quiet and shadows of dusk creating an eerie tableau. I stood transfixed. "You coming?" Phil called, breaking my reverie. I closed the door quickly and headed out to help unload our car.

The food that we had so carefully packed—the fresh fruit, the precious cheese and sweet chocolate—all of it—had melted and rotted in the heat of the trunk. Even the peanut butter had separated and turned into a hopeless, oily mess. We stood together, mouths agape, and cursed again our lack of planning. We would have to find food here in Nasiriyah or survive on crackers, the only food that had survived the heat.

Phil went in search of food and was able to buy a small cooked chicken. We ate in the dusty and decaying but surely once elegant ballroom overlooking the Euphrates River. As the sun slid into the horizon, we switched our little flashlights on, creating a soft glow that hid the worst of the dust and rubble all around us. The dinner was as sumptuous as if we'd been eating at the Ritz. At least that was what we told ourselves. Ninety percent of survival for us was attitude and humor, and we had plenty of both.

So far, despite the recent battles fought here and the fresh damage we'd seen, this journey had just seemed an excellent road trip. But we were here to work, and the next morning, we set out. Phil and I headed on foot to the city center to get a feel for the people here. We still weren't sure how they felt about the invasion and our presence.

Once we set foot on the main road that held the city's bazaars and stalls, we were surrounded by crowds of well-wishers. People were smiling, patting our backs, shaking Phil's hand, nodding to me and offering copious thanks. For what? I wondered. They had no electricity, no water, and no jobs at the moment. It was the soldiers they were really grateful to, and they expected that soon enough their lights would be on, their taps running with fresh clean water, and their pockets jingling with the money that follows aid workers. In the meantime, people were using the river water for washing and drinking. And that reality sent shivers up our collective spines. That dirty water could surely bring outbreaks of cholera and typhoid and God knew what else.

"Can you give me a job?" one man said, his eyes flashing.

"Not yet," Phil replied. "We're here to see what needs to be done."

The man's shoulders slumped and he wandered away, only to be replaced by another man.

"You know that soldier—that Jessica Lynch?" he asked.

We both nodded. She had been captured and severely wounded by Iraqi forces in late March. Held at the Saddam Hospital in Nasiriyah, she was initially reported as missing in action until she was rescued by a special ops force on April 1, 2001, just weeks before our arrival.

"I helped to get her out," the man said, pointing to himself. "It was me. I told the soldiers where she was, that she was in the Saddam Hospital. Can you let them know I'm still here? I'd like to get out, too."

Before we could answer, more came forward, all claiming to have helped in her rescue. "It was me," each declared, taking credit for her rescue. "We all knew she was being held there," one man added, pointing to the crowd around him. "We all helped in that rescue." The onlookers nodded in agreement.

"I am Dr. Said," one bespectacled man said, elbowing his way toward us. "I took care of her."

I instinctively, and carelessly, raised a brow.

Dr. Said had noticed. "No, no, it is true," he said without rancor. "Her back was broken, her legs were crushed. We planned to amputate her leg, but she cried out and resisted, so we did what we could. She was gravely ill. Do you know how she is now?"

I shook my head. We hadn't heard any details of her injuries or recovery, and had no idea if what he said, if what any of them said, was true. The descriptions the doctor and others had shared would turn out to be eerily accurate, and I wondered later how their accounts could be so accurate if they hadn't somehow been involved in her rescue. Perhaps this entire town had somehow conspired to save her. A local lawyer was the only one ever named by the United States as helping to locate Ms. Lynch; in late April, he and his family were quickly and quietly granted asylum in the United States. Perhaps he was one of several to pinpoint her exact location, though he was the only one to get the credit. It didn't seem fair, but nothing else here did either.

We continued along the street, the crowd in our wake. Shops and stalls were open, selling squawking chickens, fresh bread, rice, tea, but there were few buyers. People had no money. Offices and businesses had slowed and then stopped completely as the invasion had neared. For many, it had been months since their last paycheck. We could only reassure them that WFP would be in soon, delivering food rations, and the military was working hard to get the electrical grid back up. Once that was back, fresh water could be pumped into homes once again. Until then, people were using water from the Euphrates River and were, by their own admission, not generally boiling it before drinking. Although bottled water was being distributed by the US Army Civil Affairs (CA) group, not everyone had been able to get it, and many who had been able to get it had decided to save it instead of using it.

The people we met nodded and smiled, confident that it would be a mere matter of days or even weeks before things were back to semi-normal. Forgotten in that first blush of new freedom and hope was the fact that nothing ever really works out the way we think it will.

Nasiriyah

———◆———

W e spent the next few days doing what we were there to do. Jason spent his time evaluating the water and sanitation supply, or what was left of it. I visited the local clinics and hospitals and looked at the existing health system and its capacity, and the population in general, to determine the health needs here.

Many of the clinics and hospitals here had been looted of anything that was not nailed down. Even nailed-down items were eventually pried up and carried off. Some facilities had actually been protected by staff who had stayed behind in their hospital or clinics to prevent looting and vandalism. At great risk to themselves, they had blocked doorways with sturdy lengths of wood, and saved their equipment and medicine so that they could continue to provide care.

I spent some time trying to track down the head of the health department, but this was a town still in chaos, and to be identified as a government official now meant admitting connections with Saddam, and no one was willing to do that quite yet. One by one, they shook their heads. "I do not know who was in charge," they answered when I asked, sending me back to the drawing board to figure out what was needed here.

The lack of electricity had disrupted the cold chain—the refrigeration required to keep vaccines fresh—and countless doses had to be destroyed. UNICEF was busy ordering large and sufficient quantities of vaccines to reestablish the immunization system once the cold chain was available. Medicines, really a lack of them, were also a big problem; there just weren't enough and we had no idea when that situation would improve. We had plenty of emergency medicines—antibiotics, pain medicines, intravenous fluids—in our supply kits, but there was a critical shortage of medicine for chronic problems like hypertension, heart disease, and TB. USAID had acquired some of these drugs and would be distributing them among hospitals, clinics, and NGOs.

Chemotherapy drugs, necessary for cancer treatment, were essentially nonexistent. What little had been available had been looted or damaged or had simply expired. People who had been undergoing chemotherapy now faced the unimaginably frightening prospect of permanent interruption of their treatment.

Late one morning, while I was evaluating a clinic on the outskirts of the city, a tearful man, beads of sweat clinging to his shirt, approached me. In halting English, his words interrupted by sobs, he asked me to help his son. "He has leukemia," he said, pronouncing the word solemnly. "He needs his medicine. Without it he will . . ." His shoulders shook with a sudden burst of fresh tears. "Please," he whispered.

My heart broke for this desperate father, but there was nothing I could offer. "Baghdad will be able to help soon," I said. He was the first of many in those first days to come forward. A young woman in a smaller village, her hijab slipping carelessly from her head, begged me to get help for her sister with breast cancer. "She hasn't started her treatment yet. You are a woman. You must understand. What can we do?"

I could only swallow the hard lump in my throat. "I am so sorry. We don't have any of those meds."

A middle-aged man with skin cancer asked for medicine, not for himself but for his son, who was suffering from cancer as well. "I am old," he said, pounding his bony chest. "But my boy is young. You understand?"

I did understand, but USAID had already informed us that the only chemotherapy available for the foreseeable future would be found in Baghdad. When I tried to relay that news, the families balked. "I have no money. How can we get there? You must help."

I had no easy answers for them, yet I hoped that somehow, we could help them find transportation to Baghdad, though that was a long shot. "I'll let them know in Kuwait. I can only promise you that."

I would pass the information on, but that was all I could do. It was all a grim reminder of the many victims of war.

Aside from the disruption in cancer treatment and other chronic diseases, we were very concerned that the coming summer months would surely see outbreaks of typhoid and cholera if the water and sewer problems were not cleared up. This had been a fairly sophisticated infrastructure here with electricity, running water, and flush toilets. That was all gone now and people managed the best they could, but the potential for a public health catastrophe was certain if vital services weren't restored quickly.

When we tested the quality of the drinking water in a small village just outside Nasiriyah, it was, as expected, brimming with bacteria and would require boiling before consuming. As we stood in the midst of a group of villagers and tried to relay that vital information, a thirtyish-year-old woman with dancing eyes and a quick smile pushed her way through the crowd surrounding us and stuck out her hand. "I am Fatima," she said, crossing her thick arms. "Come," she said, beckoning me to follow. I did, and so did many of the crowd, the men muttering angrily at the boldness of this woman.

She stopped and pointed to a bucket overflowing with the murky, foul-smelling water that she'd drawn from broken pipes in the street. "This," she said, "is all we have."

"And you're boiling it, yes?" I asked, expecting a nod of her head. "No," she said softly in perfect English. "Not always."

"But . . ."

"There is not enough fuel. How can I boil it for everyone every day? Understand?" Her eyes flashed with a sudden show of anger.

"Aren't you afraid?" I asked. "You'll get sick. This is dangerous water."

Tucking a stray hair under her hijab, she smiled coyly and spoke to me in a whisper so that the watchful crowd of locals wouldn't hear her words. "I boil it for my daughter, and when she has had her fill, I take what is left. My husband," she whispered, "is an old man and I am his second wife. My life is miserable, filled with sorrow." Her chocolate brown eyes scanned the horizon, as if searching for something that was just out of sight. "I want to escape this place, and God willing, the dirty water will be the end of him."

I took her hand. "Be careful," I cautioned.

She gripped my hand and smiled. For Fatima, there was possibility in that dirty water. But there was also danger, especially for a woman with the pluck to see opportunity where others saw only misery.

On the way out of Nasiriyah, we drove through "Snipers' Alley," the lonely strip of road where the US soldiers, including Jessica Lynch, had been ambushed only weeks earlier. The US soldiers who had been taken prisoner and had been shown on television were even then missing, their fates unknown. It was chilling to be there and even more chilling to see the debris, the tanks and charred metal that still littered the road, another reminder that this was indeed a dangerous place.

Some of the team had heard that liquor was available here in Nasiriyah for the right price. There had been no alcohol available in Kuwait, so many expats were hoping to get a supply in Iraq. As always, my preferred drink was wine, which wasn't available, so I wasn't interested. One of the team made a connection and bought a bottle of gin and another of scotch. They drank the gin that last night, and we planned to smuggle the scotch back into Kuwait, an act that would make all of us instant heroes and celebrities among the expat community. We left for Kuwait late the following morning with the bottle hidden away under the driver's seat. My own bags and equipment were also under the seat, providing, we hoped, cover and protection for our contraband. We got through the first of several checkpoints without a search and were already congratulating ourselves. But the checkpoints had yet to be finished.

At the final checkpoint, the Kuwaiti soldiers ordered us all to exit our little red Mustang.

"Even me?" I asked meekly, hoping they would allow me, as the only woman, to remain inside, where I could protect the precious cargo.

The soldier frowned and motioned me out with his rifle. I stood with Salim and Phil as Jason was whisked away to check our papers. We three stood nervously as the soldiers opened the trunk and pulled everything out. Our backpacks, our camping gear, everything wound up in the dirt. Still, as thorough as they were, they seemed to be leaving the back seat alone. I felt the tension in my neck ease. Suddenly, I noticed a soldier lean in and start pulling at my stuff on the floor of the back seat. If he pulled too hard, the bottle would surely roll out.

I strolled over to him in hopes of breaking his concentration and halting the search. "It's really hot, huh?" I asked, wiping the sweat from my brow as if to emphasize the heat. He grunted and continued his search. Damn! Why couldn't I have said something clever? His hands fumbled under the front seat, and he pulled out the bottle. "Is this yours?" he asked me gruffly.

"Not ours," I said, "This is a rental car."

He marched to the back of the car and asked Phil the same. "Not ours," he said.

The soldier disappeared into a small office, and Phil and I, the only witnesses and the only ones asked about the whiskey, looked at each other. In Kuwait, this could mean real trouble—jail, expulsion, anything was possible. The soldier marched back out, looked at us sternly, and poured the whiskey into the sand.

We were not questioned further, and we were allowed to drive into Kuwait. Jason, who hadn't witnessed our close call, pulled back onto the road and turned to us.

"At least they didn't find the whiskey, huh?"

Karbala

—◆—

We spent only a day in Kuwait reporting what we'd learned and discussing options for proposals and programs. The only decision we made was that we needed to do more assessments and broaden our areas before we could submit our plans to USAID for approval. We showered and ate before heading out again, this time to Karbala and the surrounding rural areas in central Iraq. Neither the mass population displacement nor major public health disasters had yet occurred, but the fighting still raged, Iraq still faced enormous public health needs, and we knew that a catastrophe could yet develop.

We left the camping gear in Kuwait, certain that this time we were sure to find places to stay. Our food choices were better, too—raisins, bread sticks, carrots, crackers, and, as an ode to optimism, peanut butter again. We were headed to the two holiest cities in Iraq—Karbala and Najaf—and I would need to be thoroughly covered. Although I'd covered up in Nasiriyah, a

The entrance to Freedom Medicine (ABOVE) and the tents that
would be our home while working at Freedom (BELOW) in
Thal along the Pakistan-Afghanistan border, 1986.

ABOVE: Our rustic clinic.
BELOW: Irrigating a gastrointestinal bleed in the E.R.

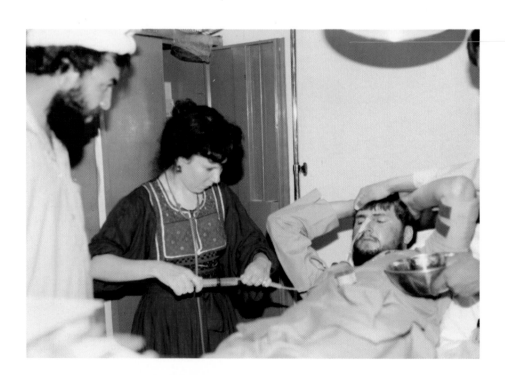

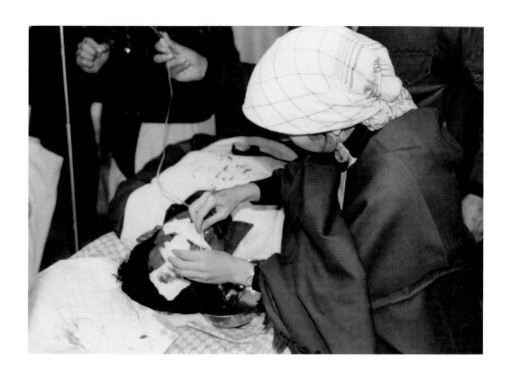

ABOVE: Working in the Freedom emergency room.
BELOW: I tend to a sickly baby in Chitral Clinic.

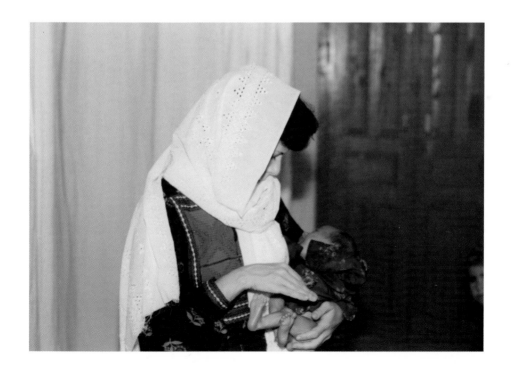

ABOVE: The staging areas in Garam-Chashma along Pakistan's northern border with Afghanistan, for both refugees and freedom fighters moving in and out of Afghanistan. BELOW: Patients in Chitral waiting to be seen.

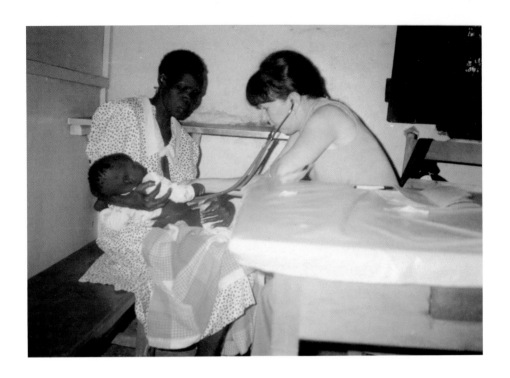

ABOVE: Seeing patients in Kakuma in 2001.
BELOW: The clinic waiting room in Kakuma.

ABOVE: Refugee huts in the Sudanese area.
BELOW: Tending to patients.

Another destroyed home (ABOVE) and a glimpse inside the
refugee camp (BELOW) in the Balkans in 2001–2002.

ABOVE: With children in Bamiyan in 2002.
BELOW: The Buddha Hollow where one of the statues once stood.
It was destroyed by the Taliban in the spring of 2001.

ABOVE: A bombed-out Taliban tank on the road to Shaidan.
BELOW: Two children outside of their mountain cave home in Afghanistan.

ABOVE: Mother and daughter with their donkey, which was their method of transport to our mobile clinic in Afghanistan in 2002. BELOW: Triaging in Afghanistan.

ABOVE: The 9/11 ceremony at the soldiers' staff house on September 11, 2002.
BELOW: The debris of war across from our first hotel in Iraq in 2003.

ABOVE: The room next to mine in Iraq. The only difference is that I had a mattress and a pillow. BELOW: Nomad villages in central Iraq.

ABOVE: Scenes from the nearby Iraqi village. BELOW: The canal in Iraq where people used this water for everything, including washing and drinking.

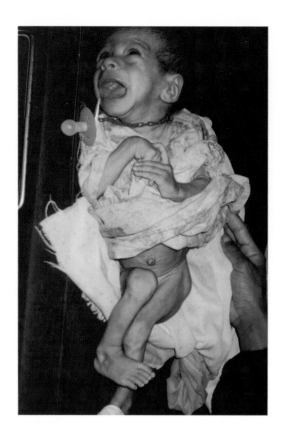

ABOVE: A malnourished baby in Iraq, one of far too many that I would see during my time as a nurse. BELOW: A makeshift camp in North Darfur in 2004.

ABOVE: Patients waiting to be seen at the IRC's clinic in South Darfur.
BELOW: An ambulance in South Darfur.

ABOVE: Greeting the children in South Darfur.
BELOW: The tailor who was burned by the Janjaweed in Darfur.

baseball cap and elbow-length sleeves had sufficed. But for these cities, I'd be required, in the sweltering, soupy heat of central Iraq, to wear a veil or full scarf to cover my head, long sleeves to cover my arms to my wrists, and long, loose pants to cover every inch of my legs. I could already feel the sweat pooling on my neck.

The team for this trip would include me, Jason again for water and sanitation, and Jen, the emergency team coordinator, out from New York, who would help in Karbala with education and child protection assessments. We would also have a journalist embedded with us—Kevin, a freelancer writing a story for the *New York Times Magazine*. We groaned at the news. "A reporter?" I whined. But whining didn't do any good. He was coming with us. No matter what.

We would travel in two rented SUVs (we still didn't have our own), and none of us wanted to travel with the reporter. It wasn't personal. He certainly seemed like a nice enough guy; we just didn't want to be "on" the whole trip. Finally, we decided we would take turns riding with him, and to our surprise, and within only hours, he seemed like one of us. It was easy to forget that he was a journalist.

We stopped in Umm Qasr, a border town in Iraq, to pick up Akram, an interpreter who could drive one of the SUVs and provide directions. Akram was big—big bones, big belly, big presence—but he was also a gentle and quiet man, and he sank awkwardly into the driver's seat. We soon learned that though he knew his country, his people, and surely the language, he didn't know the way to Karbala. Every twenty or thirty minutes, we stopped to ask directions, and then we stopped again to check and then recheck those directions. Finally, late in the day we decided to spend the night in Nasiriyah. We checked into the hotel where we had stayed on our earlier visit, but now the hotel was cleaner, it was being repaired, and there were other aid workers and journalists there, too.

Kevin and I, already fast friends, decided to leave our backpacks in the lobby and check into our rooms later. We wanted to have a look at an orphanage we had heard about, one that War-Child, an Irish aid group, would be supporting. We drove around, Kevin at the wheel, and asked for directions, which didn't seem to get us anywhere. Finally, an Iraqi man said that he would take us. He hopped into the back seat and directed us through a maze of alleys and streets until we finally arrived. The house, hidden behind a heavy steel fence, was located in a poor neighborhood. Garbage littered the streets, scraggly children poked through the debris, and hungry dogs roamed about, waiting for their turn. There seemed, at least to me, a feeling of hopelessness in the air.

We parked at the side of the road and the children instantly milled about, running their hands over the SUV's fenders and doors. Our passenger scowled. "I will watch this for you," he said, shooing the children away.

Kevin knocked at the imposing outer gate once, twice, and as he raised his hand to knock again, the door swung open. An older woman, dressed in the traditional long black dress and hijab, smiled and motioned us inside, where a crowd of shrieking, happy, healthy-appearing children greeted us. They guided us through the house and into their recreation room. Using a mixture of English, Arabic, and nods and smiles, we managed to communicate. The children were clean and neatly dressed, and they appeared to be well cared for and well loved. The staff here had had no reason to expect visitors, and it seemed to us that this must be how things always were here. Although they needed better access to health care and an upgrading of the house, the feel of this place was of a home where these children were nurtured and loved.

We said our good-byes and stepped outside the gate. Our passenger had disappeared, and the children, who'd been climbing all over the car, suddenly surrounded us. Their clothes were ragged, their skin grimy, their little arms and legs stick thin. They stood in stark contrast to the orphans we'd just left. The kids in the street tried to pick our pockets, pry off the hubcaps, and push their way into the car to grab whatever they could. When that didn't succeed, they held out their little hands, wiggling their fingers, but neither of us had brought money. We had nothing to give them, and though we wanted to stay, to linger here with these children, hear their stories, learn their names, the sun was setting and we had to get back to the hotel before dark.

We said hurried good-byes and headed back to the hotel. Electricity, we were told, had been restored only the day before, and joyous Iraqis had fired their weapons into the air, a customary act of celebration. Unfortunately, the gunfire had knocked out a central transformer, and the city had been thrown into darkness again. That meant there would be only intermittent electricity and occasional running water, so only if we were lucky would any of us get a real shower. My room held only another bucket of murky water, so that evening, it was a not unfamiliar bucket bath for me.

My room was suffocatingly hot, and, without electricity, there was no cooling fan to move the air. I was too tired to care and fell into a welcome sleep on the bed. During the night, the power came back in spurts and the overhead fan screeched periodically into life. The rare moments of cool air lulled me into a deeper sleep. In the morning I woke to sunlight streaming in through my uncovered windows. I stretched, slipped from the bed, and saw that I was covered with a fine layer of dust. I looked down at the bed and saw the only clean area was the outline where my body had lain, a kind of dirt-smeared crime scene. I'd used up my water supply the night before; there'd be no wash for me that morning.

We headed out early and made it to Karbala by late morning. The Shi'a pilgrimage to that city had just ended, and there were still crowds swarming the city center. The cities of Karbala and Najaf and their surrounding areas were Shi'a strongholds, a branch of Islam whose public traditions were forbidden by Saddam. This was the first time in many years that the Shi'a had been allowed to openly celebrate their religion, and they did it now with a fervor and intensity that was powerful and a little frightening to see. The crowds chanted, men flagellated themselves, drawing blood; their passion was palpable.

The city center held a large, golden-domed mosque, the exterior elaborately decorated with exquisite pieces of tiny, hand-painted tiles set into the wall. The only rooming house we could find was just across the street from the mosque. Even when we were welcomed into an area like this, we were still considered nonbelievers and infidels and were not really welcome around the sacred mosque. It was imperative, we knew, to keep a low profile.

This rooming house had running water, intermittent electricity, and the hardest beds and pillows that any of us had ever laid our weary heads on. We rose early, breakfasted on a boiled egg and bread provided for us by the rooming house staff, and made our own instant coffee. We had two cars but three team members trying to get assessments done.

The desk clerk, overhearing our dilemma, offered to help. "I know a woman who speaks English. Her husband has a car. You want to meet her?" he asked. When I agreed, he made arrangements for her to come to the hotel. Aliya, newly married and about thirty years old, I'd been told, arrived at the hotel hidden under the full black abaya, only her eyes, a deep charcoal black, poking through. I led her to my room, where we could speak privately, and once I shut the door, she sighed loudly and pulled her abaya back. Long blonde hair with deep dark roots spilled out. She plopped down on a chair, smoothing her midlength skirt and white blouse. "So," she said, "I need a job. Will we work together?"

"Well, let's talk first," I said.

She nodded and patted her hair down, her fingers untangling the ends, a fresh swipe of color on her lips. Crossing one knee over the other, she smiled. "Yes?"

I suddenly felt as though I was the one being interviewed. "I . . . well, this has nothing to do with the job, but your hair . . . I haven't . . ."

"I did put color into it," she said with a quick laugh. "But when I married, my husband told me he wanted my hair to be black again." She shrugged. "I made my choice and gave up the color for my husband."

I learned she'd graduated from college, spoke perfect English, and had worked for the World Food Programme until the war brought that food distribution program to a halt. "I know it will start again soon, and then I will go back to them. You agree?"

I nodded and told her what we were offering her for pay—an embarrassingly paltry sum of two dollars a day, which was in line, we were told, with average Iraqi salaries. She cleared her throat. "I know you cannot pay me what I earned with WFP, but—"

"What was your salary?" I asked, thinking maybe we could manage three or even four dollars a day, but I'd have to get permission before I made any promises.

She sat a little straighter. "Two thousand dollars a month," she said, her smile revealing perfectly straight white teeth.

I slumped in my chair. I wasn't even sure I was making that much. "I . . ."

"No worries," she said. "I want to help my people. My husband can drive us. We will start tomorrow. Yes?"

We shook hands and I walked her to the entrance, where she pointed out her dilapidated old car. The cars in Iraq were all old and barely able to sputter to life. Twelve years of UN sanctions had kept new cars, as well as the necessary parts to repair old ones, out of Iraq. Only the ingenious and lucky were driving now. They had somehow worked on and tinkered with their rusted-out, old hulks of cars. They'd jerry-rigged engines and found pieces of scrap, somehow combining it all together to make these dying cars go. This was a nation of resourceful and skilled mechanics. The only new cars on the roads were those belonging to the NGOs, the UN, or the coalition, but in that decaying old rust heap, I would surely blend right in.

The center of Karbala was like any European city—paved streets, cars with honking horns, ornate buildings, open-air shops, carts selling their wares, and crowds of people at every turn. But these days, it was a city that screamed to be cleaned, to be rid of the rotting garbage in the streets, the debris that fluttered on the slightest breeze. The invasion had halted all basic city services, and Karbala, like so many other cities, was decaying from within.

As soon as we pulled away from the city center, there was no mistaking that we were in a rural land. Bicycles were everywhere, and the bray of a donkey and the bleat of a goat replaced the cacophony of rusty engines and tooting horns. Cows and sheep were herded by children, and camel caravans made their way peacefully through village roads. Some of the camels were wild, living and hunting in packs, while many others were domesticated and were pulled along by children who tugged on the camels' ropes as they strained under their weight. The towering date palm trees for which Iraq had been famous were plentiful here and covered the road-sides and dusty earth. For many, they provided the only source of shade during the hottest time of the day, and children and others clamored to sit underneath and fan themselves with the loose branches. The scene was idyllic, almost biblical, but it hid the disease and malnutrition and dirty water that flourished here.

We were the first NGO to arrive in Karbala, the first to undertake assessments, and the first to establish a presence there. Just as in Nasiriyah, the people were excited to have us there and eager to cooperate with the assessments. On our first full day, I headed out of the city with Aliya to evaluate the rural and semi-rural clinics. The very first clinic we saw, the Al-Hur, was literally falling down. It was housed in one part of a decaying old school; even before the war, this had been a neglected area. Still, they had a generator and intermittent running water from their own water tank, though the water hadn't been treated with chlorine since the invasion and so required boiling before use, a time-consuming procedure in a busy clinic.

The surrounding area was without electricity and running water, and most people drew water from the canals. Not many villagers had the resources or the fuel to boil water, so diarrhea, particularly bloody diarrhea, was increasing, especially in children, for whom it was most dangerous. Just as in Nasiriyah and everywhere else in this country, the medicines necessary to treat diarrhea and other problems were in short supply, and no one could be sure when the central drug warehouses would be resupplying the clinics. To make it all last, the clinic staff were handing out lesser amounts of the drugs they prescribed. This meant that patients were treated inadequately, if at all, and the diarrhea or other issues would likely recur, at a more virulent level. It was a terrible dilemma for the Iraqi doctors and staff, who had been working without pay since before the war; they were dedicated but helpless without medicines.

I felt energized. I knew that IRC could help here. We could provide medicines, rehabilitate the clinic buildings, repair and upgrade water and sanitation services, work on the cold chain to restart the immunization programs, send community health workers out to teach hygiene and nutrition and general health. We saw several other clinics that first day, and they all had much in common—decaying, neglected buildings, usually without electricity, little or no medicines and supplies, and poor staff morale. As in most of Iraq, many clinics here had been looted, although many had been saved by the courageous actions of the staff.

At a time when concerns for public health disasters and dangerous epidemics loomed on the horizon and were discussed at every meeting with the UN, the ability to recognize, diagnose, and treat these epidemics was virtually nonexistent. There may not have been a public health emergency yet, but we certainly faced a crisis, and without immediate help, a disaster could result. As I evaluated the clinics and hospitals, and assessed the health of the villagers, I was already making plans for programs. These were the areas where IRC could have a real and lasting impact.

We were also learning that many women in these rural areas gave birth at home. There were no reliable statistics available on the number of home births, on maternal mortality, or complications in childbirth, and no one was even sure of the level of training of the midwives or traditional birth attendants (TBA) who helped with the births. It seemed clear to us that there was a need for midwife and TBA training. No one was even sure if these rural TBAs and midwives had supplies, or, if they did, whether the supplies were even clean.

The children, too, suffered from an inadequate system. There were no reliable statistics on malnutrition among children; our only source for that information had been anecdotal, health staff essentially guessing at the numbers based on their own observations. These children needed comprehensive screening to determine their need for nutritional supplements, vaccines, and to better understand their overall health. And then they would need the nutritional supplements, vaccines, and primary care interventions to bring them to optimal health.

Later that first day, I joined Jen and Kevin at one of the clinics, and en route to our rooming house, we three and Akram stopped at a Bedouin camp outside the city. The Bedouins are nomads who live in tents and move on or stay in a particular place according to the changing seasons or simple vagaries of life. These Bedouins had been in this spot for a long while, well over six months already, Akram told us. Their tents, tattered and worn, were clustered together for safety. On this day, only the women were "at home." Painfully thin, their black abayas covered with dust, they crowded around us, thrilled to have foreign visitors. They touched us, took our hands, and led us into the main tent, where they fluffed up old pillows and invited us to sit.

We tried to communicate through Akram, but the women, excited to have foreign visitors, spoke too quickly, and much was likely lost in translation. They were able to communicate how frightened they had been in the recent war and how they had cowered in their flimsy tents when the bombing started. One old woman, toothless and bent, described the closeness of the planes and helicopters as they swooped in to drop their weapons. She and the others reenacted what had happened during the bombing campaign by cowering together and looking fearfully skyward. The Bedouins were alarmingly close to an Iraqi army training center that had been heavily bombed, and they had been desperately afraid that they would be targeted as well. Though their physical lives and flimsy tents had been spared, they were clearly deeply affected by the war and were still alarmed and fearful when they saw soldiers.

We shared tea, sweet and sticky, and finally we had to leave. We said long good-byes and they kissed Jen and me and grasped our hands, asking us to return.

As we drove past the now crumbling Iraqi army training center, there seemed to be people living inside, so we pulled over to have a closer look. The building, a three-story cement block structure, had been heavily targeted and was now literally falling down, yet here living among the debris were about five families, each with children who were playing outside among unexploded ordnance (UXOs). We walked through the now collapsing outer walls and stepped carefully around the shattered glass, pieces of cement, and UXOs, trying to convince these children how unsafe those old bombs were. They wanted us all to get a closer look as they kicked at them and swung them about, but we declined. We would later report the UXOs to the US military here so that they could destroy them.

In the meantime, we wondered if these people were displaced from their homes, or if they'd been, like the Bedouins, always on the move. With Akram carefully translating, they told us that they were displaced, but not in the traditional sense.

"We lost our jobs," one man with a fresh growth of beard said. "Once the war started, there was no money to pay us and no work. Without money, we couldn't pay our rent and had to leave our homes. We have no place else to go."

"You were evicted?" I asked, incredulous that a landlord would behave so callously in times like these. The man nodded. I shook my head. Sometimes, the worst of times brings out the worst in people. These families planned to stay here only a short time.

Still, we were concerned for them. We reminded them to keep away from the UXOs and to boil water, and told them that they were very close to a clinic, where they could at least be seen by a doctor. Here, as in so many other destitute places in the world, people were well used to living with danger, whether unexploded rockets or surviving in crumbling buildings. It's likely they didn't heed our advice.

We arrived back at the rooming house, and there, sitting in the lobby, was an older woman with heavy makeup on and bright red lips, the color extended shakily beyond her lip line. She had a bright scarf wrapped fashionably around her head, not draped, as was the custom here, and she was smoking, all of which made her either very brave or very crazy. She noticed me looking at her, and in a clipped and proper British accent, she said, "Hello, hello."

I was drawn to her. "Oh," I said, "you speak English?"

She looked around the room and then at me and said, "Fifty-fifty."

I was dying to hear more. She was such a wonderful diversion here. "Where did you learn to speak English?" I asked.

"Oh, Paris, London," she replied as she waved her cigarette about.

She must have some fascinating tales, I thought as I sat down beside her. "When did you learn? Do you live here?" I asked.

She smiled, blew a long plume of smoke into the air, and looked me in the eye. "Hello, hello. Fifty-fifty," she said, pausing to take another drag on her cigarette. "Paris, London," she added in that clipped accent, but it was all she could say, and she repeated it over and over until the desk clerk shooed her out. Although she had been a welcome distraction, she worried me. We had no plans to care for people like her, the most vulnerable, who might not recognize danger and who could be so easily targeted.

Over the next days, I visited the remaining hospitals and most clinics—nearly nineteen—in the province of Karbala. Many clinics and even hospitals here were run by women. It seemed, too, that about 50 percent of the physicians here were women, and though many were still confined to traditional Muslim roles, many others had been encouraged, under Saddam Hussein, to go to school, become professionals, and work. At home, they were still subservient—they still cooked and cleaned and reared the children—but once they stepped beyond their walls, they worked alongside and often managed the men here. To balance the dichotomy of those roles required a degree of grace and intellect that I shall never have.

I completed assessments as I had in Nasiriyah, filled out the Rapid Health Assessment forms, and filed my trip reports. The assessments here revealed a population and medical system in desperate condition. The needs here were enormous, and I knew we could have an impact and really make a lasting difference. I met with the director of health, who was easy to find. Though gruff and excitable, he was pleased to work with us and see his health systems, which had been isolated for so long, back at capacity.

Jen and I had both been wearing scarves and long shirts, but under those shirts, we both wore jeans. On our third afternoon, we ventured out with Kevin for a walk around Karbala's center. A group of men, all wearing turbans, began to follow us.

"What are you doing here?" one shouted, a sneer curling his lips.

We three turned, and, our mouths agape, watched as another piped in.

"Look at you!" he sneered as he looked us up and down.

Despite the heat of the day, a shiver ran along my spine. Another man's eyes, almost hidden under a heavy brow, flashed angrily as we backed away. We had surely tried our best to dress and behave appropriately within the strict confines, but it wasn't enough. We learned that Coalition soldiers here were not even allowed to patrol this area around the mosque. As nonbelievers, their presence, and now ours, would defile the mosque. We headed back to the hotel and decided it was best just to leave Karbala and head to Najaf, another holy city just to the south, after some final assessments the next morning. We had been joined in Karbala by Tom, a *New York Times* photographer working on the story with Kevin, and he would accompany us for the rest of this trip.

On that last evening in Karbala, I was called to the lobby, where a young family had gathered. "They are here to ask for your help," the desk clerk said apologetically. "They heard that your group was here and insisted I call you."

"Please," a voice implored. I turned as a man, his beard freshly trimmed, his hair sleek with oil, nudged a little girl toward me. Tiny and almost lost in the ruffles of a lacy yellow dress, she stumbled forward. I knelt down quickly to catch her, the flat of my hand resting on her bone-thin chest, her heart fluttering there, a fragile butterfly beat.

"Hello," I said, smiling. She stepped back, her large brown eyes filled with fear. Her hair was gathered with a shiny yellow ribbon. The man reached down and lifted her into his arms. "She is very sick," he said, his voice hoarse. She looked like a little princess, but just a glance at her thin frame and pale skin told me she was indeed very sick. His forehead dotted with beads of sweat, his hand trembling, he handed me a manila envelope. "Please," he said, "see for yourself."

I sat down and patted the seat next to me. The girl clung more tightly to her father, but the woman, clad in the now familiar abaya, who'd stayed almost hidden in the background, sat down next to me. I opened the envelope and read the records inside. Isra, the tiny girl, was three years old. She'd been born prematurely and had been diagnosed with a heart defect that would require surgery; without surgery, breathing would be difficult for her and grow more so until her weary little heart would finally stop. I felt my own heart sink as I read. The records also indicated that Isra had a bony deformity—one of the bones of her left forearm was missing. It was then I noticed that indeed her left arm hung limply at her side.

"Yes?" the man said. "You see?"

I paused before explaining that I could not help, that we did not provide cardiac or orthopedic surgery. "You must take her to Baghdad," I said. I wrote out a referral asking for help on their behalf. I knew that before the war and the resulting chaos, specialty surgery was limited but available. These days, the military was stepping in, along with the international community, to fill that void, and I hoped that they might be able to help. Without surgery, she wouldn't survive another year.

Her family was one of many that sought us out for medical and other help. People here believed that once the invasion and war were over, America would take care of them, make their children healthy, fill their hungry bellies with food, and turn on the lights and let the water run. Although none of that had happened yet, they still had faith; they still believed that everything would be better soon.

Our three days in Karbala had been more fruitful than any of us had expected. I was sorry to say good-bye to Aliya, my interpreter, but the World Food Programme had contacted her and she was ready to go back to work. I hadn't had much of an opportunity to speak with her once her husband joined us, for then she became a good, quiet Muslim wife. She refused our offer of pay that last day, and once again, I was humbled. She and her husband had been so helpful and kind, and they wouldn't even let us pay them. "It is for our country that we helped," she said.

Amidst the devastation of war and loss, there is such generosity of spirit.

The Trip to Najaf

——◆——

J en found a small stash of Oreo cookies in one of her bags, and she and I feasted secretly on the remnants, wiping the chocolate evidence from our mouths before we met the rest of the team in the lobby. We piled into our SUVs, deciding to follow the canals that fed water to the rural villages. This would allow Jason a close look at water systems served by the canal and would give us a closer look at the lesser-known rural areas.

We packed up, split up into our two SUVs, and slipped onto the rocky, unpaved road, surrounded by swirling hot dust yet again. The weather here was now excruciatingly hot, and there was no escape. The air was heavy, the heat and humidity clinging to us as we headed south.

The villages along this area of the canal were lined with lush green date palm trees, exquisite in their abundance and beauty against the otherwise stark landscape. We stopped first in the village of Aufi, a small and quaint village that ran alongside the canal. I would find that the small mud homes, clustered together behind privacy walls, and furnished with bright carpets and pillows scattered on the floor, were not so different from the houses I knew so well in Afghanistan.

In Aufi, Jason checked out the decaying water system, while I headed to the clinic with Kevin and Jen. As we started out, we noticed two abaya-clad Iraqi women motioning to us. One of them, a tiny woman, ran toward us, her veil flying, while the other watched for a minute and then slipped away.

"You're American? You speak English?" the small woman whispered.

"Yes," we answered.

"I speak English, too," she said, "and I don't have much chance to use it. May I speak with you?"

"Of course," Kevin answered, pointing out the clinic to which we were headed.

She nodded. "My name is Halia," she said as we walked. "I am twenty-five years old and unmarried. By my own design," she said proudly. In Iraq, even for the educated and elite, marriages were still most often arranged. "I am not ready to be married. You understand?" She rushed on without pausing for an answer. "I want to see the world, get a doctorate in English, and do something important."

She was a professor, she said, at the Karbala University, but there had been no classes due to the war, and now the soldiers were using the university as a base. She had no idea when classes would start again.

We had never met an Iraqi woman quite like her. "I don't need a man right now, I am okay here," she said, tapping her forehead for emphasis. "You get it?"

We nodded in unison.

"I am happy that your soldiers are here," she said. "And Jay Garner, I like him very much, too." She was adamant that the United States stay in Iraq until everyone was sure that the political factions vying for power were neutralized. "We need help. You see that, don't you?"

She was a courageous woman. People here, though grateful to be liberated, often chose not to be seen speaking with us; they were fearful of being branded as collaborators. We met her just days after the fall of Baghdad, and people just weren't sure that Saddam wasn't lurking in the shadows, waiting to reclaim Iraq and punish anyone who'd been disloyal. Halia, so outspoken and forthright, was like a breath of fresh air, especially welcome in this oppressive land. In fact, the friend who had rushed away as Halia had rushed toward us was especially fearful of Saddam. "My friend ran off because she was afraid. It was not so long ago that her brother was murdered by Saddam's people. She is afraid to seem subversive, that the information that she had been speaking with you would find its way to the wrong people." Halia drew in a long deep breath. "I am not afraid."

It seemed clear that she wasn't. The village here was far from the main roads and the bustling cities of Iraq, but not far from the political intrigue for which this land was known. There would be whispers and lingering suspicions here for a long time to come, and no one wanted to be caught in that web. People, wisely, would choose their words and companions with care until they could be certain that Saddam and his band of thugs were gone and the danger was over.

We turned into Aufi's clinic, which, though small, was in good shape and still providing care, though with fewer medicines than they'd been used to. The people here were in reasonably good health, we were told, and this tranquil little village was doing quite well.

We said good-bye to Halia and continued along the canal. The farther we went from the cities, the more destitute were the people. One tiny village had no clinic at all, and when we introduced ourselves and told them we were here just to look at and test the water, the villagers eagerly invited us inside one of the homes. This home had one large central room, and we sat with the women and children, who asked if I would examine them. I got my stethoscope and blood pressure cuff from the car and told them we had no medicines. I did a quick baby clinic and saw several little ones. One of them, just like the little girl in Karbala, seemed to have a heart condition. She had the blue lips and fingertips, rapid irregular pulse, stunted growth, and listlessness of a baby with cardiac disease, though without testing, I couldn't be sure. I told them that her condition was serious, and that they should try to get to Baghdad for a thorough evaluation and treatment. The other children had only minor problems, respiratory and ear infections that required only basic medical treatment. Left alone, these were the problems that could fester and worsen and ultimately kill vulnerable children. Although we really hadn't done anything, the people here in this small village sent us on our way with warm, fresh bread as thanks.

At all of these villages, the people were fascinated with Jen. With her pale, delicate skin, natural blonde curls, and blue eyes, she was an object of curiosity. I had nicknamed her "Grace Kelly" because of the natural way her scarf stayed in place with blonde wisps peeking out. My veil was still dust-covered and always awry, but not Jen's. She winced every time one of us called her Grace.

We stopped last at a rural village that seemed to be stuck in the 19th century. These homes were made of the usual mud surface, and clustered together, but this village had absolutely nothing—no power lines, no water, no roads—nothing but a wonderful spirit that permeated the air here. People ran out to greet us, and we wondered when the last car had stopped here in this distant place. We were greeted joyously and guided into one of the compounds. These homes seemed the same as so many others we'd seen, but one house in this desolate place inexplicably had a real bedroom with a real bed.

While Jason looked at the latrines and tested their water, I ran another impromptu clinic, checking blood pressures, listening to hearts, examining eyes and skin as the villagers lined up to be checked. Most here had never had their blood pressures checked or their hearts and lungs auscultated, and they were eager and willing patients. They listened intently to the health advice I offered and were especially interested in comparing their blood pressures; whose was better and whose heart beat with "more force."

These people were so welcoming and so kind to us that we left reluctantly. We knew we had to get to Najaf before nightfall. It was still dangerous to be on the roads after dark. I fell asleep in the sweltering heat of the back seat of the car, amidst suitcases and work.

"Miss, miss," Akram said, his voice rising, an urgency in his words. "Wake up. You must sit up, and please cover your head. Quickly, quickly, we are in a holy city."

I woke with a start, bathed in sweat, gathered up my veil, and hurriedly covered myself. We pulled into Najaf just as thousands of Shi'a pilgrims did as well. Much like in Karbala, these pilgrims filed to the mosque, a never-ending stream of worshippers, some banging their chests, others chanting.

Shit, I thought, here we go again. Someone will be insulted by our presence here, but they barely seemed to notice us as we made our way through the city looking for a place to stay. We were waved into a hotel, where we negotiated some rooms and fell into bed. In the morning, we each hungrily ate the boiled egg and bread provided for us and explained that we wanted only hot water so that we could make our own instant coffee. Because of the pilgrimages and the thousands still streaming into this city, we thought it unlikely that we would be able to carry out any useful assessments here in Najaf. We decided it was best to head south and stop at villages along the way.

Tom, the photographer who'd joined us, asked that we make a detour to an area where he and other journalists had been ambushed, their cars set ablaze or stolen just weeks earlier. With some difficulty, he directed us through the maze of similar-looking roads until finally he pointed out a deserted stretch of road. There in the distance was one lonely charred hulk of a car, the surrounding landscape scorched black.

"It belonged to a *Newsweek* magazine reporter," Tom said, looking through the lens of his camera and snapping away. "When our cars were attacked, we jumped out and rolled onto the ground and into the brush, any bit of shrub to camouflage us, and it did. No one was seriously injured—a few scrapes and minor burns, but otherwise . . ." He lowered the camera, his gaze resting on the burned-out remains of the car. He stood there quietly, perhaps remembering how close he'd come, perhaps reminding himself how quickly things can change. He heaved a sigh and turned. "We'd better get going, huh?"

We headed back along the main roads and stopped at a large village along the canal. Even in the unbearable heat and sweltering sun of the day, women clad in black abayas were bent over the dirty water, scrubbing clothes and pots, a never-ending cycle of work for them. Children and some adults, likely alerted by the hum of our vehicles, poured out of every nook and cranny in this village called Al Diseem.

They surrounded us. When Akram asked about health care, they guided us to a crumbling and long-abandoned clinic. Akram and one of the village men pried the door open, and we stepped inside to the musky scent of old dust and older rodents. The rooms were in disarray. Long-expired pills and medical supplies covered now in layers and layers of dust, pieces of smashed equipment—lights and desks, exam tables, a cabinet—littered the floor. We stepped warily over the debris, broken shards of glass crunching under our feet. I reached for one of the hundreds of pill bottles—a quick look revealed that all had expired, some were antibiotics, some for blood pressure—but it was hard to tell. The bottles had been opened, most of the pills spilling out. This place was a disaster waiting to strike.

I groaned and turned to the people who had gathered behind us. With Akram interpreting, I tried to explain the dangers here. "This isn't safe," I said gently but firmly, remembering that this was their village, not mine, and it was important that they not feel I was insulting them. "This is the government's responsibility," I added for good measure. "But until they clean this up, I hope that you might try to keep this place safe, maybe sweep up the debris, gather the pills and destroy them. Just to keep everyone safe, you know?"

While Jason had a look at the water system, I wandered about the village with countless children in tow. For my own diversion, I taught them to sing "Maria" from *West Side Story*, but I substituted *Haliya* for *Maria* and had them serenade Kevin. They were incredible little showmen, all gestures and big voices, and though the English lyrics were unfamiliar to them, the language of song is universal.

Before long, our impromptu musical was interrupted by a thin Iraqi man, a gray blanket draped over his shoulders in this heat, a worrisome sign in this land where battles still raged and suspicion still lingered.

"Hello," he shouted. "American?"

We hesitated. Akram spoke up. "Why do you ask?"

The man stepped closer, a wide smile revealing a row of rotted teeth. "I like America," he replied, standing a little taller. "I have friends, you know, you understand?"

We didn't, but we nodded anyway.

The man tapped his own chest. "I was an Iraqi soldier."

My heart pounded in my ears. Shit! Everyone here had seemed so friendly, but was it only a ruse?

"One of Saddam's soldiers?" Akram asked warily.

"Yes, yes," he exclaimed proudly. "I was a prisoner of the Americans. They were very good to me." He was so pleased with the treatment he had received and the warm blanket they had let him keep that he proudly showed us his prisoner badge, issued by the Red Cross, as he extolled the virtues of the American soldiers. "Very good men," he proclaimed. "Do you know them?"

"Well, some of them."

"Do you know—?" He rattled off a list of names—Bob, Jim, Curt—continuing until he paused to take a deep breath. "Look," he said as he lovingly fingered the gray army-issue blanket, "even this blanket is of the finest quality. And they gave it to me. Do you think you can help me? I'd like to see them again."

We shook our heads. Though he seemed genuine in his praise of all things American, who knew if he wasn't in fact a saboteur? War makes you suspicious of everyone.

We reluctantly waved good-bye to the children, the village, and to the lonely former POW, and then we were on the road again.

We saw several other villages, all similar, some with clinics, some without, all in some degree of need. None had electricity or running water, but they expected that those would soon be restored. After all, the United States was here now, and they always brought miracles—or so these people and everyone in Iraq, it seemed, all believed. At one village clinic, the female doctors spoke softly and asked if they could speak openly with me. I assured them I was here to listen with an open mind.

"We are grateful that the United States came into our country, but now we are weary and tired of the empty promises to deliver help and electricity and water. Your armies must leave, leave Iraqis in peace to clean up and take care of ourselves." They were unyielding in their demands. "Foreigners, all of you, must leave. You aren't helping us here. You are only bringing trouble, and we will have that for years to come. Tell your people to leave us alone!"

My cheeks grew red with embarrassment, or maybe it was a flash of resentment. We were here to help, after all. "I'm sorry to have bothered you," I said, stepping quickly away from the clinic. Aside from the men by the mosque in Karbala, these were the first hints of anger I had heard, the first grumblings of discontent. I didn't know then how true their predictions would be; things indeed would only get worse, and sooner than any of us had imagined.

We knew that we couldn't possibly make it to Basrah before nightfall, so we stopped at our now-favorite hotel in Nasiriyah for the night. The hotel was barely recognizable now with all of its improvements. The plywood and stacked-high furniture that had protected the blasted windows were now replaced with bright, clean clear glass. The lobby furniture, no longer necessary to protect the window area, was now arranged for comfortable seating. The whole place seemed clean and there was electricity, as evidenced by the rotating overhead fans and the bright chandeliers now lit and glowing. A lot had changed here in Nasiriyah. Akram went to the market and came back with a hot, plump chicken and fresh bread, and we feasted on that in the still dusty, decaying, and dim ballroom. It would be, we were told, the last room here to be restored, and the lights were not yet working. I was grateful that the ambience of our first visit to this elegant old room remained intact.

This would be our last night together. Tom would head back to Baghdad in the morning, and once we arrived in Basrah, Akram would find his way back to Umm Qasr. The rest of the team, including Kevin, would be heading back to Kuwait after meetings in Basrah.

My room this time had electricity, a fan, a light, and, now that I could see them, the largest cockroaches I had seen since my latrine in Africa. I had been blissfully ignorant of their existence on previous visits, but now they seemed to be everywhere—on my bed, the walls, spinning around on the ceiling fan, in my shoes, under my pillow, sitting on my backpack. The electricity sputtered and died, and with it, all evidence of my roommates. I took a real shower, though with scant water, by flashlight, accompanied by the roaches, which somehow avoided the water as they scurried about my feet in the little globe of light created by my flashlight. I dried off with a crusty and slightly smelly towel the hotel had provided. We had all determined that although they were open for business now, they had neglected the laundry, and these were the same sheets and towels that had been used by countless other guests. No matter, I was still clean. I slept peacefully, and in the quiet, I realized that the cockroaches did, too.

We left early the next morning, breakfasting on jam, crackers, and instant coffee before saying our good-byes to the hotel staff. We were headed to a Marsh Arab village that we had hoped to see earlier. The Marsh Arabs of Jebbayash had been especially persecuted under Saddam Hussein's vicious regime and had been isolated and forgotten for years, not unlike Afghanistan's Hazara population. The Marsh Arabs had historically relied on the marshes for their livelihood; they fished, they wove mats and rugs and even homes from the reeds that grew in lush abundance along the water's edge.

During the Gulf War of 1991, the Marsh Arabs had supported the coalition. Post-war, Saddam retaliated by draining the marshes upon which these people's very existence so relied. With UN sanctions in place, they were isolated and struggling just to survive. Some revolted, according to the people left there, and some managed to escape. The rest managed to get by on the UN WFP food rations, while others eked out a small living by farming the soil.

The children here who were lucky enough to attend school—mostly the boys—walked barefoot along rocky roads, for a distance of about three miles. They were considered the lucky ones. In Iraq, education had always been important, allowing children here the opportunity to read and learn and grow, though most texts contained flattering portraits and likely untrue stories of Saddam's benevolent leadership. Nonetheless, Saddam controlled his people by controlling access to the outside world. UN sanctions had prohibited most outside contact, and Saddam further tightened his grip by forbidding satellite transmission of foreign programs. All that people here could view was Saddam's own programming, which further extolled his own charms and derided the world as infidels and enemies of Iraq.

When we arrived in Jebbayash, we were the first foreigners many of them had ever seen. We were cheered and mobbed, touched and fussed over. We were movie stars. Amazingly, these people had fared pretty well; they had weathered Saddam's brutal regime, and now, since his fall, the dams had been removed and the water was flowing into the marshes once again. People here had great hope for their future. Although they had one small clinic and one small hospital, they had survived in good health and hopeful spirits.

We headed to Basrah in the highest heat of the day. As we pulled into the city, a camouflage-clad British soldier motioned us to pull over. "Where are you headed?" he asked, leaning into the car, his eyes sweeping over all of us and the contents of our vehicle.

"To a house just up there," Jen answered. "We're with IRC." We pulled out our IDs and waved them in the air.

"Be careful," he warned, his soft British accent somehow tempering his message. "Two cars were just ambushed here at this intersection. The passengers were robbed at gunpoint. Keep your eyes open," he said. "Crime is on the rise, and they're targeting foreigners. We can't be everywhere. You have to take care of yourselves and each other. Understood?" He tapped on the driver's door and waved us on our way.

The soldier's warning wasn't really a surprise. In every country I'd been to, people know that aid workers have the nice cars, the money, the jewelry, and we don't fight back. Easy targets, easy rewards for those daring enough and willing to commit the acts. Chaos, crime, and lawlessness were the order of the day in Basrah and Baghdad; other cities were tense but quiet. Iraq was on edge, but we continued on, certain that the danger wouldn't touch us.

In Basrah, we had a staff meeting, where we met up with some new staff and presented our assessments, ideas, and program proposals. It was obvious that we had found the right niche for IRC's expertise; we had completed the rapid assessments, identified the most pressing needs, and started the program design process.

We had been on the road for much of the day. We were hungry, but there was no food in the Basrah house, and, because of the crime and danger lurking literally right outside our door, we had no way of getting food. The electricity was out, so without food or light, we simply collapsed into bed, limp, hot, and sweaty in the thick night air. The sound of gunfire and dogs barking right outside the house started and then continued intermittently throughout the night. Still, somehow we slept. Barking dogs and gunfire, the night sounds of Iraq.

Najaf

——•——

We left for Kuwait early the next morning and arrived tired, hot, and hungry. But here in Kuwait there was electricity and water and shops and a restaurant in our building. We attended a flurry of UN and other meetings, worked on our program ideas and proposals, and prepared to move into Iraq to implement our programs. Phil headed back to New York, and reluctantly we said good-bye to him. Jen would be leaving soon as well. Kevin was working on his article; he really hoped to hop a bus to Baghdad and profile the people he met along the way. We were all heading in opposite directions, and we were all far too busy to be pensive or reflective.

It was about this time, in early May, that we learned that a new civilian administrator, L. Paul Bremer—a former State Department bureaucrat—had been named to head up the interim government of Iraq. I wondered what that meant for the popular Jay Garner. Everywhere I'd been I'd heard the chants

"Jay Garner! Jay Garner!" His name represented hope to the people here. I also learned that the appointed medical administrator, a vibrant, experienced respected physician who'd headed up the interim Ministry of Health in Iraq, had been replaced by an inexperienced political donor to the president. Just when stability was needed, instability seemed to be the order of the day.

We wrote reports, called or emailed family, and said good-bye to civilization once again. We also stocked up on food—nonperishables like instant coffee, jam, peanut butter, crackers, whatever we could think of to supplement whatever meager diet we would get in Iraq—and headed back to Najaf, which would be our base of operations. The team included Jason again, Adam—the Australian field coordinator—and me, for health.

In Najaf, we checked into the same hotel where we had spent one night during the Shi'a pilgrimage just days earlier. Once again, the night was punctuated with bursts of gunfire and what sounded like return fire. My window overlooked a deserted alley, and with nothing to see, I went to bed and dozed in between the staccato bursts. The next morning, I feasted on my only guaranteed meal of the day, my precious boiled egg and bread. I sliced the warm egg lengthwise so it would seem as though there was more of it and made an egg sandwich with part of the bread. I slathered jam generously on what remained of the bread and washed it all down with sips of hot, strong, black instant coffee.

We headed that first morning to the CMOC in Najaf. The Marines were pulling out and the US Army soldiers were just getting CMOC and the Civil Affairs (CA) office organized. We learned that the gunfire we'd heard the night before had been the sounds of a battle between the US Marines and local insurgents right outside our hotel.

We met with the mayor of Najaf, who had an office in the same complex as CMOC. He was an enthusiastic, willing leader and eager, he assured us, to help usher in change for the people of Iraq. Just as in Karbala and so many other places, IRC was the very first NGO to show up, and here, we were literally moving in. The mayor helped smooth our way to meet with department heads and others with whom we hoped to work. He seemed an impressive man, but within days, we heard grumblings that he was a Saddam loyalist, a criminal, and a man who had been responsible for countless vicious acts against his own people. The US Army investigated, and shortly thereafter, he was removed from office. It was yet another reminder that we had to be careful here; everyone had a history, and there were plenty of Saddam loyalists still lurking about.

As we departed the CMOC building that first day, we were surrounded by a crowd of Iraqi men who hoped to get jobs as interpreters with us. Several slick, handsome, well-dressed young men were told to come the next day, and as we were pulling out, a tall, reed-thin man with heavy black eyebrows and a line of sweat clinging to his forehead leaned into the window. "You must hire me," he said with unmistakable urgency.

With a wave of his hand, Jason dismissed him, but there was something about him, an honesty and openness that I liked. "Come tomorrow!" I shouted as he turned away.

"My name is Amir," he called as we drove off.

The next morning, the two polished interpreters and an older Iraqi, rather full of himself, showed up and were hired. We would each have our own interpreter and an extra for administrative work. I wanted someone who would be willing to work and to learn with me, someone who would literally not hesitate to get his hands dirty. These guys we'd just hired were all too self-absorbed, too clean, too smooth for me.

Amir strode nervously through the door, almost tripping, his anxious eyes darting around, and I smiled.

Our interview was short. "Are you willing to learn medical terms, work long hours, and help me in any way necessary?"

"Oh yes, yes, I am," he assured me. "I need this job to feed my family, my parents and brothers and sisters." There was no shiny veneer to Amir; he was straightforward and uncomplicated and I liked him. I hired him and we went to work that very first morning.

I continued my assessments in the areas around Najaf, and Amir and I made the long trip to Karbala several times a week. We went to each of the hospitals in Najaf and Karbala to keep in close contact with the medical system here, and we attended weekly meetings with the health directors in each governorate as well. I frequently sought out the advice of Dr. Sayed, an energetic young pediatrician I'd met at the Women's Hospital in Karbala. He became a valuable asset to IRC. He'd been trained as a primary care physician in Baghdad, then the government had sent him to Karbala to work. His background was impressive—primary care, pediatrics, administration. He seemed to have done it all.

I knew I would be finishing up my contract with IRC in June, and that meant I had to find an Iraqi physician to take over my programs. The sooner I found someone, the better prepared he or she would be to manage everything and to work with me before I left. I was sizing up every physician and administrator I met. We wouldn't be able to get a health manager with international experience, but as long as we could find someone who would be a good fit for us and IRC, the programs would be fine. I thought about discussing it with Dr. Sayed but decided I would have plenty of time in the coming weeks. In the meantime, I had plenty to do, program proposals to research and write, and several more assessments in and around Najaf. People often assume aid work is glamorous and exciting, but much of it, though vital, necessary, and ultimately life-saving, is boring and involves endless days of writing and voluminous research to support what you've written. There are only rare moments of excitement and drama, but among those was the nightly gunfire.

The staccato rounds of gunfire pierced the heavy night air; a silent night was rare now. Still, we all managed to sleep through most of it, only occasionally complaining about interrupted sleep. We were all well used to those sounds and went about our business barely noticing the chaos of gunfire. We had to move from our hotel/rooming house to another, since we had been informed that Al-Hakim, a Muslim cleric who had been exiled to Iran under Saddam, was returning home to Najaf and his entourage would be housed here in our hotel. It was feared that Al-Hakim would stir up anti-American fervor and violence, and CMOC advised us to keep a low profile.

One morning, before Al-Hakim had even arrived, and before we'd moved from our hotel, I waited alone in the lobby for Amir and the driver to return from an errand. Two Muslim clerics dressed in the full black robes and white turbans that marked them as Shi'a mullahs came into the lobby, sat, and proceeded to enjoy a breakfast of yogurt and bread. They motioned with their hands as they invited me to join them, but I politely declined. I had work to do.

They seemed to be kind and engaging men, and when one asked where I was from, I foolishly never hesitated before saying, "I'm an American."

They looked at each other and then at me, their eyes blazing. "The filthy dogs," one snarled as he stood and moved toward me. The other, his forehead one long, angry line, frowned. "Get out," he said in a whisper so fierce that at first I wasn't sure what he'd said.

"Get out," the first one added, his voice shaking with anger. "You are all criminals; here to steal from us!"

No one else was in the lobby, no one to intervene, no one to help. With my heart flapping furiously in my chest, I gathered my papers.

"Americans get out of Iraq. We don't want you here!"

The blood drained from my head as a knot of fear bubbled up in my stomach. I knew it would take a millisecond to kill one of us, to emphasize a point, or to gain world attention if only for an instant. I hurried out, their shouts ringing in my ears, and stood in a small alleyway so that they couldn't see me. It seemed forever before Amir and the driver returned.

"What?" Amir exploded when I told him what had happened. "We will go back," he said.

"No," I answered. "I don't want any more problems. We'll go to CMOC and report it, and I'll tell Adam. That's all." I did report and discuss the incident with the soldiers, who could only remind me to be careful. That same day, Adam found a family-run hotel/rooming house close by, and we moved in. As with each of the other places where we'd stayed in Iraq, a room consisted of a small, wood-frame bed with a pad thrown onto it—no mattress, no comfort, but at least it was like a bed—and a squat latrine/shower combination so we could shower when the taps worked. We would still get the boiled egg and bread breakfast, and I was grateful, since it was still my only sure meal of the day. We were often too busy to stop for a bite, and it seemed when we had the time, the area was not the safest. Though I tried at the end of our day to pick something up, it didn't always work out. I would feast on bread and jam later if I was able to get the bread; otherwise I went to bed hungry, dreaming of the morning's hard-boiled egg. I was running low on instant coffee and was rationing my precious morning cups; since there was no instant coffee available in Iraq, I was down to a half cup in the morning. I would need to resupply soon, coffee and food.

I carried out assessments in Najaf and the more rural areas away from the city center. Just as in Karbala, the city of Najaf, though not quite as modern as Karbala, had paved roads, buildings, shops, and a central mosque. The outlying areas were just as destitute as those around Karbala. The people were in a fragile state, barely surviving on the food and resources they had available; with the added insult of diminished health care, life there seemed to be hanging by a thread. We had to have our programs approved by USAID/DART in order to draw down the money necessary to implement them. We worked to put together a Quick Impact Proposal (QIP); I wrote the health QIP, Jason completed the water and sanitation QIP, and a child specialist, new to IRC, worked on child protection.

My QIP included demographic data, thorough problem analysis, and the number and needs of the beneficiary population. The proposals also included an implementation plan with timeline, detailed activities, and expected results and impact. We also included a plan to monitor performance.

We drove to Al-Hillah to meet the USAID/DART representatives and present our proposals. Al-Hillah was also home to the ORHA representatives, and all were housed in what had once been an elegant, four-star hotel. As we approached the area we saw, in large red neon letters on the roof of the hotel, the letters O-R-H-A for all to see. That sign courted danger. Better to maintain a low profile until you could be absolutely sure that you were accepted and safe. The garish sign was almost an embarrassment, but the ORHA staff didn't seem to notice how odd and out of place it was. Jay Garner was still there, and though we didn't meet him, we did notice how well received he was by Iraqis. He walked through the lobby in his rolled-up shirtsleeves, smiled, shook hands, made people feel important.

No wonder Iraqis liked him.

Hell, *I* liked him.

We met with the USAID/DART team and presented our proposals, answered their questions, and, finally, gained their approval. Now we could finally implement our ideas.

First, we would head back to Kuwait to resupply, make arrangements to have our pre-positioned supplies moved into Iraq, and tidy up final program details. There would be no work for the interpreter staff in our absence, and I had to convince Amir that I would be back and so would he.

We left Najaf early, before the sun rose, hoping to make the trip before the sultry heat of the day was upon us. Suleiman, an IRC employee from Tanzania, had joined us for a short stint to help with logistics. He would drive us to Kuwait City, and from there, he would catch a flight home to Africa. Suleiman had a wonderful and gentle nature but a terrible sense of direction. It took hours before we realized we'd been driving in circles. The heat was indescribable; hot enough, we thought, to truly fry an egg. We'd all brought our bottles of water, but they quickly became as hot as the air and offered no relief from the sweltering breeze.

When we finally arrived in Kuwait some twelve hours after we'd left Najaf, we rushed for the air-conditioning our hotel offered.

An Emergency

—◆—

I t was late May, and I planned to resupply, attend some meetings, and
see what equipment and medicines we could access from USAID (they
were still here continuing emergency assessments, looking at proposals,
and arranging for distribution of medical supplies they had brought), as well
as UNICEF and WHO. Almost immediately after returning to Kuwait
City, I just didn't feel well. A day or so later, I developed a fever, nausea,
and abdominal pain, all signs of appendicitis. Although I had gone to the
US embassy when I'd first arrived in Kuwait with the express purpose of
developing an expat medical plan and had in fact created a list of satisfac-
tory doctors, clinics, and hospitals, I wasn't sure if I had insurance to cover
any of it. Meanwhile, I attended the meetings, arranged for supplies, wrote
reports, and wished whatever this was would go away. After two full days,
when I couldn't stand the pain and discomfort anymore, I quietly told
Adam that I was going to the clinic "to be checked" before heading back

to Iraq. He was busy and involved in mounds of work and barely heard me as I left the office.

I went to the clinic I'd chosen as part of my expat plan. "How much will it cost to see a surgeon?" I asked the receptionist.

"A surgeon? Cash?"

I nodded. The cost would be fifteen Kuwaiti dinars, about forty-five US dollars, not bad at all, but it would take most of my money.

I waited for only a few minutes before I was ushered into the surgeon's office.

"What seems to be the problem?" he asked.

I told him that I believed I had appendicitis.

He raised his eyebrows and said, "Really?"

I told him about my background and my job here and just why I thought I had this. He examined my tense and tender abdomen and wanted to do some tests to confirm the diagnosis.

I asked him for the prices of the tests and said I wasn't sure I could afford all of them. We negotiated the tests I'd have. He wanted liver function tests, and I said no; I agreed to a white blood count (to check for the degree of infection) and electrolytes (to determine my overall condition); he wanted to order a gallbladder study, and I said no, just an ultrasound. All in all, considering how I was directing my own care, he was very reasonable and very kind to me.

The tests confirmed the appendicitis, and he said, "We must admit you right away."

I told him I wasn't sure about insurance and that without it, I couldn't pay for surgery. I told him I had to return to the IRC office and talk to Adam, and then I would come back.

The doctor, a middle-aged Syrian man with a soft voice and gentle manner, was reluctant to let me leave; he wasn't sure I would return, and he didn't want to let me go. "You must promise to return, otherwise, well . . ." He stroked his beard and bobbed his head. "Well, you know."

I promised that I would return. He said he would take me to surgery that evening. I made him promise that if I felt fine after surgery, he would release me. I was sure that I would not need to stay in the hospital, that I would be fine and ready to leave right after surgery, and leaving would save money.

The surgeon smiled. He seemed to think otherwise.

I returned to the hotel and went to the IRC office, which was also Adam's room. I walked in and sat down, resting my hands and my gaze on my lap. Adam looked up, his brow wrinkled. "What's wrong?" he asked.

All of my control over the last days broke down and I started to cry, my shoulders shaking, my nose running, my fingers twitching. Adam came around his desk and knelt in front of me, taking my hands in his. "Tell me what it is. Please."

In between my sobs, I told him. "I have appendicitis and need surgery and I have no money to pay for it."

He smiled, his eyes dancing with relief. "Love, you have insurance with IRC. What's all this fuss?" His smooth Australian accent made his words that much sweeter.

The sense of relief was overwhelming. I started to smile and then laugh, but that made the pain worse, which made me cry all the more. I wiped my nose, my eyes, and my mouth on my sleeve as Adam patiently explained that he would take care of it all. He would call the IRC office in New York—we were seven or eight hours ahead of them, so the office wasn't open yet—and he would take care of everything.

"First," he said, "we'll get you back to the hospital. Tell me who you want New York to notify at home."

"No one," I said, my voice firm. I didn't think it would be fair for my family, my sister, my friends, to know that I was undergoing emergency surgery in a place they still believed was backward and dirty. New York was understandably eager to notify someone. I understood how it was for them, but I couldn't bear for my family to sit anxiously and helplessly so far away and imagine the worst. I promised Adam and New York that I would call home after surgery.

I reassured Adam that I would be okay, that there was nothing for him to do at the hospital, and that I would have the doctor call him. I returned alone to the hospital, where I was admitted and sedated and given intravenous antibiotics. I slept for the first time in days. Through a haze, I heard someone say that Adam was calling. The doctor spoke to him, and later I was transferred to the main hospital for surgery. I didn't get to see much of the hospital, but it seemed clean and modern to my drugged eyes.

The nurses took my jewelry, but I wouldn't let them take the metal cuff bracelet that had been given to me in Afghanistan almost one year earlier. I had promised never to remove it. The nurses were determined to get it off, but I told them it didn't come off. Finally they relented and covered it with gauze and tape. They took my clothes and gave me a paper hospital gown. I hadn't a smidge of dignity left, but by then I didn't care.

I was given another sedative and wheeled into the operating room. I hadn't seen the surgeon in several hours, so I was relieved to see him lean over and reassure me that I would be fine. "Hello, hello, my dear. Everything will be alright," he said.

The anesthesiologist came in, and I heard him, through my heavy haze of drugs, order anesthesia doses that I thought were far too much for someone my size. An oxygen mask was placed over my face; I tried to remove it, but my wrists had been secured.

I tried to speak, to say, *"No, that dose is too high for me."* I wanted to say, *"Take off the sheet, see for yourself."* But I couldn't get the words out; I didn't feel panicked or afraid, and that is the last thing I remember.

Next thing I knew, someone was waking me, and I felt like hell. I was in pain, I was vomiting, my head felt as though it would explode, and they were making me move from the OR stretcher to a bed. I had been wheeled to a room where Jen was waiting for me. I had never felt worse in my life, and I told her she should just go back to the hotel. All I wanted was pain medicine and something to stop the vomiting. God, I had never been so sick.

I was in a bed, but I slept fitfully; I was tangled up in the IV (intravenous) tubing, my paper gown was torn, my skin was stuck to the plastic sheet I was lying on, I was vomiting into a small basin, the room was pitch black, I was alone, and for the second time that day, I cried, but softly this time and only to myself. Although there were nurses here, in this part of the world, family members were expected to stay and take care of the patient; I had sent Jen home, so I was on my own. In the middle of the night, I had to pee desperately. I was unable to sit upright, so I slid sideways out of bed and literally crawled to the bathroom, dragging my IV pole.

For the first time in my life, I was grateful for a squat latrine toilet; there was no way I could get myself fully upright to sit. I was not grateful though for the lack of towels, soap, and even paper towels. (I learned the next day that families were expected to provide those.) I crawled back to bed and slowed down the rate of my IV (which would slow the rate at which fluids were delivered to my bloodstream and kidneys and would decrease urination) so I wouldn't have to go through that miserable ordeal again.

The next morning, the surgeon returned on rounds and gave me a knowing smile as he asked how I felt. I had been vomiting all night; I was sweaty and still stuck to the sheets. I was in pain from my head to my abdomen, which throbbed with every move I made.

"Never felt better," I said. "When can I leave?"

He looked very serious as he reminded me that I still required IV hydration and medicines, not to mention that I would have to stop vomiting and actually eat before discharge would even be considered. I could try drinking water later, he said, if my vomiting had stopped. He increased the IV drip rate before leaving my room.

The nursing staff here didn't come around in the morning with fresh towels and soap and clean hospital gowns. I had no family here to do that, so I asked for a bar of soap and paper towels and crawled back to the bathroom to try to wash up. Doubled over, trying to use the soap and then dry off with paper towels was too much work to ever be worth it. I peered at the mirror and was startled by my own reflection, my greasy, slicked-down hair, my ghostly-pale, shiny skin, and the bruises on my face, probably from intubation, I assumed, and the array of bruises covering my arms, abdomen, and hips. Surgery sure was rough business in Kuwait. I crawled back to bed, no longer caring that I was dirty; it was too hard to get clean here.

Later in the morning, Jen returned, laptop in hand, to spend the day by my side. I hadn't even known her just a few weeks earlier, and already she'd been a loyal friend. How could I ever thank her? Well, for starters, I knew she had work to do before she left for New York the following day, and although she professed that she could get it done sitting here next to me, the truth of it was she couldn't, and so once again, sadly, I told her that it really was okay to go. She brought me flowers and arranged them in a tall glass of water. "From IRC," she said as she kissed my sweaty brow and wished me a swift recovery.

I slept fitfully through the morning, buzzed the nurses to say that I hadn't vomited, and asked for a pitcher of water. I drank small sips; I dreaded the thought of dragging myself to the bathroom again.

Adam came in later, smiling. "God, I hate hospitals," he said, passing me a small package wrapped in old newspaper. I slipped my finger under the corner and began to unwrap it. "I'm really awful at presents, but I wanted to get you something," he said as I pulled the paper away.

He was grinning proudly, his fingers restlessly tapping the bedside table. It was the first time I'd seen him without a cigarette clutched between his fingers and a cup of steaming coffee at his lips.

I pulled off the last of the paper, and there, nestled within, was a line of plastic-wrapped dried fish. I started to laugh just as he began to explain. "I didn't know what to get, and then I saw these and thought, 'Ahh protein! Sick people always need protein.'"

That only made me laugh harder, which made the pain worse. He passed me his mobile phone and said, "Call home, I'm going out for a cigarette."

I called home, shared scant details, and said I was fine.

"So you'll be coming home?"

That was the first inkling I'd had that anyone might think I should go home; my only thoughts had been about when I could get back to Iraq.

"No," I answered, "I still have work to do here."

"They'll let you stay?"

"Sure, I'm fine." I was anxious to end the conversation. "Tell everyone I'm fine and I'll call soon, okay?" I hung up and waited for Adam to return.

He walked in, more relaxed but now reeking of smoke. "All set?" he asked.

"I think I can leave here later today or tomorrow if all goes well. When are we going back to Iraq?"

"Even if you're discharged from the hospital tomorrow, which I doubt, I don't know about Iraq. What does the doctor say?"

"That won't be a problem," I said.

He raised a brow. "Make sure to ask for a permission to return to work note," he said. Adam stayed for a bit longer, his fingers fidgeting, eager for another smoke. To his great relief, I said I wanted to rest and he should go back to work. What I wanted was to be alone, to curl up into a sweaty ball and sleep.

Later that day, I told the nurses I was able to drink water and I would try to eat. I assumed my first meal, which would be dinner, would be something light and simple, like broth or Jell-O. Dinnertime came, and an aide arrived with my tray, sliding it onto the small bedside table before leaving. I wiggled around in bed and managed to lift the cover from the tray. There, on a white plastic dinner plate, lay the full carcass of a shiny gray fish, one eye staring up at me. I started to laugh—more protein—and I laughed harder still. My abdomen burned with the pain of it. I finally replaced the tray cover over the still-staring fish and told the nurse later I had eaten. No one questioned me.

I slept on and off, sweating more, my hair matted to my forehead, my skin stuck to the plastic sheet. Occasionally I crawled to the bathroom and then back to bed for another restless night.

Morning dawned and rounds started, but only a junior doctor appeared. I asked about discharge and getting a return to work note. He said I shouldn't return to work, and certainly not in Iraq. But I was determined to get back there—I had work to finish, programs to implement, a manager to hire, too much to leave undone or hope that someone else would do later. I had worked too hard to let it lie idle or simply languish and be lost in the myriad of other work that was being done. I'd had an appendectomy, not brain surgery. I was going back, but I knew I couldn't argue the point here.

"Well then," I said, "how about a back to work note for when I go home?"

"We can manage that," he replied easily.

The senior doctor came later, and he, too, said that heading back over the border to work in Iraq was out of the question. "Too dirty," he added for emphasis.

I thought, but never said, that I was plenty dirty here. I said I still needed that back to work note, knowing full well that he wouldn't write out that I could not return to Iraq. He allowed me to dictate what I needed on the note, no mention of restrictions or comments on where or how I worked. I was discharged later that day. Adam picked me up and deposited me at the rooming house, where I slid into a warm bath and then slept, finally clean, for fourteen hours. I woke refreshed and hungry. I had bread and hot instant coffee for breakfast. Nothing could have tasted better.

Well, maybe pizza and a glass of wine.

A Night of Terror

——◆——

I spent a few more days in Kuwait, and finally, Adam and I headed back to Najaf. The drive was hot, the air heavy, the road as dusty as ever. As we drove through one dusty village, a young boy, as so often happened, ran to the side of the road and raised his arm, in greeting, I thought. The sides of the roads had often been lined with children who, recognizing the uniqueness of a foreign vehicle, would run out to wave and greet us. In the pickup's front passenger seat, I started to wave back, when I realized his arm had drawn back, not in a wave but to throw something—deadly weapon or rock. I ducked and yelled for Adam to do the same. He swerved, and we avoided the brunt of the hit. As that rock and then more rained down on the car door, we saw the boy run into the maze of alleys in the village. We were lucky; his aim hadn't been good enough, and we had realized at the last moment that something was wrong. It was a sobering reminder of where we were. Things had changed in Iraq in the days I'd been recovering in Kuwait. The tension here was thick, the cheering crowds gone, the air heavy with heat and anger.

Paul Bremer was directing Iraq now, and he was in full charge. With a heavy, authoritarian hand, antiterrorism (he had been an antiterrorism expert at the State Department) and rigid security seemed to be his primary goals. Electricity, water, health care for the average Iraqi seemed to languish somewhere lower on the list, and the military civil affairs experts and NGOs struggled to fill the gaps. One reservist sergeant based in Karbala, a literal rocket scientist at home, was busy designing a reliable power grid that would turn the lights on here in Iraq.

But the lights weren't on yet, and the situation had changed significantly in the days since I'd last been here. People were still without money, food, water, and reliable electricity in much of the country. They had lost faith and grown impatient; their tempers flared, and they weren't quite so happy to see us now. We were no longer heroes—we were the people who had ruined everything and delivered nothing. The waving, cheering crowds were gone, replaced by watchful eyes, suspicious minds, and people—like the boy with the rocks—who wanted to take their anger out on someone. Added to that was this new administrator with the perfect hair, fancy suits, and squeaky-clean construction boots. More image than action.

We arrived at the rooming house in Najaf, where the team would now consist of me, Adam as the coordinator, and Azad, a tiny Armenian man who replaced Jason on water and sanitation. I sent a message to Amir, my interpreter, and he appeared early the next morning at our rooming house. We set off early to Karbala to reconnect with the medical system and staff there, who likely thought that my plans and I had turned to dust. There was no reliable or consistent communication in Iraq, no telephones, no internet; there had been no way for me to get a message to them that I was in a hospital in Kuwait, so it was important that I get back to work quickly to explain my absence and implement our programs.

In Karbala, we reconnected with the director of health, the director of primary care, and Dr. Sayed, while I made plans to get our programs off the ground. I would be leaving Iraq soon and needed to make arrangements for national staff to fill my role so that the programs would continue. Dr. Sayed agreed to take over my position as health manager.

The sound of gunfire still broke the stillness of night here, but mostly we'd adapted and normally slept straight through till morning. One night, I was startled awake by a sharp rapping on my bedroom door. I looked at my watch by the bright moonlight streaming in and saw that it was almost midnight. I assumed it was a hotel or IRC employee with a silly message; they frequently knocked at my door late, since they knew I'd answer. Adam and Azad would simply ignore it. I decided not to answer and got up to use the squat toilet in my room instead. On my way back to bed, I glanced out the window, my mouth dropping open. There were four US Army tanks lined up directly in front of the hotel, still more across the road, all with their gun turrets pointed at our windows. Soldiers, too, lined the road with weapons at the ready. I was puzzled but not really afraid; I was sure that they were here on patrol or searching for terrorists or saboteurs. Another series of hard knocks shook my door. I took the time to brush and pin up my hair and run some gloss over my lips before I opened the door.

I heard a quick hush of voices and rustle of movement, and I hesitated. "Step away from the door," a harsh, unseen voice commanded me.

My heart flapped furiously in my chest. This was not what I'd expected, not at all. "Can I come into the hallway?" I asked timidly.

Several rifles appeared, all trained on me. Other than the rifles, which seemed to glisten in the moonlight streaming in, the hallway was black, the men holding the rifles invisible. Bathed in deep shadow, their identities remained obscured, which made the moment all the more sinister. I hesitated, my breath catching in my throat, my lungs seizing up. Were these men the ones the soldiers were after?

"Show your hands!" a voice demanded, and I put my now trembling hands into the air. Motioning with their rifles, they directed me into the hallway, where the glare of lights shone on a cluster of US soldiers, some of whom I was sure I'd seen. I relaxed and dropped my hands; though no one had given me permission, no one shouted to put them back up either. This was okay after all. "Who else is here?" a voice barked.

"Adam," I answered, completely forgetting Azad.

"Is this his room?" they asked as they pointed with their weapons to his door. I nodded that it was. "He's not answering," the soldier sneered.

"It's the middle of the night, he's sleeping." I shook my head. "Want me to wake him?" There was only silence as they motioned me forward with their guns. I walked quickly to his door and knocked. "Adam," I called, "there are soldiers here to see us." I could hear him moving about; the soldiers positioned themselves on either side of his door with me still directly in front, so that when he opened it, he'd see only me. And then I realized that was the point. It was a kind of ambush. But why? Everything seemed to stop; a shiver ran up my spine. This was going terribly wrong. We hadn't done anything wrong and yet . . .

I wanted to shout a warning to Adam to be careful, but just then he opened the door, pulling on his jeans as he did. He was quickly surrounded by soldiers; two hung back with their rifles pointed at me. Oddly, now that Adam was here, I began to relax a little. I was certain that there would be a great story behind this midnight raid, terrorists or some evil element lurking about, with the soldiers dispatched to see to our safety.

The soldiers asked Adam if the new white Toyota trucks parked outside belonged to us. We'd finally gotten our own and had driven them happily into Iraq.

"Yes, they belong to us," Adam answered, a hitch in his voice.

And with that simple reply, there was a distinct shift in the air. Adam was pushed roughly to the stairwell. I was told not to move. Three gun-toting soldiers escorted Adam, and three stayed with me. As he was taking his first steps down, Adam realized I was not behind him. He stopped and turned. "I won't go down without her." They prodded his back with a rifle. "Roberta, are you alright?" he shouted, his voice cracking.

I tried to answer, but they were pointing their weapons at both of us, and my voice was thick and almost a whisper. "I . . ."

The soldiers prodded Adam down the stairs, and when he tried to resist, they barked, "Move or we'll be forced to hurt you." I knew that this was not a rescue.

The soldiers searched Adam's room, tossing everything, opening drawers, pulling his suitcase out and going through his belongings. They had probably searched mine as well, but I was too numb to notice. Minutes later, I, too, was escorted down the darkened stairway at gunpoint. I was marched to the street, where the tanks and a squad of soldiers stood about with their guns pointed at us. Adam was sitting on the street with his hands clasped on top of his head. I was motioned to do the same. I turned to Adam and opened my mouth to speak. "No talking," a voice barked. Though we weren't allowed to communicate with each other, I could feel his unease; we were each lost in our own fearful thoughts.

I could see people crowded around their windows watching the drama play out, and I knew that no matter what happened, this would be bad for us. If not even the soldiers trusted us, why should they? But, as I squatted on the road, it finally occurred to me that some terrible mistake must have brought them to us.

"Excuse me," I said. "We know the commander here." I couldn't grasp his name from the confusing maze that my brain had become. A soldier glared at me; it was clear that I shouldn't speak unless asked a question. All eyes and weapons were trained on us, our skin moist with sweat and fear in the heat and uncertainty of that deep night.

One of the soldiers finally spoke up. "We have reliable intelligence that some terrorists have just moved into the area, a man and woman driving new white Toyotas. You two match that description perfectly."

I swallowed the hard lump that was in my throat. Trouble was, we weren't terrorists, but this was how mistakes were made.

"Check us out with your commander." Adam spit his words into the air. "We're aid workers."

The soldiers mumbled an unintelligible reply. One of them was on his handheld radio, the hum of static breaking up his words.

"Alright, that's it," one of them finally said as the soldiers pulled back their weapons and seemed to relax. "Your story checks out. You can go." He motioned back toward the rooming house, then trained his gaze on me. "The next time we knock—answer. We were just about to kick your door in."

We'd been in custody for less than an hour, but an eternity in a situation like that.

Back in the rooming house, Adam was angry and chain-smoking. "They could have killed us; they were so young and inexperienced, with nervous trigger fingers."

I was just happy that they had released us. My arms ached from holding them on top of my head, and my thighs burned from the long squat. I was already seeing the humor in the episode, too. *Me, a terrorist?* I thought. I had brushed my hair and applied lip gloss.

Adam was relieved that neither of us had mentioned Azad, our impatient, Russian-accented coworker, for his accent would surely have aroused further suspicion. The Russian breakaway Republic of Chechnya had been fighting for independence from Russian rule for almost a decade, and the Chechnyans had gained recent notoriety as a particularly vicious and bold terrorist group. Azad's accent, so similar to that of a Chechnyan, would surely have aroused suspicion and prolonged our confinement. It wasn't that we'd been protecting him; we'd simply forgotten him.

By morning, I was ready to get to work and move on. It was over for me, but I knew that the tension continued for the soldiers, who lived every minute of every day under a cloud of unrelenting pressure and fear; danger lurked everywhere for them. Their suspicion and weapons were always at the ready; to relax for a moment could mean death.

Azad had slept through the entire incident and only learned of it the following morning, when, over coffee, Adam related the story in tense detail.

In his heavy accent, Azad brusquely replied, "That's nothing; once in the Congo I had to dance for my freedom as rebel fighters with guns took shots at my feet. They were laughing so hard, I was sure I'd be crippled."

He shrugged. "So, you didn't have to dance? No problem." There'd be no sympathy from Azad.

And no rest for the weary. I had too much to do. The events of the night before did not affect my appetite and longing for my morning boiled egg. Once I'd devoured every crumb, I was ready to go, and there was still plenty to get done.

Final Days

—•◆•—

Typhoid, an early concern, was rearing its feared head around Karbala and Najaf. It wasn't an epidemic yet, but we knew we had to get medicines and, more importantly, clean water on line here. It was the children who were suffering.

One tiny, stick-thin little girl I saw in a clinic hallway was suffering from typhoid, and there were no antibiotics yet to treat her. All the clinic could offer was IV fluids, and she lay quietly as the fluid dripped into her arm, her eyes open wide, her lips dry and cracked, her skin ghostly pale. Her mother rose, her hands held out toward me as if I could drop the antidote into her hands. "We're working to get the medicines here," I said. That much was true, but Customs in Kuwait was holding up our supplies. If only we could get the bureaucrats to see what we saw, maybe then they'd release our equipment and medicines without the required song and dance.

There were still assessments to complete in Najaf, decisions to be made about exactly which clinics we would support. I spent many of my last days in the long, hot commute to Karbala, revisiting the clinics there. Karbala, home to the mosque from which we'd been shouted away, had suffered further in the weeks since I'd been there last. The unrelenting heat, the lack of running water, reliable electricity, and city services all seemed to conspire to make Karbala a desperate place. Trash was everywhere, rotting food lay in the streets, buzzing, disease-infested flies covered sides of beef strung up in open butcher shops. Weary, bent, abaya-clad women picked through the rotted food, looking for edible scraps to take home. People had been too long without. Karbala was a desperate province in desperate need of relief. We struggled to get our programs on line, set up priorities, decide what was urgently needed, and determine what we had available to meet those needs.

Our WHO Emergency Health Kits had made it through Customs in Kuwait and to us in Iraq and we had delivered them, each carrying enough medicines and supplies to treat ten thousand people for three months, to the medical warehouses in both Najaf and Karbala. There, the kits would be broken up and supplies and medicines would be distributed based on consumption history and current need in the area. Finally—we were delivering help instead of ideas and promises.

We also managed to find the village of Aufi again, in search of Halia, the Karbala University professor we'd met there. I'd hoped to speak with her about the possibility of working with us occasionally as an interpreter. A young neighbor directed us to the "professor's" house, and Halia, fully clad in an abaya, shyly emerged and invited me in for tea with her family. She lived in a typical, one-story, Eastern-style mud and plaster home furnished sparely with a carpet and floor pillows.

Her female relatives and two small children joined us. They sat perfectly still and expressionless, all eyes on me until the quiet was broken by one fussing child. "Don't be nervous," Halia said, touching my hand gently. "They have been afraid of being too near Americans, but I convinced them to meet you and see one for themselves. Understand?"

I nodded. Halia poured tea for all of us and we sat. The children ambled about, coming closer to me. A tiny girl plopped down next to me and smiled, and with that simple gesture, the women seemed to relax. "Please tell them," I said, "that I'm very happy to meet them."

Halia translated for us and served the tea in tiny porcelain cups. "My cousin," Halia said, motioning to one of the women, "says you are very nice, very friendly." I smiled. One small victory, followed by another. Halia was going back to her position at the university. She'd have no time to work with us. Classes would be starting soon, a bit of normalcy finally returning to at least one small piece of Iraq. We sat and shared the sticky sweet tea, and then it was time to say good-bye, though I expected that I'd see Halia at the university, where some of the soldiers still worked.

Other solders lived and worked in an old, abandoned, and now crumbling school building. There was no electricity, though they were getting generators for their computers. They slept in the sweltering heat of the closed-in rooms and bathed in makeshift showers outside. I stopped there occasionally to get information on areas and roads to avoid. The soldiers worked long hours, wrote long reports, and gave me short weather updates.

"It's one hundred and fifty degrees today. Can ya feel it?" a cigar-chewing sergeant asked me one day.

"Jeez, are you sure?" I knew it was hot, I was bathed in sweat, but one hundred and fifty degrees seemed more than I'd imagined.

"Yeah, I'm sure," he answered, fanning himself with a sheaf of papers.

Another soldier, dressed in layers of camouflage and protective gear and guzzling water, piped in. "It sure feels about that to me," he said in a cool Southern drawl. I suppose it could have been one hundred and fifty, at least for them. Clad as they were in layers of military-issue clothing and gear, the heat wove itself into everything they carried and wore—a reminder once again that I had nothing to complain about.

I was back on the road, running from the hospital to clinics to offices to Dr. Sayed, who would be our interim health manager once I left Iraq. There was so much to do and so little time left for me here. I was polishing up my final reports and handing over details of our work to Dr. Sayed. In the meantime, Adam had been looking for a small house for us to move into, and he announced, shortly after the incident with the soldiers, that he had found one. He had been eager to get out of the rooming house, but I felt safe there, certainly safer than I would in a house with just the three of us. I accompanied Adam to have a look at the house. My shoulders sagged at the sight. Though it was a perfectly acceptable-looking place from the outside, there was no running water and only intermittent electricity. The two squat toilets were really just outdoor latrines placed inside the house. Without a flush mechanism, we'd have to pour water in after use. Since there'd been no running water for a while, the rank smell of the toilets permeated the house; the heat of the day baked the scent into the very walls.

There was a generator, but none of us knew how to use it. There was an ominous warning the day before we moved in. Someone had painted anti-American slogans on the gate and outside walls. It seemed clear that we weren't welcome here. Reluctantly, I packed up again and said good-bye to the family who ran the rooming house. They'd tried to convince Adam to let me stay there, but to no avail.

We moved into the house. Adam and Azad chose the only two downstairs bedrooms, so I climbed to the second floor to find a habitable room. As hot as it had been on the first floor, the second was worse. The heat seeped in through the roof and was inescapable. Even the toilet smell was worse up there. I went back downstairs and claimed the floor of the common room as my own.

That first night was to be my only one in the house. Although we had no water, we did have electricity for a time, and it seemed that it might last. I slept on the floor, an overhead fan turning, taking away some of the day's heat, the whir of the blades lulling me into sleep. I was jarred awake by the sweltering heat of the night once the electricity died. The silence was broken by the barking of dogs, and then by the unmistakable sound of gunfire just outside.

"Shit," I murmured.

Although the volley of gunshots had become common night sounds here, they seemed more sinister now that we were in a house without protection, without communication, hidden behind great walls where anything could happen. The gunfire finally slowed and then stopped, but the miserable heat lay heavy in the night air. I lay with a loose shirt covering me and desperately tried to sleep, but I finally gave up and rose for the day at 4:00 A.M. The propane tank for the stove was empty; there would be no coffee this morning, and no food either.

I washed my face with bottled water and sipped the warm water as I dressed, but it was coffee I needed. My eyelids were as heavy as the air, my brain fried, a jumble of loose wires and poor connections. I wrote some final reports by flashlight and sat, waiting for the house and the city to wake.

Finally, Adam, who so required the jolt of coffee and a cigarette in the morning, appeared and brought the last of the propane to life. He boiled some water, and we shared blissful hot coffee.

We piled all of my stuff into one of the SUVs. Today was Friday, the holy day, and our only day off. Azad would remain in the house alone for a day or two until Adam returned; he was not the least concerned. I worried for him, especially after the gunfire of the night before, but he insisted that he wanted to stay there. We said good-bye, and Adam and I headed to Kuwait.

The ride was another hot, dusty one. We were caught several times in the midst of US Army convoys, and we struggled to get around or avoid them. We knew even then the dangers of being caught up in an attack on a convoy; they were such easy and obvious targets, though they at least had the resources to fight back. If we were caught with them in an attack, we were doomed. We darted in and out of the single-file convoy on the single-lane highway and finally broke free, only to run into still other convoys later.

We arrived in Kuwait to beds, electricity, plumbing, heaven. I made some final preparations, finished up reports, and packed my suitcase for the trip home. We got word the next morning that eight armed men had tried to break into the Najaf house. Azad was fine but was moving back to the rooming house until Adam returned.

Security would only worsen in the coming days and weeks, and the tension we'd felt would erupt into further and unimaginable violence just weeks after I left. A car bomb exploded at the Jordanian embassy, killing eleven. Najaf, too, would be the site of a horrific suicide bombing at the central mosque that killed over eighty-five, including the Shi'a cleric Al-Hakim. It would later become the site of heavy fighting with forces loyal to yet another cleric, Al-Sadr.

The car bomb, the popular tool of terrorists, was introduced into Iraq. That summer of 2003, a car bomb exploded at the UN headquarters in Baghdad, killing twenty-three. Seamus, my friend from the Balkans who had guided me around Dublin en route to Bamiyan, was in Baghdad at the time, working with the UN. It took several nerve-wracking days before we learned that he was fine but that many of his coworkers and friends had been killed.

In April 2004, an IRC staff member from Canada was kidnapped from the Najaf house and held for ten harrowing days, threatened again and again with beheading before he was finally released. IRC closed its Iraq programs shortly after that incident. For the first time ever, I felt the fears of *what if.* What if I'd been there? What if it had been me? What if, what if, what if? But I wasn't there, it wasn't me, and I quickly shook off my what-ifs.

Once IRC left, there was no way to know how Dr. Sayed, my interpreter Amir, and so many others fared, or if they'd even survived the last agonizing years, when death hovered so closely.

But there was some good news. Not so long ago, I received an email from Halia, the Iraqi professor, who'd been so determined not to marry. She had met and married an American and was living in Virginia.

The world really is growing smaller by the day.

Homecoming

———•◆•———

I had a one-night layover in Dubai on my way home. I'd been booked into the airport's palatial hotel, and once I dropped my bags off, I combed my hair, swiped some color on my lips, and headed to the Irish pub I'd seen on my way to Iraq, hoping that my luck with free drinks in Dubai would hold out. All I had in my pocket were some Iraqi dinars and my credit card, which I was loathe to use here. The bar was as smoky and enticing inside as it had seemed from the outside. I slid onto a stool, my elbows on the mahogany bar, my eyes on the price list. Shit. This place was too rich for me.

"What'll ya have, miss?" the bartender asked, buffing the shine on a crystal glass. "I . . ." My fingers fumbled in my pocket and slid over my credit card. I hesitated. And the gods intervened.

"What do you fancy?" a tall, sandy-haired man asked, sliding onto the stool next to me. "On my tab," he said to the bartender. My luck had held. God, I loved Dubai, a place where drinks were forever free.

I had two glasses—alright, maybe three—of white wine before slipping back into the maze of the airport and into my room in the hotel, where I slipped into a blissful bubble bath and between clean, crisp sheets in a real bed. Then I fell into the deep and satisfying sleep of the truly weary. I woke early; I was already wondering how the crisis in Liberia was faring. . . .

As it turned out, it was to Sudan that I would head the following winter when the government there backed a silent genocide against the rebels and the villagers who supported them in a remote, barely accessible region called Darfur.

VI

DARFUR

2004

A Secret War

‑•‑

Sudan, the largest nation in Africa, is a country that seems forever plagued by war. It boasts a tormented history of conflict, turmoil, and support for terrorism. It was to Sudan that Osama bin Laden fled in the late 1990s when the heat was on. He was sheltered there until world pressure and the American bombing of a government pharmaceutical factory forced the government of Sudan to reconsider the wisdom of hosting bin Laden. They finally ousted him in 1996. Sudan had also been the sight of a particularly vicious civil war for over twenty years, producing refugees like Grace and the others I'd met in Kakuma in 2001.

By 2004, the world had lost interest in the interminable scuffles and posturing in Sudan. Our distinct lack of interest allowed another far more heinous and corrupt conflict to develop in the distant western part of Sudan known as Darfur. The remote Darfur district of western Sudan, one of the world's poorest and most inaccessible regions, was then home to approximately six million people, representing 20 percent of Sudan's total population and comprising a complex mix of tribes.[1] A mixture of Arab and Christian, they had, for the most part, contained their ethnic and tribal rivalries over the years and had even managed to live side by side.

The people of Darfur had long been isolated in its unforgiving and harsh environs—bone dry and blisteringly hot for most of the year, until the flooding rains came and invariably washed away crops, animals, possessions, and hopes. Only the hearty and determined could survive there, and survive they did, even growing bountiful crops that helped to feed the region through the dry, dusty, and barren months. The year 2002, however, saw the start of a worrying drought, and the meager food resources, already in danger, had essentially disappeared by late 2003. The long war in the south had left the Darfurians far from the central government's focus; that conflict was taking much of the government's resources and attention and fostering a growing sense of animosity, in addition to a literal, as well as figurative, distance between the government and this remote region.

This was a region and a situation that were ripe for exploitation. In February 2003, two rebel groups—the Sudan Liberation Army (SLA) and the Justice and Equality Movement (JEM)—took matters into their own hands. Claiming to represent the oppressed people of Darfur, they launched attacks against Government of Sudan (GoS) garrisons in the region. The Sudan military retaliated with attacks on rebel positions and an aerial bombing campaign against villages suspected of sympathizing with or harboring rebels. The bombing raids reportedly included cargoes of scrap metal, rusted automobiles, discarded appliances, and more heaved out of military airplanes onto unsuspecting villages below, resulting in several deaths.

The government also activated an independent militia of Arab horsemen, known as the Janjaweed (literally, 'evil men on horses'). Those militias were like a pack of feral wolves, but they were far more dangerous because they had been trained, armed, and supported by the Sudanese military. They adopted brutal tactics in their conquest of villages and were efficient in their cruelty, even coordinating their gruesome attacks on innocent villages by assigning groups for looting, for burning, for raping, and for killing. In addition to the pillaging of villages, the Janjaweed militias abducted boys, murdered men, stole livestock, poisoned water supplies, and raped girls and women. Their brazen strategy included branding the hands of the women and girls they raped, an evil maneuver intended to prolong the humiliation and torment of their victims. But they were perhaps best known for the fear they instilled in the hearts and minds of the citizens of Darfur, for even the whisper that the Janjaweed were nearby emptied homes and villages and created literal ghost towns of once bustling villages.

Darfur, a vulnerable, chronically underdeveloped region with precious few reserves in the best of times, was not prepared to cope with these worst of times. In late 2003, disease, starvation, and death loomed on the horizon. To keep news of the scope of this devastating situation from filtering out, the government actively restricted visas and travel permits to journalists and aid workers. The remoteness and relative inaccessibility of the Darfur region, along with the government's control of regional travel, fostered the development of a silent humanitarian crisis that for many months went almost unnoticed, delaying the response from the outside world and limiting media coverage of the plight of Darfurians. The result had been scant news of the crisis; what little trickled through came mostly from the Chad border, where just over one hundred thousand Darfurians had fled. Still, the greater number, over one million, were displaced within Darfur, far from the world's eyes and attention.

The usually staid UN, finally angered by the constant obstacles placed in the path of those trying to help, went so far as to call the horrific hidden conflict "ethnic cleansing." The chief UN humanitarian official, Jan Egeland, described the situation in Darfur as "the worst humanitarian crisis in Sudan . . . and one of the worst in the world at the moment."[2]

The government's complicity in the carnage in Darfur was well known, but without the obligatory hard evidence of atrocities, it seemed that there was no government, no world leader with the courage to stand up for these tortured people and put a stop to the genocide. Ten years after the horrific genocide in Rwanda and the pledges of world leaders that "never again" would the world stand silently by, stand silently by they did. Their pledges rang hollow and empty in the deserts of Darfur, where those fleeing the carnage made no sounds, no cries of anguish, no labored breathing as they ran for their lives. The touch of their bare feet on the sandy earth elicited no sound, no warning to the marauders who were mercilessly hunting them down. A silent escape was their only hope, for they were being hunted, killed, raped, maimed, and tortured by the thousands, their panicked flight invisible to the world, but not to the aid groups who'd been quietly waiting and watching and planning their moves.

In February 2004, the International Rescue Committee (IRC) asked if I would be part of an emergency team they were sending to Darfur in order to assess the situation and provide assistance to the displaced and war-affected people there. This would be another *first in* assignment, more meetings, more waiting, but I was ready, and it was into this political and humanitarian quagmire that I headed in early March 2004.

Back to Africa

———•◦•———

With a trusty lipstick in my pocket (I had long since realized the value to my own fragile ego of a sturdy all-day lipstick whenever I was mired in the mud and muck of a desolate place) and summer clothes in my bag, I headed to Sudan on a cold, rainy afternoon. I flew from Boston to Frankfurt and from there to Khartoum, the capital of Sudan. As seemed always the case, I arrived late in the evening after a full day and a half of travel, so I simply fell into bed in yet another IRC guest house. The night was warm, and the fresh scent of hibiscus wafting in through the open window, along with the sounds of barking dogs, trilling birds, and the crunch of footsteps on gravel, were sweet reminders that I was back in Africa.

On this team, I would manage health. Adam, my coordinator and friend from Iraq, was field coordinator again, and we were joined by Jack, the director of the Emergency Response Unit, out to provide advice and support in those first days. He would only remain for a short time before returning to headquarters in New York.

When I had been in Africa for only a few days, Adam asked me to complete a "proof of life" questionnaire. For all of my experience in aid work, I'd never been asked to do this before.

"Proof of life?" I asked, hovering over the paper. "What is it?"

He hesitated, as though mulling over his words. "Well, you know this is a dangerous place. There's a real threat of kidnapping, rape, murder, and we just want to be prepared. If you go missing and someone says they have you, with this proof of life information, we can ask them to prove it."

He went on to explain that I would provide an answer to a question that I chose—not unlike an online banking question. The question and answer required that it be private, something that only close family or friends would know. If a group claiming to have me could provide that answer, then presumably they did have me, otherwise I was likely dead, or at the very least not with the group claiming responsibility.

The importance of the moment, the question was not lost on me. My first instinct was to be funny. "Just ask them if I'm wearing lipstick. That's the real proof of life for me."

Adam remained stone-faced. "This is serious."

I decided on a question and answer and completed the form. I thought often over the next two months of that "proof of life" statement and its implications. It seemed that the proof of my life had come down to a secret phrase, but the proof of my life, or of any life, would never be found in a secret phrase, a whispered question, a final moment. The proof of my life was in my precious memories of the incredible refugees whom I'd met over the years. They'd given me proof of my own life and in the magnificence of all our lives, and they did it with simple acts of kindness toward each other and to me, a shy smile, an unrestrained giggle, a soft touch, a lingering tear. They encouraged my spirit to soar and my dreams to take flight. They are the ultimate proof of my life.

The envelope with my question and answer, my blood type, and my immediate next of kin remains sealed to this day.

There was little time to linger over my proof of life forms. There was work to do here. The United States Agency for International Development (USAID), with whom I'd also worked in Iraq, was involved early in the Darfur crisis. Keenly aware that time was running out and urgent interventions were needed, we weren't surprised to learn that the mortality rates in Darfur were expected to rise far beyond emergency levels. The cumulative death rate could potentially rise to 30 percent of the vulnerable population[1] once the rainy season began in earnest in May. That's an incredible number; think of 30 percent of the people in your town dying of starvation or untreated disease. The undeniable fact of the government of Sudan's active attempts to effectively hinder life-saving aid from reaching the region made the situation all the more critical.

Aid work had changed; it was no longer a simple and straightforward job. It seemed that every site then, and even now, was fraught with complex political barriers. With all of that in mind and the absolute urgency of the situation guiding us, we started right away, researching, writing proposals, drafting papers, attending meetings, the boring and sometimes deadly dull prerequisites for successful interventions.

Mayo

—◆—

The government of Sudan, though loudly proclaiming their willingness to help the victims in Darfur, continued to place endless obstacles in the path of harried aid workers eager to get to Darfur to provide aid. While we waited in Khartoum for travel permits, we actively sought, much to the dismay of the government, displaced Darfurians who could provide us with the only firsthand accounts available of the atrocities in Darfur. By speaking with them, we hoped to learn exactly what the situation was and what we could do to help.

Mayo, a dusty, destitute, and long-forgotten area of Khartoum, lay far from the city center and was home to internally displaced persons, or IDPs—those who are forced to move around within their own country in search of safety—from the civil war in the south, as well as recently arrived Darfurians. The government housed several thousand IDPs from Darfur in a crumbling and dusty old municipal building in Mayo. It was a dismal place. Children and stray dogs ran together here in packs and scavenged together through garbage, searching for scraps of anything edible, or worthwhile to sell.

Jack had been to the Darfur IDP camp there and had been amazed at the number of women and girls who stepped forward to tell him that they had been raped by the Janjaweed. Here in Sudan, as in so many places, rape had always carried with it a stigma that hung about the victim like a haze announcing that she was no longer clean. As a result, victims here had hesitated to come forward; there were few if any available services, and to proclaim oneself a victim carried the risk of further victimization and abandonment. However, the prevalence of the crime and the sheer number of victims actually helped to erase the stigma, at least here in Mayo, and these women wanted people to know of their plight; they wanted help and they were no longer ashamed to ask for it. They'd eagerly raised their voices and hands to get Jack's attention; each had a story, and each wanted to tell it. The fact that he was a man did nothing to deter them; they were determined to be heard, and they jostled for space in the crowded quarters. Unfortunately, Jack hadn't been able to stay and speak at length with them that day, but he knew that I had plans to get to Mayo, and he promised that I would be there soon.

Days later, I drove out to Mayo with a local staff member. As we waited at the gate for permission to enter the camp, we could see the IDPs huddled just inside, peering out at us expectantly. I smiled, confident that I would be speaking with them shortly. A beleaguered-looking Sudanese official leaned around the heavy wooden gate and asked in Arabic where our papers were.

My escort answered him. "What papers do you mean?"

"My travel permit?" I asked.

He looked me up and down. "No," he said. "You need papers now to come in to Mayo."

"Since when?" I asked. "Jack was just here and he didn't have any special papers."

"That's all changed now. You need papers, or you don't get in."

So we asked tiredly where to get the papers and how long the process might take.

He looked at us and sighed. "I don't know how long, maybe a week."

Arguing the point was out of the question but begging was not, so I tried that. "Please," I said, "we just want to help, and to do that, we have to talk to these people. We won't be long, I promise."

But he was steadfast in his refusal, and finally we gave up and turned to leave. Just then, an International Committee of the Red Cross (ICRC) vehicle showed up, and two workers got out. I decided to wait and see if they would get in. ICRC is considered to have a universal mandate to gain access to the persecuted, dispossessed, and displaced, and if anyone could get in, it would surely be them. I hoped to sneak in right behind them. Instead, I watched as they, too, were turned away.

The ICRC delegate, a skinny, redheaded woman with a cigarette in her nicotine-stained fingers, moaned and said in a clear French accent, "Oh shit! I don't have time for this!" She took a lazy drag on her cigarette and blew out a long plume of smoke, waving away the haze as it reached her eyes. Without ever acknowledging us, she hopped back into her shiny SUV and they pulled away, leaving us all in a cloud of dust and dirt.

It was no surprise that the government was trying to contain the news of their atrocities in Darfur, since here in Khartoum, several NGOs had arrived and we were all heading out to speak to these battered victims. But the savvy government would have none of that, so we were all turned away. But the government was way ahead of us even then. They ordered the IDPs to move from Mayo camp and either return to Darfur, or otherwise manage on their own. Twenty-four hours after our attempt to visit, authorities sent soldiers and police to clear the camp.

Word of the soldiers' arrival and the trouble spread quickly. Many IDPs fled the camp just as they had their villages not so long ago. Some cowered in fear just beyond the gate. Others decided to resist and were joined by local university students. What happened next would never be clear, for chaos overtook the scene. Shots were heard, military tanks appeared, and a bomb was rumored to have gone off. Fighting raged through the night; fires erupted and deathly screams were heard throughout the area.

Finally in the stark light and eerie quiet of morning, the carnage was evident. There were bodies strewn about and pools of blood drying in the sun. IDPs, police, and probably soldiers as well had died here.[1] The numbers of dead and injured were disputed; some reports put the total dead at fifteen, others said eight, including IDPs and soldiers. The government steadfastly denied it all.

The following morning, when representatives from OCHA, the United Nations Office for the Coordination of Humanitarian Affairs, were finally allowed into the area, there was no evidence that Mayo had ever housed anyone, for it was entirely bare; no furniture, no possessions left behind. It had been cleared of all signs of life. The only proof that people had ever lived, and ultimately died, here were drying pools of blood and bloodstained walls riddled with the scars of bullets, undeniable evidence that tragedy had occurred within them.

The UN finally did find some of the IDPs in the middle of nowhere, just outside Khartoum. These victims of Mayo reported to the UN that they had been rounded up on buses, driven out there, and simply abandoned. The UN angrily made the usual complaints to the usual deaf ears of the government.

Meetings

———◆———

U nlike Iraq, where the UN had delayed their involvement, the UN was here in Sudan, and they were here with a vengeance. Although they were more outspoken and involved than I had ever seen them, the UN leadership still failed to step into the murderous quagmire and demand an end to the vicious hostilities in Darfur. There were no calls to send in UN peacekeeping forces. As if to underscore the UN's lack of vision and courage, in April 2004, Sudan was nominated for voting membership to the UN Commission on Human Rights in Geneva, and membership was quickly granted. Only the United States protested the obscene image of Sudan voting on and guiding international human rights issues while it waged a murderous campaign against its own people.

Many UN agencies were represented here: the United Nations Office for the Coordination of Humanitarian Affairs (OCHA); the United Nations Children's Fund (UNICEF); the World Food Programme (WFP); the

United Nations Population Fund (UNFPA); the World Health Organization (WHO); the United Nations Development Programme (UNDP); and the Food and Agriculture Organization of the United Nations (FAO), with more still to come. Most of these agencies had been based here for years, involved in the intermittent wars and misery that had plagued most regions of Sudan at one time or another. For the Darfur crisis, the various UN agencies were gearing up and trying to respond to the needs there, which seemed to increase by leaps and bounds every minute of every day.

We attended endless meetings with the UN while we waited for travel permits. Aside from the overall informational meetings, we also attended sectoral meetings for planning in health, water and sanitation, food and food security, protection, shelter, and education. And when those were done, we attended planning meetings intended to plan still more meetings. There were days I thought my head would explode. The World Health Organization (WHO) had informed us at one of the endless meetings that there was essentially no primary health care in Darfur. For this devastated and diseased population, health care was nonexistent, and without rapid interventions, thousands would die needlessly, just as USAID had predicted. We were here and ready to help once allowed into the region, but without the necessary drugs and equipment, our presence in Darfur would be worthless.

I met with UNICEF, and they donated enough essential drugs to cover our anticipated needs for six months. As described by WHO, essential drugs are those that will provide curative care for expected diseases in a region. We signed an agreement that would require us to provide regular reports regarding the distribution of the medicines. With the supply of medicines, we were ahead of the game, and even if we obtained nothing else, we could function effectively.

IRC headquarters had reminded me before I'd left for Sudan that gender-based violence (GBV) and reproductive care are often neglected in disaster situations and that I should make every effort to initiate a reproductive health program. Women in Darfur and throughout Sudan were still routinely victimized by circumcision, or female genital mutilation (FGM), and would require special care to overcome the multiple complications associated with that practice. The women of Darfur were also being abducted, tortured, and raped in growing and alarming numbers. We had to provide care for all of these tormented women.

Female circumcision is traditionally carried out on small girls, usually between the ages of two and nine. The motivation behind FGM includes prevention of intercourse prior to marriage, promotion of cleanliness, and diminishment of women's sexual pleasure, thereby ensuring faithful wives. Though cleanliness is reportedly a basis for FGM, the practice is anything but, and it often results in lingering infection and, sometimes, death.

There are two main categories of FGM. The *suna* form of FGM involves removal of the clitoris; the *pharonic* form involves removal of the clitoris and labia minora, and excision and sewing together of the labia majora. To check the efficacy of the sewing, nothing larger than a match should be able to be inserted into the vagina once the pharonic procedure is completed. This latter procedure allows only the flow of menstrual blood through the vaginal opening. Reversal of the procedure is said to be rarely undertaken, and these girls are allowed to later marry without reversal of the procedure, resulting in excruciatingly painful intercourse. Once a girl conceives, only surgery can release the glut of vaginal and perineal scar tissue so that a vaginal delivery can ensue. Without surgical release of the scar tissue, vaginal delivery will be impossible, and unless an emergency Cesarean section can be arranged, death for the mother and baby is inevitable. The maternal mortality rate in Darfur was among the highest in Sudan, at least in part due to the continuing practice of FGM.[1]

Reproductive health care was therefore vital in this region, and to implement it effectively, we would need special obstetric equipment to help us provide routine pre- and postnatal care, in addition to ensuring access to clean deliveries and emergency obstetric care when necessary. We would also be providing rape counseling and providing routine women's health care in this very un-routine environment. UNFPA had special kits for use in emergency situations, so I met with the director and his staff in Khartoum and presented them with a long list of equipment that IRC would require to provide effective and sustainable health care for women in Darfur. Initially, UNFPA was so bogged down with the bureaucracy of the UN system that it looked as though I would have to sign away my firstborn to access anything. After several meetings, we finally broke through the endless list of requirements and UNFPA donated valuable reproductive and women's health equipment, which would cover the full spectrum of reproductive care in the coming months. On a handshake and a nod, our agreement was sealed.

I submitted a list of basic equipment needs, including blood pressure cuffs, stethoscopes, suture kits, and the like to WHO in Khartoum. They, too, quickly opened their cupboard and donated what we needed. No bureaucracy there; nothing to sign or even later report on. WHO only wanted to help, and help they did.

We were ready; now we just needed to get to Darfur.

A Place to Call Home

───•◆•───

I never did get an opportunity to speak to the IDPs who'd been forced out of Mayo, but I did finally get my travel permit for Al Fasher, the regional capital of North Darfur, where we would base our operations. It was now home to well over forty thousand IDPs; some estimates had placed the number at seventy-five thousand. I was desperate just to get to work—not the work of meetings and reports and never-ending statistics but the time with refugees that I'd had so little of in Iraq. Here, I was determined not to repeat that cycle.

Early one morning, I finally boarded a shiny WFP plane and flew to the rugged region of Darfur. Al Fasher was a dusty, crowded town, filled with haggard people with drawn, tired faces, goats and donkeys contentedly meandering about, and markets selling tomatoes and onions just on the verge of rotting. There was an ever-present fog of dust in the air. Although there were schools and a military base there, it was a town that had never been properly maintained. Plaster homes were crumbling, electricity was limited to the military areas, and water was a precious commodity. The influx of tens of thousands of IDPs into this decaying scene placed Al Fasher's delicate balance at risk.

Adam had found a small office/house on a dusty main street and moved in quickly. Resources and habitable property here were limited, and we knew that we were lucky to have this place. He'd even managed to find a propane hot plate for cooking, since we would have no real kitchen. We'd been promised electricity, but the town's power was diverted to the army garrisons, leaving us, and much of Al Fasher, in the dark.

Our bathroom was another crumbling mud, two-room outhouse located behind the office; one room held a freestanding latrine and another housed a small room for washing. To wash, we had to lug our water in from a large standing container in our front yard; bucket baths were the order of the day. Without light, washing took great effort, and since the water was dirty to begin with, I always felt dirtier after washing.

The latrine was a tiny dark room filled with more of the marauding, menacing cockroaches that seem to own Africa. When I needed to use the latrine, I was always swifter than I believed I could be, but any foray into the latrine required a delicate dance with the roaches; a run, a dip, a desperate shuffle to get in and out quickly. The enormous insects were stalwart defenders of the latrine and seemed to delight in terrorizing me. Many times, I wound up saying "the hell with it," just peeing anywhere and then running like crazy out of there.

The desperate heat in Al Fasher enveloped the town; the bright blue sky was utterly cloudless, and the sun bore into the dusty land and into all of us for at least fourteen hours of every day. The heat was so intense that it never really wore off; it stayed tucked into everything—clothes, food, even our skin. Without electricity, there was no hope of relief. Because I was in another Muslim post, I was expected to dress conservatively. A head scarf wasn't required, but I usually wore my baseball cap to try to keep the sun at bay. Once again, there was no wine. It seems that the things I crave when

I'm away are the things I can't have—wine, bubble baths, electricity—but the truth is I was too busy to miss any of it.

I slept on a roped metal cot with a pad over it. Tucked underneath my bed was an old fashioned chamber pot, a gift from Adam so that I could avoid cockroach run-ins in the middle of the night. It was far easier in the middle of the night to roll out of bed, feel around for the pot, squat quickly, and then roll right back into bed. In the morning, we would each carefully balance our pots as we carried them to the latrine to be emptied.

Because time for cooking and buying food was limited, I usually wound up eating tomatoes, onions, sometimes even cucumbers and bread if I was really lucky. We had no complaints about our living conditions. Considering where we were and how the IDPs were living, we knew that we were lucky to have a bed and the promise of tomatoes. The team was now just Adam and me. We rarely saw each other during the day; after morning instant coffee, we each headed in different directions to get our work done. In the evening, we saw each other briefly; I headed to bed early so that I could rise with the sun and start work, and Adam often stayed up and worked by flashlight.

I fell asleep those first nights in Al Fasher to the unmistakable sounds of shelling off in the distance. (I easily slept through the sounds now, only waking when the noise was especially loud. Quite a change from that first night in Thal several years earlier, when I literally cowered in my cot.) I knew now that these sounds of war signaled continued terrors for the people they targeted. For us, it meant that the steady stream of desperate refugees into Al Fasher would not ease.

My first destination in Al Fasher was the IDP camp called Al Mashtel, which housed tens of thousands of gaunt, tired refugees in a space meant for less than five thousand. They were huddled together when I first saw them—not for warmth, for they sat under an unforgiving and blistering sun, but rather because there was just not enough room on this patch of land for all of them. An endless sea of people, as far as the eye could see; over sixty thousand by some estimates, held hostage first by the Janjaweed terrors perpetrated back in their own villages and now held hostage here, forced into this crowded, squalid, depressing camp. They survived here with little food, little water, no shelter, and few prospects for anything better.

The scenes were mind numbing, the politics unsettling, and the victims filled with a quiet dignity that was impressive for its infinite hope against all odds or common sense.

The women, though dressed in literal rags, which were covered by the now grimy, fraying, torn veils required by their religion, were almost elegant in their small movements. Just as with the African women I'd met several years earlier in Kakuma and the returning refugees in Bamiyan, these women, too, though encumbered with hellish burdens, were as graceful and poised as though they'd been sitting at afternoon tea instead of on filthy ground amidst misery and squalor. The children—at least those who were covered—wore fraying rags. The few men here, mostly old and milling about in small groups, wore the traditional white robes and turbans of the region. All of them—men, women, and children—wore expressions of sad resignation: tight mouths, loose slumping shoulders, and wary eyes. They had seen the worst of humanity, and they were lucky to have come through it with their lives, even if nothing else. The women here had survived rape and torture and mayhem, the men had escaped certain death, and the children had witnessed it all.

Here in Al Mashtel, they were existing on barren, dry land with occasional sticks of thorn brush pushing through the earth. They had gathered scraps of rags, ragged brush, and, if they were lucky, torn pieces of discarded cardboard, and with these remnants, they had constructed small shelters and borders, a hopeful attempt to create a place they could call home. Women and children made up the vast majority of IDPs here; the men had been murdered or were missing or in fearful hiding from the Janjaweed. The women sat or squatted on their tiny plots of space, seemingly resigned to their plight. The children, dirty and ragged, ran about in search of brush, or just sat quietly drawing lines in the dirt.

This camp was a miserable place to call home. The ground here was littered with feces, both human and animal. Although some latrines had been constructed and more were planned, these rural dwellers weren't used to latrines and so resorted to their familiar habit of squatting wherever the need overtook them. For those who did attempt to use the latrines, their inexperience was clear, for the ground surrounding the latrines was covered with feces. We would either have to teach them the proper use and cleaning of latrines or else dig defecation fields where they could squat and not worry about correct use. Here in this teeming environment, one of our first concerns was the prevention of disease, and to that end, creating better defecation areas or helping people use what was available would go a long way in preventing disease and dysentery outbreaks. Adam and I had already discussed the possibility of just going out and digging the defecation fields ourselves. No fuss, no proposals, no research to back it all up. Just do it. However, there were people here to do just that. It seemed we'd have to wait to avoid stepping on others' toes. In the meantime, I tried to watch where I put my open-toed-sandal-clad feet, but I somehow never really paid enough attention—I was busy writing notes or speaking as I walked—and, no surprise, I often wound up with literally shitty feet.

In addition to the feces, the ground was littered with the rotting, decaying carcasses of dead donkeys, goats, and other small animals. Those lucky enough to escape with their animals had been unable to feed them or provide them with water, and they had withered and died, as so many of their owners soon would here in this fierce wasteland. Combined with the ever-present feces, the stench was overwhelming; it filled the air and attracted flies and birds of prey, giving the scene its final terrible indignity.

Throughout the camp were freestanding hand pumps for water so that people could fill up jugs for cooking and cleaning. The containers were filthy, long-used plastic jugs and were usually carried by small children, who stood in never-ending lines to fill their jugs, though they could barely carry the heavy containers once filled. They didn't complain, for their time at the pump was playtime, a chance to meet other children and be childish while waiting their turns. Once they reached the tap and filled their jugs, they struggled to balance the heavy containers, but the water invariably splashed out onto the ground. By the time they made it home, much of their precious cargo had been lost.

The lines for water were also remarkable for the presence of animals. The donkeys, goats, dogs, sometimes a camel, lingered about in search of water, too. The problem was they would surely spread disease through the open water taps. The children and people here didn't seem to notice or mind the animals in their line for water, for they were used to sharing. It was the health teams who watched in horror as goats drew a drink from the open tap.

As wretched as this place was, it was home for now, and the truth was these people here in this squalid camp were the lucky ones. They had survived, they had a place to stay, some food for their children, the beginnings of health care, and finally they had some semblance of protection. Protection was the one thing that the IDPs and villagers consistently identified as their primary need.

"If you do nothing else, at least protect us," was the commonest refrain.

"What we need is protection from these evil men while we are here and a guarantee of safety in our own villages," one man said, his fingers scurrying over his prayer beads. "You understand? We want to return home, plant our fields, and continue our lives."

The Janjaweed, who had so brazenly attacked the IDPs' villages, later attacked their camps, from which they looted recently donated items such as food, blankets, and shelter materials. The IDPs were so terrified of the Janjaweed that they asked aid groups not to distribute these items in hopes of preventing another attack. It was a conundrum. Our very presence here afforded these haggard and besieged displaced victims a semblance of protection, and they felt sure that even the bold Janjaweed would hesitate to attack under the eyes of international witnesses. However, it wasn't long before several aid convoys were ambushed as they traveled about, the Sudanese workers shot or injured by land mines. But the Janjaweed reportedly failed to show their faces and quickly retreated, blaming the attacks on rebel elements.

The government of Sudan, a military dictatorship with a well-earned reputation for torturing its own citizens, was finally, and with great reluctance, allowing international aid into the region. But once allowed into Darfur, our movements were restricted, our activities and interventions confined to specific areas, usually the provincial centers. As a result, we had access to only about 15 percent of the population of Darfur, leaving the vast majority of the victims of Darfur still without help of any kind. The government seemed determined to thwart our efforts at every turn. By controlling our movements, they manipulated us and the situation to their own advantage. It was the most politically charged, bureaucratically boondoggled area imaginable. If ever I needed a glass of wine to get past the bureaucracy and the bullshit, it was then. But there was no wine to be had.

Time was running out, not just for the IDPs in Al Fasher but for the still hidden, who were so adversely affected by the conflict here. One million people were on the move, searching for safety, protection from their tormentors, help to reclaim their lost lives. Some would find their way to IDP camps, but many more, still terrified, would stay hidden and alone, starving and dying, afraid to venture into the camps.

There were also too few NGOs with just too much to do. Together, with our best efforts combined, we could only hope to slow the coming disaster, not prevent it. We needed more of everything—food, medicine, equipment, and experienced personnel. The rains were imminent, as we'd heard at every meeting, and it was imperative that we have our resources in place. Adam worked furiously to get our WHO emergency kits through Khartoum and into Darfur before the rains came and transformed Darfur into an impenetrable wall of mud and water. We felt overwhelmed some days by the scope of the unfolding events. Without world attention on Darfur, it was a battle that, we were acutely aware, we could well lose.

Hawa and the
Terrors of the Janjaweed

———◆———

T he stories of the Janjaweed's barbarous acts were swiftly becoming the stuff of legend. They were the cruelest militia imaginable. There was no basis for this war of atrocities beyond the original rebellious and pathetically ineffective rebel attacks on government garrisons in 2003. The government's retaliatory attacks on civilians in the area were clear violations of international law and basic decent behavior. This seemed to be a government of thugs. The proof of that lay in the stories of their victims.

Hawa was thirty-two years old when I met her in the health tent in Al Mashtel. She wore a faded pink dress and head scarf, a perfect complement to her shiny, nut-brown skin. Through an interpreter, I learned that she'd only recently escaped an attack on her village in Tawila, about a three-hour drive from Al Fasher. She'd been a busy midwife in Tawila, delivering babies, caring for women, often with only a bag of feed or grain as payment for her services.

"My life was good," she said, a sudden light swimming in the deep black of her eyes. "My husband farmed a small piece of land, where he grew cucumbers and tomatoes, sometimes onions or even beans if the last year's harvest had been good. My three girls were growing strong, and all attended school in the village center." She smiled, a sad, lopsided lift to her mouth, as though she was struggling with the memories. "Life was better than it would ever be again. I just didn't know how lucky I was."

They'd lived, she said, in a small mud plaster house surrounded by their treasures. Her greatest treasure, aside from her children, had been her UNFPA midwife bag, which she'd received at her graduation from the Ministry of Health (MoH) midwifery school in Al Fasher many years before. It had contained everything she'd needed to care for the women and babies of her village. She and her husband had been respected members of the community of Tawila. They'd heard of the Janjaweed attacks in other nearby villages and had even spoken to victims as they'd stopped in Tawila en route to safety in Al Fasher. But, as is common for all of us, they'd never expected that they would be attacked, that their lives would be turned upside down and that they would have to struggle simply to survive. "That was the kind of thing that happened to other people," she said firmly. "Not to us. Not in Tawila."

She was quiet then, sitting perfectly straight in one of the clinic's wooden chairs, her long, graceful fingers playing with the edges of her dress. I waited, afraid to interfere, wanting her to have the time to tell me what she'd come to say. After a time, she cleared her throat and began.

"The day was warm," she remembered. "I had delivered a baby in the very early morning and I'd planned to return to check on the baby and mother later that day. My girls had just gone to school, my husband was in the fields." She paused again, seeming to roll the memories over in her mind.

I touched her arm. "Are you okay?" I asked. "You don't have to finish."

Her eyes were moist. She smiled wanly and continued.

"I'd been paid for the morning's delivery, so I planned to go to the market to buy some eggs for dinner. I counted out my coins, placed them in my small purse, and started out."

Just then, three small girls, all dressed in the traditional gauzy veil and brightly colored dresses, shuffled in, their eyes searching until they rested on Hawa. "My girls," she said and smiled warmly as she greeted each with a hug and whispered endearments. The three avoided my gaze and shyly looked down, pushing the sandy earth about with their sandaled feet. She motioned them to sit on a nearby bench and she continued.

"I walked to the market in the center of the village," she said. "It seemed somehow different that day, a kind of tension in my quiet village. A crowd had gathered," she remembered. "But they were quiet, almost solemn; I thought someone important had died."

She'd watched, puzzled, as people had whispered to one another while still others had seemed to be leaving the marketplace, their donkeys straining under the weight of bags of grain and household items. People had been in a hurry in a place where there was nothing to hurry for. "Something was very wrong; I could feel it, and I was suddenly afraid." She'd seen a friend standing in the midst of the crowd and approached her.

"What is it? What is wrong?" she'd asked her friend Zeinab.

Zeinab's eyes had grown wide with terror. "The Janjaweed," she'd whispered. "They are near."

"Those words could only mean one thing," Hawa declared. "Tawila was about to be attacked. I have never known such fear or confusion."

I could see the pain of that moment in her red-rimmed eyes and in the fine tremors of her hands as she relived those hours. She spoke softly, quietly, so her girls might not hear. "Everyone was consumed with fright that day, afraid to move, afraid not to."

Some men had planned to fight, she said, and they'd raced for their weapons; others had known that the only sure way to survive was to escape the village or to run and hide in the *wadi*, the drying riverbed. Hawa had

259

hesitated, unsure if she should escape to the fields or gather her children from the school. The Janjaweed had answered her hesitation by galloping toward the village center; the unmistakable sounds of the horses' hooves and the cries of the villagers had filled the air and destroyed all hope of getting to the school. She'd joined others in the desperate race to the *wadi*, and as she and countless others had crouched there silently, they'd listened helplessly to the agonizing screams of terror coming from the village. They'd watched in horror as clouds of black smoke had drifted into the clear blue sky. She'd hunkered there for what seemed an eternity until all sounds of distress had faded. She didn't know how long she'd been there, but on that day in late February, the sun had been high in its full heat of the day as she and many others had emerged tentatively from their hiding places.

She'd been filled with dread as she'd run to the schoolhouse, stumbling and falling several times, tearing her veil as she'd hurriedly picked herself up. Her hands were balled into tight fists as she continued her story.

"I passed bloodied bodies in the road, many that I knew and had called friend, but I couldn't stop to help. I had to find my children." She'd reached the school just as many others had. The sobbing and terrified teachers and students had poured out of the small building, some wounded and covered in blood, others' clothes torn. All had appeared somehow disheveled and unlike the laughing girls they'd been just hours earlier. Something terrible had happened here. "I rushed ahead, pushing people out of my way. I had to find my girls," she said, her voice cracking.

She was lucky; she'd found her girls, gathered them up quickly, and told them they had to leave Tawila. They'd raced to her husband's fields, but the fields had been smoldering and smoking, and there had been no sign of him; no sign that he'd even been there. His scorched crops had been abandoned. He seemed to have just disappeared.

"We could not wait," she sobbed. "We couldn't even go back to the house to get anything. I was too afraid the Janjaweed would be there, and so we fled. For three days and nights, we walked; we hid in the *wadi*, we hardly slept, so desperate was I to reach Al Fasher."

She'd had no word of her husband, but she knew it was likely that the Janjaweed had killed him, for it is the men they target for death, the men who might one day rise up and fight back and defeat these vicious thugs.

Many others had disappeared that day as well. Hawa had had no word of Zeinab, her lifelong friend, no way to know if she'd been murdered or kidnapped, or somehow escaped. She had no idea either of what had happened to the tiny baby she'd helped to deliver that morning; surely he and his mother, still weak from the delivery, would have been trapped in their tiny house during the attack. Hawa did not want to think of what might have befallen them.

When I asked her, Hawa said she would not return to Tawila. "It is not safe there," she whispered out of earshot of her children. "I cannot return until I know that we will be safe, and that may never happen. Our journey here to Al Mashtel was long, and we were tired and hungry and thirsty and filled with fear for all of the three days we traveled. We feel safe here for now."

Seventy-five people died that day in Tawila, among them several local merchants who were known to be vocal in their opposition to the government. It was presumed that those men had been singled out for death and purposely hunted down that February morning. Eyewitnesses reported that the Janjaweed were aided in this cruel and well-organized attack by uniformed members of the Sudanese military. There has been no government investigation of military involvement, just the usual, well-rehearsed denials.

Over ninety-three women, including forty-one schoolgirls and their teachers, were raped and tormented; one hundred and fifty women were reported abducted; an unknown number of men and boys were also kidnapped. Their fates are still not known.

Tawila became a ghost town on that bloody day filled with death and horror.[1]

Tawila

◆

On a hot, hazy morning, a month after the assault there, we finally had permission and permits to assess Tawila, the village from which Hawa and her children had fled. What had been a three-day escape on foot was a three-hour drive over rough, sandy roads. The drive was remarkable for the dust that covered all of us and for the empty villages we saw en route. Once-bustling settlements were now abandoned, all signs of life destroyed, the earth scorched. In the quiet of morning, you could almost hear the echoes of recent screams still lingering in the haze and dust.

Fields were abandoned, no harvesting or planting in this, the planting season. Without a fresh harvest to feed Darfur in the coming months, the future would be even bleaker than the present. This was a dead and empty land, courtesy of the Janjaweed's reign of terror. The landscape just beyond Tawila on the road to Kebkabiya was even more desolate, village after village razed to the ground. The only signs that life of any kind had existed there were the scattered shards of clay pottery, only because the fires had managed to just singe the rugged clay. Entire communities had been decimated, almost as if an eraser had simply wiped everything clean, leaving barely a trace of the villagers and their lives.

Tawila, too, had changed from Hawa's initial description of the carnage, which had been confirmed by so many others. It was eerily quiet on our visit, not the bustling, crowded village of people's memories. There was still evidence of the Janjaweed's brutality in the burned-out homes, smashed property still lying about, and scorched fields. I wondered which had been Hawa's fields. Many houses remained; they'd likely been looted of everything of value, but still they stood, erect sentinels in their own defiance of the Janjaweed. Where there were homes, there was surely hope.

These rural villages consisted of simple mud plaster huts and homes; sometimes in the larger, more prosperous villages stood a few wooden structures—schools, a clinic, a municipal center. Electricity was rare, although some villages had acquired it; wells and boreholes had been dug to provide water. It was those water supplies that the Janjaweed had targeted and destroyed or poisoned, leaving the fragile population without the necessities of basic survival. Water now could only be drawn from drying, contaminated streams, placing the population at great risk of contracting one or another deadly disease.

Although most residents of Tawila had abandoned this place, there were budding signs of life once again, as perhaps one thousand IDPs whose villages had been attacked had stopped in Tawila on their way to somewhere, anywhere else. These IDPs were unsure if they would wait here in Tawila or just push on to Al Fasher. Here in Tawila, aid groups were starting assessments, trying to determine if aid was needed here, or if these displaced would simply move on. WFP arrived the day we were there as well. They were planning food distributions for the people staying here, good news for these starving families.

The British branch of the NGO Save the Children (SC-UK) opened a clinic in Tawila the day we arrived to assess the situation. The clinic was held in an old, dilapidated two-room schoolhouse in the village center. IDPs lingered nearby, many spending their days inside another old school building but hiding in the *wadi* at night, fearful of further attacks.

While at the SC-UK clinic in Tawila, I had an opportunity to speak to one of the staff there. Ibrahim had been a medical assistant and a resident of Tawila until the attacks there. He, his wife, and his two small children had escaped the massacre and fled to the safety of Al Fasher the day of the attack. Once he was sure his family was safe, he'd secured a job with SC-UK and returned to Tawila to help. Under the watchful eyes of the Sudan security forces, he told me what he knew about Tawila.

"You must be careful," he whispered. "The Janjaweed are not far from here. They are camped out just beyond the village, and they are watching us. I fear that they will attack again. The SLA are nearby as well." His eyes darted about as he spoke, landing first on the security men and then on his coworkers. It would be bad for him if he was found to be sharing this information with me. He was brave to speak so openly.

"Won't the SLA provide some protection?" I asked.

He shook his head. "The SLA cannot protect us, but their very presence here convinces the Janjaweed to stay and harass us. We are pawns in the middle of their fight."

No wonder the IDPs here planned on continuing their journey to safety. Ibrahim said that each day, countless IDPs headed to Al Fasher with loaded-up donkeys or goats in tow. Some were able to arrange rides on trucks going that way, but the outcome would be the same—Tawila would be abandoned and empty again if it were not protected.

"The Janjaweed are living openly in Kabkabiya," he said. Kabkabiya was a town about four hours by car from Tawila. It was a large town housing an army garrison. If the Janjaweed were there, they had to have the permission of the army.

"The Janjaweed do nothing without the authorization of the military," Ibrahim declared. "The military guides their attacks, sometimes sending in helicopters first to guide the offensive. Sometimes the Janjaweed even wear military uniforms, and they all carry military weapons."

Ibrahim was not sure how long he would stay, for he was certain that Tawila would be attacked again and what had not been destroyed, ultimately would be. He wasn't sure if the next attack would come from the Janjaweed or the rebels. For people living with paralyzing fear, either was an ominous proposition.

By July 2004, SC-UK considered closing or scaling down their clinics here. The Sudanese military had moved into Tawila and right into the clinic, ostensibly to protect the IDPs, but their very presence interfered with the clinic's work by intimidating patients and staff, and placed the workers and IDPs at great risk should an attack occur.[1]

But Ibrahim had not lost hope for the future of Tawila; he believed that the town would recover one day, and that his friends and family would return home to bring new life to this devastated region.

He just didn't know when that would be.

Disease and Disaster

Hearing Hawa's and Ibrahim's words and seeing Tawila for myself infuriated me, but as an aid worker, I was required to at least maintain the appearance of neutrality. There wasn't really time to linger over their stories or the ongoing tragedies, or let my anger boil over. There was too much to do. The health of these people was precarious at best. Most were in some stage of chronic or acute malnutrition. Few would likely survive even a minor illness. Their bodies hadn't the strength to fight off respiratory infections or diarrhea; they needed medical care, immunizations, nutritional screening, access to clean water, sanitation facilities, and a roof over their heads, even if only a plastic one, to protect them from the harsh rays of the sun and the coming rains.

Sudan's Federal Humanitarian Aid Commission (HAC) decided to move the ever-increasing population of IDPs from the poorly equipped Al Mashtel site to a new, but even more desolate, site called Abu-Shok, on the outskirts of Al Fasher. Adam was involved in designing shelters for the new camp. I would be involved in setting up a health system for the new camp, since it had been decided among the involved NGOs here that IRC would take the lead in health in Abu-Shok.

The endless meetings I'd so dreaded in Khartoum had paid off. I already had a complete pharmacy, supplied by UNICEF, with enough essential drugs to last us about six months. We also had reproductive health equipment, supplied by the UNFPA, and basic clinic equipment, courtesy of WHO, so that we could establish services without delay.

We had many health concerns for this vulnerable community. First among those was the potential for, and intermittent reports of, a measles outbreak in Al Mashtel. Although hard to believe, measles was and continues to be a scourge causing hundreds of thousands of deaths among displaced, dispossessed, and refugee children.[1] It was still the leading cause of childhood death from vaccine-preventable disease around the world. Due to the IDPs' already precarious health, the spread of measles in a refugee setting is perilously swift and often deadly, not unlike throwing a lit match onto dry brush in a forest.

This region was also part of Africa's "meningitis belt," where every year an outbreak of the deadly infection occurs, whose swift spread can be readily prevented or halted with vaccines. Meningitis season was just around the corner; it consumes the summer months when rains make access to health care near impossible. UNICEF had a supply of meningitis vaccine but not enough to cover the region.[2] Rationing vaccines and ultimately health care was an issue that faced us if more was not made available in time.

And still there was more. Polio, a waterborne disease that usually infects young children, attacks the nervous system, causing paralysis, muscular atrophy, deformity, and sometimes death. It was reemerging, according to WHO.[3] Although previously eradicated in Darfur, recent conditions and lack of vaccination campaigns had allowed the devastating disease to reemerge and attack the most vulnerable of the population here.

Aside from the vaccine-preventable diseases, there were other worrisome ailments here in this region. Dysentery, malaria, leprosy, leishmaniasis, guinea worms, river blindness—the list was endless, but most were familiar to me now; long gone was any anxiety on my part when I encountered those diseases. Others, though, would require my full attention. River blindness, another form of filariasis—which results in filariae—the migrating worms I had seen at Kakuma, the refugee camp in Kenya—is transmitted through the bite of an infected fly or mosquito and can cause blindness. It is most commonly found near rivers in Africa where the *Simulium* fly breeds, hence the name river blindness. There was treatment available, but the government of Sudan controlled that drug supply.

Guinea worms are another form of filariae, although guinea worms are the largest of this species, and the females can actually grow to three feet in length. Guinea worms are contracted by ingesting them, usually in contaminated freshwater. Once they are in the stomach, digestive juices release the infected larvae into the body, where they mature. The presence of female larvae in the human body provokes an allergic and inflammatory response, forcing the worms to break through the skin. They are most commonly seen on the legs but can emerge from any site, including genitalia, arms, and breasts. There are multiple complications, including systemic infection, but they can also emerge without fanfare and fuss, causing only aesthetic distress. There is both drug treatment, which is readily available, and the alternative treatment of making small incisions over larvae sites to allow the worms to migrate out, which is what we had done for filariasis in Kakuma.

Leprosy is another disease indigenous to Sudan. Transmission is insidious and swift—it can be passed by breathing in the droplets of an infected person's sneeze. As easily as it can spread, few people actually develop the disease. There are several diverse strains of leprosy, each with multiple presentations and symptoms. I only knew that if I thought I was seeing leprosy, I would refer the patient to a center capable of making the appropriate diagnosis.

For now, simpler, more ordinary diseases were our primary concern. Health data revealed that diarrhea, respiratory infections, malaria, and eye infections were the commonest complaints. These seemingly simple diseases could easily prove fatal to this already vulnerable, debilitated population. Access to quality health care and medicines was the remedy, and we were designing our health programs to respond to that need.

Aside from designing the programs, we literally had to design and then construct clinics in the new camp. They would need to be functional in this austere desert environment, and they would have to be erected quickly, literally within days. We had neither staff nor materials to get it done, but fate was with us. One morning, a jovial, potbellied, laughing German arrived at our door and volunteered to help.

Viktor was an amiable fellow who seemed able to do most everything. He sat down and, in a heavy German accent, asked what I needed to run the clinic. He then made some architectural-grade drawings and proceeded to incorporate all of my needs into a simple reed-and-steel structure. He and Adam arranged to purchase the materials, and they hired local workers to build it. Henry supervised and then joined the crew to guarantee the project's swift completion. In just forty-eight hours, we had a beautiful reed structure, functional, sturdy, and ready to use, but although we had medicines and equipment, we needed staff—local doctors and nurses to staff our clinics. Other NGOs and even Adam, a sudden pessimist, said we would never get staff; I disagreed. I knew we could find well-trained staff to join us. I went to the Ministry of Health (MoH) in Al Fasher with my wish list, the number of doctors and nurses and support staff I was looking for. We were, to everyone's surprise but mine, inundated with applications and crudely written resumes.

Halima—Dignity and Desperation

———•◆•———

We had the necessary equipment and drugs for our planned clinics, but we needed local staff to run the clinics on a day-to-day basis. The MoH and the local government labor office arranged interviews with potential staff. On a hot, cloudless day, we met the candidates proposed by the MoH.

One of these was a tiny, bone-thin woman applying for a nursing position. Considering that most Sudanese women were tall and stately, this woman stood out due to her diminutive size. Dressed in the traditional full veil, she was lost in the plentiful folds of fabric. Her skin was a rich cocoa brown, her eyes the deep sparkling black of a freshly polished onyx. Her delicate features, her thin brows, the slant of her nose, gave her an almost regal appearance. She stepped forward slowly, a hesitation in the shuffle of her feet, her eyes firmly on the ground in front of her. Through the interpreter, and after introductions, I motioned her to sit across from me. She stumbled, her foot catching on the folds of her dress. She caught herself and slid onto the seat, busying herself with smoothing the fabric of her dress. Her anxiety was palpable.

"*Shwaya*," 'Easy,' I said gently.

Halima had come a long way for this interview. She was from Kabkabiya, the village beyond Tawila, about seven or eight hours away if the roads were good on a given day. Kabkabyia usually had a relatively small population of about sixteen thousand but was then home to a population of sixty-two thousand IDPs who had fled attacks on their own nearby villages. The newcomers were straining the meager resources of that already isolated town. Food and medical supplies were dwindling, and there were no job prospects. Starvation was near at hand until the WFP, Action Contre La Faim (Action Against Hunger, or ACF), and other NGOs stepped in to actively assess the situation and begin food and health programs.

Although Kabkabiya was home to a Sudanese government military garrison and should have been safe, the Janjaweed, acting on behalf of the government, had identified, attacked and killed rebel sympathizers there. They also continued to strike nearby villages, likely with the help of those soldiers stationed in Kabkabiya. The IDPs there had hoped to find protection from the Janjaweed in the soldiers' very presence, but it was those same soldiers who often directed the when, where, and how of the Janjaweed attacks. The Janjaweed attacked two IDP camps in Kabkabiya in December 2003 right under the nose of the Sudanese military.[1] Those IDP camps had been abandoned; the fearful inhabitants had sought refuge with family and friends in the area. The Janjaweed continued to be positioned right outside the town, ready to attack anywhere at the government's direction.

Halima knew, as most in North Darfur did, that the government was still confining NGOs to the provincial capitals. In North Darfur, we were all based in Al Fasher, and those looking for help, food, medical care, protection, or just a job came to Al Fasher for help.

"Are you a nurse?" I asked her.

She smiled tentatively and started to speak. "Well, I studied to be one but only finished one year of school."

She paused, drew a deep, steadying breath and continued. "I married," she said softly, "and so I had work to do at home and then quickly I had babies. I could not finish school with babies at home. My husband, Ismael, took care of us. He worked repairing motors and he earned enough to support all of us; even my mother lived with us." She smiled at the memories.

She was describing what was surely a cozy life in this bleak region. No fields to plow or cultivate, a steady source of income, no "hungry season" in her house.

"My Ismael supported the SLA against the Janjaweed and government, and once the government had his name, he was a marked man. I begged him to stop, to leave Kabkabiya so that he would be safe."

Halima hesitated, taking time to catch her breath and compose herself. In a rush of words, she continued her story. "Ismael refused to leave, and one day, not so long ago, the Janjaweed caught him. I was told that he tried to run, but the Janjaweed shot him in the back and he fell, bleeding and dying, and still the Janjaweed tormented him in his last moments." A sob caught in her throat. "Their horses surrounded him and they kicked and stabbed him until he finally died."

Fresh tears welled up in her eyes, and she dabbed at them with the end of her veil. "We have all moved here, to be safe," she said softly. "We are staying with my cousin's family, but their house is small and the food is not enough. If I can get a job, I can support my own children and my mother."

She looked at me with pleading in her eyes. "I am not a nurse," she said, "but I can learn. I will do anything." She leaned toward me and grasped my hands in hers. "Please," she whispered, "help me."

My heart broke for her. I looked at my list of jobs and saw "registrar" among them. "You can read and write?" I asked.

Halima smiled broadly. "Of course," she replied.

"I will see what we can do," I said, hoping that Adam would agree to hire her.

Her eyes filled with tears and she hugged me. "*Shukran*," she murmured.

Her thanks humbled me; I had done nothing aside from giving her hope, yet to her it was everything.

But we had to place her hiring on hold; the clinic was delayed again.

Abu-Shok

———•◆•———

The move from Al Mashtel to Abu-Shok was initially scheduled for early April, but the details of the new camp had not been worked out. Finally, after rounds of new meetings, the move was scheduled for late April. IRC, ICRC, Oxfam, the UN, and other NGOs worked furiously and dug latrines, drilled for water, and designed simple shelters constructed of plastic sheeting so that the residents of Abu-Shok would have the basic necessities of life. A small village was springing to life and bursting through the barren desert landscape. In the months ahead it would grow far beyond capacity, unable to hold all those who needed shelter.

I worked with Adam and Viktor to get our clinic constructed, stocked, staffed, and ready for our first patients. The clinic was ready for the move, with Halima at the registration desk. We saw almost fifty patients on moving day. The daily patient census continued to grow as more IDPs flooded into Abu-Shok. A second clinic was constructed and staffed, and it, too, became well utilized, each clinic seeing over three hundred patients a day. As we expected, diarrhea and malnutrition were the commonest complaints.

Action Contre La Faim (ACF), a French NGO, agreed to undertake a nutrition survey in Abu-Shok and discovered that the malnutrition problem was growing and reaching crisis proportions despite the food rations and medical care. They opened feeding centers to provide vital nutritional support to starving babies and children, but for adults and older children, the options were few; they relied on the food rations supplied by WFP. Most people here suffered some degree of starvation; some would die, and, as I'd seen so often around the world, many others would linger, their bodies slowly wasting, their hopes fading. Starvation remains, to this day, the toughest disease to treat.

Fuel became a problem as well, for there simply wasn't any. Women and children went out beyond the camp's perimeter and foraged for scraps of brush or sticks of wood, but it was then, when they were alone and most vulnerable, that they were often targeted for rape and violence. There was some semblance of protection within the boundaries of the camp, but just beyond its unseen walls, danger lay in wait.

Abu-Shok offered at best an austere existence, a fact that made it easier for the government to coerce these desperate people into returning to their own villages. Although the government promised protection, these were the same thugs who were in cahoots with the cowardly Janjaweed. The IDPs' terrifying experiences made them wary of the loose and empty promises of the government, and most simply stayed put. Abu-Shok would not be closing anytime soon. It actually quickly grew to hold more than we had originally anticipated. This tiny camp-village that had sprung from infertile earth was bursting. Without a solution to the Darfur crisis, a solution that would allow these haggard people to return home, another camp could well be needed.

We had been instructed by the government, even threatened, that under no circumstances were we to speak with the refugees or take pictures. We could be expelled, they warned, or jailed, if caught doing either. But how else to tell a story, to get the international community involved without the words of the victims and the devastating pictures that truly tell the story? I was determined to do both, and I was often in trouble for my attempts.

I did manage to speak with many refugees, for it was only through their words that we could know the horrors they'd experienced. Pictures would prove to be far more difficult, but I resolved to at least try. I practiced holding my camera under my baseball cap and snapping pictures through the opening in the back of the cap. After many attempts and pictures only of the lining of my cap, I finally mastered the technique. I thought I was pretty ingenious, ready for anything.

One morning as we walked through the new camp at Abu-Shok, I was struck by the desolation of the scenes and the hopelessness on the faces of the refugees. I surreptitiously took my camera out, turned it on, and had it cupped in my hand when a local government official approached Adam and me. It was clear from his purposeful stride that he was angry about something, so I hurriedly stuffed the camera into my shirt pocket and hoped he wouldn't notice.

The official proceeded to berate us for a series of imagined infractions, the worst of which was that we had brought a "foreign woman" in to speak with the refugees. None of this, at least this time, was true, unless he meant me. As he continued his tirade, I began to look around at the heart-wrenching scenes and wished he'd just wrap it up. I had things to do.

Suddenly, without warning, the unmistakable whir and click of my camera going off filled the air. My eyes grew wide as I glanced in horror at my pocket. Adam's jaw clenched and his eyes flashed as he cast a sideways glance at me. My stomach churned. I waited for the inevitable threat from the government official. And waited. But our visitor kept right on talking, with nary a glance at me. And then I realized that he was so enamored with the sound of his own voice that he hadn't noticed my discomfort or Adam's anger. We might not have been standing there at all. I felt such relief, I started to smile, and then to laugh. Adam raised a brow, and I coughed to cover my laughter.

How lucky was I? Another bullet—so to speak—dodged.

The Continuing Genocide

— ⋅◆⋅ —

I spent over two months in Darfur, assessing the health of the displaced and conflict-affected, and implementing health programs to forestall a health disaster, but a health disaster was imminent anyway.

While White House lawyers pored over material to determine if Darfur met the international legal criteria to be called a genocide, the genocide continued. The war was one of semantics for Washington power brokers. The genocide in Srebrenica had occurred almost ten years earlier, yet it was only in 2003 that the World Court in Geneva ruled that in fact a genocide had taken place. Too little, too late for the dead of Srebrenica. I feared the same for the people of Darfur.

The horrific stories from Darfur continued to trickle out. The tormented stories of Halima, Hawa, and Ibrahim were terrible even if they stood alone, but their stories portrayed only three of the more than one million terror-filled experiences of that place and that time. Their anguished stories barely scratched the surface of the misery that was, and is, Darfur.

In June 2004, US satellite photos identified over three hundred decimated villages in Darfur, villages that were plundered and burned, nothing left but scorched, tired earth.[1] The rapes and murders and torment of the innocent of Darfur continued at an alarming pace despite assurances by the government that they would ensure that the vicious activities of the Janjaweed would cease.

The recurring theme of military helicopters circling villages only to be followed by vicious attacks by Janjaweed continued. Women who survived reported abductions and repeated rapes and torture. There were similar stories of rape camps, areas where women were held and raped and tormented again and again until their captors tired of them and either killed or released them. Men reported seeing others in their villages murdered or taken by force, their whereabouts still unknown, although they were likely dead as well. Children continued to suffer the most; their displacement was a literal death sentence, for it is they, the most vulnerable, who die first of starvation, disease, and neglect.

Inexplicably, the rebels in Darfur who'd been fighting the Janjaweed joined the fray and attacked aid convoys and harassed and detained aid workers. Sixteen UN workers were abducted and held for two days by the SLA in a village in North Darfur in June 2004.[2] The rebels were purposely disrupting the very aid process that the people they vowed to protect so desperately needed. Their brazen actions gave credibility to the government's claims of rebel abuse and provocation and surely helped to prolong the Janjaweed's reign of terror.

The government responded by accusing NGOs and the UN of supporting rebel activities and actually expelled a UN worker from Darfur. The UN angrily protested, but there was little else they could do. The government also targeted several NGOs as complicit with the rebels and took steps to limit their activities. The government was stepping up their bizarre rhetoric and strange accusations in response to increasing pressure from world leaders. They would continue to deny any involvement in the Darfur tragedy despite the obvious blood on their hands.

On the last day of June 2004, Colin Powell, the US secretary of state, made an official visit to Sudan to protest the horrors of Darfur and to urge the government of Sudan to stop the carnage there. As part of his mission, he traveled to Darfur, to the camp at Abu-Shok, to see the refugees for himself.[3] The usually stoic and subdued inhabitants of Abu-Shok, I was told, crawled out of their tiny plastic huts and cheered his arrival.

That image, that powerful and tender description of cheering, waving refugees gave me such hope, until I learned that the government had forced the healthiest among these war-ravaged people to appear, to cheer and wave and smile and prove to Colin Powell and the world that they were healthy and happy and well fed indeed. The sickliest were told to stay out of sight. To beef up the appearance of the IDPs, the government infiltrated the camp with its own workers, their trickery evidenced by the men's shiny leather shoes and the women's obesity. Colin Powell's entourage was reported to have noticed the interlopers and knew that they were government plants. The government continued their heinous games.

Within days of Colin Powell's visit, the head of the UN, Kofi Annan, made an official sojourn to Sudan to protest the government's villainous actions in Darfur, and he, too, included a visit to that beleaguered region. His itinerary included a stop at Al Mashtel, the camp which, though it had seemingly been emptied and its inhabitants moved to Abu-Shok, then housed some four thousand desperate arrivals for whom there was no place else to go. They lived there in squalor, without food, without water, and without shelter. It would have made for a compelling meeting, but when Annan arrived, the camp's inhabitants had disappeared; all that remained were some stray donkeys picking through the rubble. The government had purposely moved these squatters to avoid any embarrassment.

Annan's delegation moved then to Abu-Shok and spoke with several inhabitants there. The government watched the proceedings with heightened interest, as only certain IDPs had been chosen to speak, the better to contain information. Names of others who spoke were written down, and several days later, three of those IDPs who had dared to step forward and be heard were arrested by the government for interacting with the delegation.[4]

Despite the government's attempts to depict a rosy situation in Darfur, the reality was that the situation was deteriorating for the IDPs. Malnutrition was increasing, and, without fuel for food preparation, it would increase further despite food rations being delivered by WFP. Dysentery was rising and medicine that we had hoped would last for many months was running out. Malaria, too, was on the rise, and the disease burden on this already fragile population could prove deadly.

I was asked to return to Darfur, and, lipstick in hand, returned there in August 2004, just a few short months after my departure, to resume my role there.

Return to Darfur

—•—

When I returned to Darfur in the summer, the newest statistics indicated that almost two million had been forced from their homes and seventy thousand had been killed. Those numbers had doubled in the short time since my earlier visit. The people of Darfur were accustomed to deprivation and misery, but not on the scale that consumed them then.

In September 2004, Colin Powell, speaking on behalf of the US government, declared that a genocide was taking place in Darfur.[1] He urged the world to act, to stop the killing, but the world was strangely silent.

On this trip, I would go first to Nyala in South Darfur, where fighting still raged, trouble still brewed, and where the refugees were in desperate condition. Many new arrivals had barely escaped with their lives, and they were living in the open, without food, shelter, or protection. IRC would be opening two health clinics, and I would be responsible for getting the larger one up and running.

A mortality study designed to calculate the death rate between June and August of 2004, carried out under the guidance of WHO, revealed an alarming trend. WHO determined that the death rate in Darfur was alarmingly high and well above the emergency threshold. North Darfur had a mortality rate three times the expected rate for Africa, while West Darfur's rate was six times the expected rate for Africa. South Darfur (where I was headed) had a rate seven times the expected rate for Africa, all of which confirmed that the emergency in Darfur continued to unfold.[2]

I spent my first days in the sultry summer heat of Khartoum securing a press pass, which would ensure my ability to take pictures. I couldn't believe how easy it was to acquire the precious pass. For a government with so many rules and restrictions, it was easy enough to maneuver around them with a smile and a nod.

The following day, I was scheduled to fly to Nyala, but that same day, eighty Eritrean refugees who were being forcibly repatriated to Eritrea from Libya hijacked the plane they were on and forced it to land in Sudan.[3] The Khartoum airport was surrounded by soldiers, and we were sent away and told to return in the night. That night, the drama continued to unfold as the refugees demanded that a UN representative be sent to the scene to hear their demands. We arrived as instructed but were sent away again. The next morning, we ventured back and sat around while officials decided if they would allow us to fly. In Khartoum, things only happen if an endless number of officials and bureaucrats agree to it. The vagaries of life there are endless. After a second full day of waiting, we were finally allowed to head to Nyala.

Unlike the arid desert landscape of Al Fasher, Nyala is a soggy and damp place, and I arrived in the first days of the rainy season. That term does not even begin to describe the horrific storms. Shortly after my arrival, a dreadful squall battered South Darfur. For five long hours, the night was marked by torrential downpours, howling winds, and bursts of lightning. I was certain that all the fragile camp shelters would be blown away, but the following day, as I drove through a camp in the murky mist of early morning, I stared in amazement at the shelters that still stood, sturdy little sanctuaries against the harsh life there. The roads were now streams and gullies, and mud was plentiful, making it difficult to navigate on foot or vehicle. These people seem destined to endure one indignity after another.

My home in Nyala was a shared room in a typical Sudanese plaster house. I shared the house with several other expats from Africa, England, and Europe. We had a generator, which allowed occasional electricity. The bathrooms were another story, dirty and damp with squat toilets and water taps at midwaist. My bed was a rope cot covered by a mat. On my first night in Nyala, I threw myself onto my bed, exhausted and eager for sleep. But within minutes, it was clear that I was not alone. My paper-thin mattress was infested with bedbugs. They were voracious attackers, and within minutes, every inch of me was blotchy and sore. I sat up and tried to scratch my misery away. It became my nightly routine until, only days later, I'd adjusted and slept peacefully each night. The bugs were still there, but we had learned to coexist. There were also skinny rats and feisty cockroaches sharing our quarters. They scurried about at night in search of food. Since I had none, they never really bothered with me.

There's always a silver lining. That was mine.

Kalma Camp

———◆———

There were no meetings here, at least not at first. My role was to get IRC's clinic in Kalma up and running. There were approximately seventy thousand refugees in Kalma, a large and miserable plot of land dotted with UN tents and water pumps.[1] A few days before my arrival, there were fifteen reported deaths in Kalma—not so unusual, considering the circumstances, but those were only the reported deaths; the real toll was likely higher, as there was no system in place yet for following the mortality rate. Of those who'd died, five were children under age ten who'd succumbed to diarrhea. Of the adults, it seemed, at least by the anecdotal reports I received, that several had died of respiratory infections. These people were so fragile that minor illnesses were killing them.

Kalma was large, covering miles and miles, almost a village really. Bits of green shot through the brown earth, and though few trees remained, a few were visible just beyond the camp. The smell of wood fires filled the air as people prepared their food rations. Children, filthy and dressed in rags, played on a large pile of incinerated garbage, sifting through the ashes. Other children played in the puddles of standing water that had collected after the recent rains. Still others milled about the small bazaar where enterprising refugees were selling food and wares, and anything they could.

Sadly, Kalma already had a violent reputation. It had been closed to aid workers just before our arrival after a CARE employee was killed by IDPs. We learned that a Sudanese national staff member working for CARE was identified by an IDP woman as Janjaweed. She incited a riot when she started to yell that he was the one who had killed her husband. The IDPs, eager to take revenge on the hated Janjaweed, surrounded him, beat him with sticks and stones, and then dismembered and beheaded him. His body lay in the road for six hours before police got through. Once through, they closed the camp. It turned out the victim was not a member of the hated Janjaweed. He was an aid worker just trying to help. But in a volatile situation, no one can be sure who to trust.

The clinic in Kalma was busy from the moment we opened. The Ministry of Health had provided us with staff—one physician, several clinical assistants, nurses, midwives, and a pharmacist. We had medicine and supplies from UNICEF and WHO, and we were treating over three hundred patients daily. Aside from the usual diseases—malaria, fevers, diarrhea—there were exotic diseases as well, such as typhoid, cholera, polio, and meningitis. Added to that, we were mired in an outbreak of acute jaundice, called hepatitis E.[2]

Hepatitis E had invaded the camps of Darfur, turning young eyes a bright neon yellow and making the weakest even weaker. Tracking the disease was vital in preventing and stopping its spread. We spent our days like detectives, investigating the regions from which the hepatitis seemed to spread. Because symptoms started some six weeks after exposure, we had to find out where people had been six weeks before their symptoms began. Were they in camps, or villages, or on the move? Had they had access to latrines and soap and clean water? With the right information and tools—chlorination, soap, and plentiful latrines—we could halt the spread of this miserable epidemic, which had a 20 percent mortality rate among pregnant women.

Still, even with the emergence of acute jaundice, it was malaria, diarrhea, and malnutrition that were the primary diseases and killers of both young and old, and those would be our main concerns. Having enough medicine to treat our fragile patients was always a problem.

It was always early morning when I arrived at the clinic, but the people of Kalma were already well into their day. A line of people, mostly women, sat quietly on the ground, waiting to be seen. For most, it was likely their only chance to just sit, to rest, to look around. Once we opened the doors to the clinic, the queue for registration seemed endless. As one after another registered to be seen, the complaints seemed a poignant litany of their lives here: diarrhea, fever, weakness. To my eyes, they all appeared frail and sickly. Even the healthiest appearing among them would give us pause at home, but in Darfur, we had learned to accept the sight of these brittle-boned, weary people.

As in every clinic I worked around the world, we saw women and children first, men later. Tradition in so many of these places required that men be first in everything—food, shelter, education—but these women and children would always come first for me. Once registered, they were vaccinated and tested for malaria, then their physical complaints were addressed. Bellies were poked, chests were listened to, fevers were investigated, eyes and ears were examined. For perhaps the first time in their lives, they were the center of attention. Each was given a diagnosis and medicines, a validation of their maladies. The severely malnourished children were referred to feeding centers. For those older children and adults who were malnourished, there was no special center, no treatment, just a quiet understanding, an acknowledgement of their frailty.

People streamed into the clinic throughout the day, but the sickest seemed to come later in the day. They were carried on the back of donkey carts or in the arms of family, and we tended them with an urgency unfamiliar here. We shouted for intravenous fluids and medicines and watched for miracle improvements. Sometimes that happened, and sometimes it didn't.

A ten-year-old boy, Ali, was carried into our clinic with a fever, vomiting, and abdominal pain. I leaned over his tiny, frail form and palpated his rigid abdomen. He jumped when I pressed in, and I quickly removed my hand from the right lower quadrant of his abdomen. There was nothing exotic about this diagnosis. He had the signs of a straightforward appendicitis, and we transported him to Nyala hospital, where an appendectomy was carried out. Ali was soon home, though home was a plastic-encased hut here in this camp.

Although the appendicitis was not one of them, there were exotic diseases here that we had to consider. Typhoid fever was a distinct threat, as was cholera, though I had not seen either yet. Meningitis and polio reared their feared heads in other areas of Darfur, but not then in Kalma. Our days were filled with the now mundane—malaria, diarrhea, and sometimes acute jaundice. But sickness is never mundane to the people it strikes.

The Janjaweed

I saw two Janjaweed one day while driving out to Kalma. They were sitting atop mangy, thin camels. Each had a rifle slung over one shoulder and an odd piece of weaponry—a large wooden cylinder with a leather rope fastened to one end—over the other shoulder. They appeared as terrifying as I'd heard. They were unkempt, snarly-looking characters who sauntered along atop their camels, their eyes scanning the road and the people. I slumped down a little in my seat and angled my camera just so. I snapped away but got only a fuzzy photo of men on camels. I was afraid to be bolder, to sit up straighter, to get clearer photos. If just these two could create an atmosphere of such fear, I couldn't even imagine the terror created by the usual fifty or more attackers.

The Janjaweed of Darfur were, and still remain, infamous for the brutal acts of cruelty that they foisted upon innocent victims. Their villainy was well known, but perhaps their most heinous act, among all their evil acts, was the purposeful burning of babies and children. Their victims reported that the Janjaweed threw babies and children into blazing fires and watched as they screamed for help that would never come. The images these acts evoked are still almost too horrible to imagine.

One victim was a ten-year-old boy named Hossein. In 2003, the Janjaweed rode into his village, where they plundered and robbed the helpless townsfolk. Before they were done, they set a fire in the center of the little town and committed one final act of madness by throwing several small children into the fire. Most would die that day. The attackers grabbed young Hossein and threw him into the raging fires. His legs were ablaze and his face crackled as the skin and muscle there burned. But little Hossein was lucky. The Janjaweed retreated, and he was pulled from the flames before they claimed him as a victim. His luck, however, stopped there. For an agonizing year, he underwent painful treatment in a rural hospital and then was discharged to the care of his family and the misery of Kalma.

Although his burns had long healed, I was told, he still had disfiguring facial scars and a thick glut of scar tissue on his legs that prevented him from bending his knees. That simple loss prevented him from being a boy. He walked stiffly and could no longer run or play, but perhaps his most serious scar was the one we would never see, the damage to his young spirit and heart and mind. He was a child traumatized; he would never be the same.

This sad and compelling story was reported in the United States, and a generous donor, eager to help Hossein, asked IRC to locate him. Since he was last known to be in Kalma camp, the area of my new clinic, I was asked to help in the search. There were over seventy thousand refugees in the camp at the time, and I was certain it would be a long and tedious process, a search for the proverbial needle in a haystack. After all, this camp was enormous; there were no addresses, no streets or numbers, nothing to guide me.

But this place was far more organized than I'd dreamed. It turned out that people migrated to the areas of the camp where others from their own towns and villages had settled. I checked with our clinic staff, and they quickly pointed me in the direction where people from the boy's village had settled. We asked the village elders and they guided us to the child's straw and mud hut. After endless questioning, we finally learned that he was gone.

"To Nyala," they said. "Someone came for him." Damn it. Had the government discovered that his story was attracting attention? Were they going to punish him? I contacted the IRC office in Khartoum and learned that the someone who'd come for him had been a Sudanese staff member who'd taken Hossein to Nyala the previous day, hoping to have him examined.

The villagers, eager to seek help for their seriously wounded neighbors, quickly produced another victim of yet another horrific attack, and they guided me to his hut. Mohammed was thirty years old when the Janjaweed rode into his small village. He had been a tailor, known for his detailed needlework and delicate pieces. The father of three small children, he and his wife had created a comfortable life. When the Janjaweed rode in, Mohammed watched in horror as people ran, only to be chased down and executed. Desperate to escape the carnage, he searched for his family but was unable to find them in the running throng. He panicked and raced for the outskirts of the village, but the horsemen saw his flight and were upon him in an instant. Without warning, they shot him in the back. He fell to the ground, helpless and without any chance of escape.

As the horsemen rode by on their way out of the village, they used their blazing torches to set his hands and feet afire. He saw the flames consume his hands, but, until the Janjaweed rode past, he could not dampen the flames. Finally, another villager came to his rescue and smothered the flames. After several months in a local hospital, he, too, made his way to Kalma.

When I met him, he was as helpless as the day the Janjaweed attacked his village. Though he can walk, his hands have scarred and formed into frozen claws. He is unable to feed, bathe, or dress himself. He cannot even dry the tears that invariably fall when he recounts his day of terror. He sniffled his tears away while his wife produced a tiny, lacy baby dress, tiny seed pearls sewn intricately into the bodice. I ran my fingers across the silky dress. It was an exquisite piece of handiwork.

"The last piece I made with my own hands," he said, sadness draping his words. "I will never sew again. Not now." He dropped his hands to his lap and sighed. But more than the sewing, he would never hold his babies tight, never feel the touch of fabric in his hands, or the handshake of a friend. "When we go home, and someday we will, I don't know how I will support my family."

I had no soothing words, ho hopeful promises to share, so I placed my hand over his gnarled one and nodded.

It wasn't long before the villagers pulled me away and steered me to another small hut, the plastic sheeting that covered it fraying and loose, the small space inside cluttered and close. I stepped inside. "This is Talya," a woman said, motioning to the thin woman sitting cross-legged on the damp earth floor of her hut, her hands hidden in the folds of her dress. A small child sat nearby, her fingers making lines in the dirt.

"When the Janjaweed tore through her village, Talya grabbed her small baby and ran," the woman said. And all at once, everyone rushed to tell the story, though Talya sat quietly. The facts of that day, the utter cruelty of it, sicken me still.

She'd cradled her crying baby in her left arm, and with her right hand, she held tightly the hand of her then eight-year-old daughter. In terror they ran, but not fast enough. The Janjaweed's bullets flew all around, one tearing off Talya's left hand before settling in the heart of the baby she held so tightly and loved so dearly. Her precious baby died instantly. Her other child was not spared. She suffered a gunshot wound to her right chest, collapsing her little girl lungs. The three fell together to the ground and crouched there until that attack was over and help arrived.

Talya's baby was buried, and she and her little girl were taken to a small local hospital. The stump of tissue where Talya's hand had just been was sewn up quickly, and the girl's lung was reinflated.

The woman who'd brought me lifted Talya's scarred stump from its hiding place. Talya squirmed and pulled her little girl close, lifting her dress to show me the scars in her chest where the bullet had struck. The girl smiled, glad of any speck of attention. She watched while I wrote it all down. I wasn't sure what I could do, likely nothing, but I wanted, at least, to remember every detail of these people and this day.

Their physical wounds had healed, and both, I was told, were lucky to have survived. But luck is relative in Darfur. Talya, who struggled with adjusting to life with only one hand, was tormented with thoughts of her lost baby. Her little girl pulled away from her mother and stood in front of me. "When can we go home?" she asked softly. The woman who'd brought me translated as the little girl and Talya held my gaze. I could only shake my head and bite back the tears that welled up in the corners of my eyes.

And still there were more people to see, more stories to hear. I was guided next to Aliha, a young widowed mother of ten when her village was attacked in the spring of 2004. During the attack and ensuing chaos, she was separated from seven of her children. She had not seen them since that terrible day and had no idea if they were dead or alive.

"But she is not always sad," the interpreter said. "On her best days, she imagines they are alive and perhaps living somewhere in Darfur. On her worst days, well, on those days, she tries not to think of the other possibilities. She lives here now in Kalma." Aliha had angled her head and listened as her story was told, and when the interpreter went silent, she pulled her three remaining children close.

No wonder the government had forbidden us to speak to these victims. The truth was more shocking than any of us might have guessed.

The Women of Darfur

———•◆•———

D awn always seemed to break swiftly over Darfur. There was no
easing into the day, no lingering over tea, no time for morning
reflection. The women were up and working long before dawn.
Their silhouettes, an endless line of single-file figures, could be seen on the
horizon as they strode out at dawn to gather the day's firewood.

Although the women of Darfur had been the traditional firewood
gatherers and water collectors, here in the camps, away from the safety of
their own villages, those acts were filled with great danger. The gathering
of firewood required the women to leave the relative safety of the camp
and venture further beyond to find fuel. The greenery that I'd seen when
I'd first arrived grew scarcer each day, and as the women wandered farther
out, they were targeted, for it was then, when they were alone or in small
groups, that the Janjaweed and others came out of hiding to rape and torment these women.

Rape, a traditional weapon of war, had been used in Darfur to further frighten and dominate this already fearful and vulnerable people. There was little they could do to protect themselves, which was why they cried for protection as their first need. The refugees sent out the elderly and "ugly" to collect wood, thinking that they would not be raped. But rape has nothing to do with attraction, it has everything to do with creating an atmosphere of fear, a strategy at which the Janjaweed excelled.

Each morning, as I arrived at the clinic, I caught sight of the women as they filed out of the camp in search of fuel. I feared for their safety and wished we could hire escorts. To be honest, I'm not sure why we didn't. It seemed such a simple solution, though things, I suppose, are never as simple as they seem at the time. Early one morning, as we drove along the long, windy road to the camp, I saw a lone elderly woman struggling to cut limbs from near-naked trees. I cringed, knowing the risk her solitary figure represented. I asked if we could stop. The driver shook his head. He had other staff to ferry.

For the women, there was more than firewood to be gathered. They collected the day's water from tap stands located throughout the camp. The taps were sturdy, stand-alone mechanisms that required great effort and great strength before the first drops of water could be coaxed out. Once the collection cans were filled, they were hoisted onto thin, bony shoulders or stooped heads and carried back to little huts, where there was still more to do. Food had to be prepared for hungry little mouths. There were children and clothes to be washed. There was always something waiting to be done.

It was the women of Darfur who, through relentless suffering, struggled to create a life for their families here in camp. These extraordinary women had been terrorized during this cruel war. They had been forced to watch as their children and husbands had been murdered, as their homes had burned to the ground, as friends and family had simply disappeared.

Their lives had been decimated. Everything familiar was gone. They lived in crowded camps where everything—where they lived, how they lived, what they ate—was all decided for them. Yet for all the horrors they'd witnessed, they still managed a smile, a wave, sometimes a hearty handshake when they met newcomers or greeted old friends. There were tens of thousands of women in that camp. They struggled each day to gather firewood, collect water, cook their rations, wash their clothes, and give hope to their children. For most, there were no extras in their tiny huts.

But some, like Seetna, saw opportunity where others saw only misery. I met her when she came to our clinic looking for work. Though dressed in the fresh, bright colors of her village, her mouth was drawn, her eyes firmly on the ground, her step slow and measured. Through an interpreter, she timidly asked about work and explained that her husband had been killed during an attack on her village. Her eyes filled up as she described a sadly familiar story of how he'd run until a bullet had torn through his back, killing him instantly. She'd had no time to mourn, and though her home and her very life had been reduced to ashes that morning, she'd had three small children to save. She'd quickly gathered them up and fled to this refugee camp, where she was provided with shelter, food, and water.

And nothing else.

Her family's food rations consisted of sorghum, beans, oil, sugar, and tea. There were no eggs, no plump chickens, and no meat—nothing special to feed a young family. Every day had been, as it was for everyone here, a dreary recitation of the day before. Only a job would allow her the chance to get some small extras for her family. She was one of hundreds who would appear at our clinic hoping that a job awaited them, but Seetna was among the very first. After we spoke, I asked her to come back in a week or so, when I would have a better idea of the clinic's needs.

I watched her leave that day, her back a little straighter, her step a little brisker, and it occurred to me that for the first time in many months, she likely felt as though she had something to look forward to, something to wish for. She returned exactly one week later. She must have counted the days and minutes until she could return.

She was shown into our rustic clinic, where we greeted each other warmly. "I need someone to clean the clinic," I asked through an interpreter. "Can you do that?"

The silver flecks in Seetna's deep black eyes sparkled; she took my hand in both of hers and smiled. She never asked about her salary or her responsibilities. She started that day and continued long after I had gone. With a broom, she swept, with rags she dusted, with joy she carried out her duties. She became one of our best employees. Even the earth floor of our clinic was spotless. She was lucky to have found us, and we her, but luck is elusive for most people in Darfur.

We had many other impressive female staff, as well as patients. Though Darfur was easily the world's most tormented region, there were moments of pure magic there, and it was often the women who quite literally delivered them.

I remember one dreary morning when a young woman, visibly pregnant, came to our clinic in the throes of labor. She was young, perhaps just twenty years old, and, aside from her pregnant belly, she was all bones and hard angles. She'd already given birth to four babies, of whom only two had survived. She came to our clinic to deliver this newest baby in the hopes that we might help this one to survive.

We ushered her into our midwife's room, where she curled onto her side and quickly fell fast asleep. I smiled each time I passed her there, for sleep was surely blissful to a young refugee mother. Perhaps she was dreaming of her village, her lost babies, her life before the madness set in. We expected fairly swift progression to birth, since these babies are so often so tiny. But the hours passed, the young mother only occasionally stirred, and still no baby. Then, finally, late in the afternoon, the young mother called to us and the lusty wail of a baby filled the air. She had delivered, with our midwife's help, a healthy girl.

With hardly a moment to spare, we were called to the latrine just outside the clinic, where another young woman had given birth to a plump boy. Both babies appeared to be healthy, and both shrieked in protest at their new surroundings. The staff and patients in the clinic all smiled at the news and the sound of healthy newborn cries. There is no joy quite like that of the promise of a healthy newborn, especially in a place like Darfur.

Our senior midwife, a warm and smiling woman named Zina, her gray hair peeking from under her veil, supervised the care of these women and their babies, a role for which she was well suited. "Come," she said one day, throwing her arm over my shoulder, "I will show you my room." Her room was the small space cordoned off with canvas sheeting, which allowed women to labor and give birth in privacy. With little more than forceps to help, she'd been delivering babies long before there was trouble here, and she still expected that one day, the fighting would end, the residents of Kalma would go home, and all would be well again.

"You will see," she said. "The government will tire of this. It will end soon." Perhaps she'd forgotten the civil war in the south that had raged for years, and she had no way of knowing that years later, the unrest and misery would linger there. For Zina, it was the new mothers and babies that mattered, and I followed her one busy day as she made her rounds.

One young woman, about twenty-five years old and six months pregnant, presented to our clinic bleeding profusely. She was clearly losing this baby. She had already lost three other pregnancies and had yet to bring a baby to term. Beads of sweat dotted her brow as Zina scurried about and helped the woman deliver a tiny stillborn baby. She draped a sheet about the lifeless infant, then quietly wrapped the young woman in a compassionate embrace. The young woman finally gave way to her sadness and cried softly in Zina's arms. I stepped back, not wanting to break the chain of love in that tiny room.

Amidst the dirt and dust and darkness of Darfur, Zina brought a kind of magic and endless optimism to her work, to those people. The lives she welcomed, saved, influenced, or prayed over were all the better for her very presence.

I've always included myself in that number.

The Children of Darfur

A reporter for ABC News arrived to do a follow-up on little Hossein, the boy who'd been so scarred by the burns he'd suffered. The doctors in Khartoum had decided there was nothing to be done for him, so instead of heading to the United States, as the donor had hoped, he was back in the camp, his scars like ropes around his legs, no surgery in his future.

The reporter and cameraman arrived at the camp, took their equipment from the back of the SUV, and began to set up for an opening scene. The reporter donned a fresh shirt, ran a wipe over his face, climbed to the roof of the vehicle, and began to speak into a microphone, the view of Kalma as a backdrop. Within minutes, almost as though they'd been lying in wait, the authorities and camp policemen appeared.

"Stop," they shouted, motioning for the reporter to climb down and the cameraman to stop filming. "You need papers, you need permission. You cannot just come here and take pictures." The policeman, a scowl on his face, looked at each of us in turn. I wanted to scowl back, but I stood there politely instead.

The man who'd been introduced to me as the producer quickly pulled out a cell phone, punched in some numbers, and began speaking in a mixture of languages, throwing in a little Arabic for good measure. "Hmm," he said, nodding his head before passing the phone to the policeman. "He wants to speak to you."

The policeman, his brows raised, took the phone and held it to his ear. "Hello," he bellowed. "I am—" But whoever was on the other end cut him off. I could just make out a raised voice barking orders. The policeman shrank a little as he held the phone tight to his ear.

"Who is it?" I whispered to the producer.

"The head of the government commission," he answered loudly so that the other policeman and authorities would hear.

What government commission? I wondered. The phone was handed back to the producer, who tucked it into his pocket while the policemen and authorities conferred. "Well, then," one of the men said, "let us know if you need help." Another motioned to the camera and then to himself.

The producer shook his head. "Another time, maybe."

The reporter climbed back onto the SUV and resumed his report. When he was done, they followed me on foot to Hossein's hut. Already a crowd had gathered, most of them children, and they began to trail us along the alleys and roads of the camp.

"So, I have to ask," I said to the producer as he walked alongside me. "Who did you call?"

He laughed. "A friend in Khartoum."

"But . . ."

"I'm more *fixer* than producer," he said. "My job is to fix problems however I can. Today, it meant calling a friend who never actually told them who he was. He just shouted that we had permission to be here, and if they wanted to keep their jobs, they should leave us alone to do what we came to do."

I don't know if I'd ever been more impressed.

We arrived at Hossein's hut, but he was on his way to school, and despite the crowd and the presence of the cameras, he didn't want to be late. He spoke to the reporter quickly. A clinic interpreter shared what he said.

"I want to be a doctor someday," he said shyly, a tight smile stretching through the scars on his face. "But first, I'd like a soccer ball."

That was an almost impossible wish. There were no toys here in Kalma, no soccer balls, no toy trucks. The children had learned to fashion their own playthings from the trash that lay in piles around the camp. Kites, crafted from worn and fraying colored plastic bags, were tied to simple bits of string. As the children ran, the little kites took magnificent flight and colored the bleak landscape.

But Hossein's wish would come true, thanks to the reporter, who left money behind—a soccer ball for Hossein and a little help for the tailor, he said. That simple generous gesture changed things for both—Hossein took to running after his ball, one small step at a time, and the tailor learned to smile again. The reporter had only one stipulation—that no one be told it was he who had provided the gifts.

I kept his secret and the truth of his kindness to myself.

Until now.

The Truth of Darfur

The UN, on the other hand, had no time for secrets or sitting around, and as if they'd just remembered that they survived on meetings, by late September, the endless summits were on again. I spent much of my time flying back and forth between Darfur and Khartoum on the rickety planes of a small local airline. The Russian and Eastern European pilots sat in the cockpit in full view of the passengers and smoked incessantly, dropping their cigarette stubs into old two-liter plastic soda bottles filled with murky water. They were always the first ones off the plane, cigarettes still dangling from their lips, fatigue streaking their eyes. They never looked back at us, never acknowledged us. It was as though we weren't even there.

In Khartoum, the meetings took on a sense of urgency not unlike the earliest days of our intervention here. By October, conditions throughout Darfur were as miserable as ever despite the government's attempts to depict an improving situation. New arrivals to Kalma reported that government tanks were razing their villages even as the government continued to deny any involvement in or knowledge of the atrocities. The government, perhaps weary of all the attention paid to Darfur, announced plans to forcibly send thousands of refugees from Kalma back to their destroyed villages. The logic of that mandate was beyond reason, and the refugees refused to go. Through their elders, they announced that the government would have to shoot them, for they would not leave Kalma. This was a government though that would indeed shoot its own people. The prospect of a standoff cast a pall over our meetings and heightened the misery of Darfur. Few of us had ever witnessed a more volatile situation, and we held our breath as the tensions increased.

In October, while I was in Khartoum, two policemen were murdered in Kalma during a food distribution. The food rations allotted for each person had been reduced yet again, and the NGO responsible for distributing those rations was late at getting the food out. People were on edge, fearful that they would not get food and that they would be forced out of the camp without warning. In that frenzy of fear, anything could happen. And it did—two policemen were killed. The facts of the killings were never clear. We were not allowed into the camp for several days, until the furor had died down. By then, the truth of the incident was lost somewhere in the thick, hot, dusty air.

October also saw a troubling rise in incidents aimed at the international community working in Darfur. An expat with World Vision was arrested in Nyala. He was held overnight, but the charges were never established and he was released. Two Irish aid workers with Save the Children UK were killed in North Darfur when their vehicle rolled over a land mine. That incident had its intended effect; aid workers were not allowed into that region until safety could be assured. The roads to our remotest camps were plagued by robberies and banditry. The insecurity made the work of helping that much more difficult.

The Sudanese Liberation Army (SLA, the rebels fighting the Janjaweed) approached the UN and asked for food. They said that they were literally starving and would be forced to rob aid workers if they were not fed soon. It was a dilemma, since the UN mandate says you cannot feed combatants, but these people were starving. Unlike the Janjaweed, the SLA had no government backing or contributors. There seemed endless problems, all without solution. The SLA rebels were never provided with food aid. The attacks on aid workers continued.

Meanwhile, Khartoum was the site of a serious coup attempt. Though there were countless opponents to the government, they had yet to raise a successful strategy, and many of the instigators of this failed attempt were arrested. Perhaps to reassert itself after the failed coup attempt, the government destroyed a shantytown just outside Khartoum. The area was poor and was inhabited by many of Darfur's and South Sudan's displaced. They had built small houses and lived there in relative comfort and safety, but in Khartoum, comfort and safety could not be relied on. A friend of mine from IRC's Khartoum office lived there, and I went out with her to see the remnants of her neighborhood. There was little left to see.

Once sturdy homes had been razed by bulldozers and had been reduced to dust and rubble. Many of the residents rebuilt makeshift shelters, but they essentially lived in the open and were forced to tramp over unsteady piles of rubble to get about. Many people did not have the resources to build even a makeshift shelter and simply lived among the rubble. The conditions were miserable. Kalma seemed comfortable in comparison.

None of us could speak up. We had been told that the government would likely expel any of us who did. I asked Eunice, my friend from South Sudan who was living amidst the rubble, how she managed not to be angry.

Her eyes filled up with tears. "We are just helpless here," she said. "We are without hope."

Tears pricked my eyes but I held them back. "Don't lose hope," I said softly. It was the only reply I could muster, but the truth was, I had lost hope, too.

Death in Darfur

I n Darfur, the endless rains continued. Great sheets of water fell from the sky, making roads impassable and creating stagnant pools of water, perfect breeding grounds for deadly disease. And though I'd hoped to spend my days in the clinic with patients, I spent much of my time chasing the paperwork that held the statistics we were collecting. We needed the numbers to know what we were up against.

We were already consumed with the ominous approach of cholera, which had caused death and disability just across the border in Chad. This army of bacteria was stealthily making its way to Darfur. Cholera is furtive and fast and required us to be on the alert, so we gathered equipment and statistics to prevent disaster, tracking the flow of the cholera as it crossed the border into our regions. We formed our own armies and equipped ourselves with fluids and rehydration salts and plastic sheeting.

Meningitis season was also near, as it invariably arrived once the rains were finished. We hoped to be involved in a vaccination campaign to prevent that potential disaster. This, too, was the thick of malaria season, when the bite of a mosquito releases killer parasites into a waiting bloodstream. The parasites attack fragile red blood cells, and without treatment, death may be the result. And death was our most formidable foe, for it hovered around these camps, ready to claim the weakest and most vulnerable despite our efforts.

I will never forget one little girl whose life seemed especially harsh. She was eight years old when her bony, frail body was carried into our clinic. She weighed, at best, forty pounds. She was said to have cerebral palsy, perhaps from a birth injury or maybe a result of chronic starvation. Either way, she neither spoke nor interacted. She appeared lifeless long before the final remnants of life seeped out of her. Her name was Maryam and she did not respond, not even when I whispered into her ear. She'd been brought to us in the final, deadly stages of malnutrition, when there is little left to do, when not even hope is an option. It seemed that in all of the years I'd tended people like Maryam, starvation had remained our deadliest enemy. We referred her to the therapeutic feeding center in the camp run by MSF and learned the next day that she had died. Maryam was laid to rest just outside the camp.

Most people in Darfur were in some stage of starvation, and most had suffered from one disease or another in the last few years. These once-hardy people were starving, disease ridden, and dying. Malnutrition claimed many under the age of five and more than a few over five. In this age of pandemic obesity in the developed world's wealthy nations, starving to death seems the cruelest end.

There were reliable reports that thousands in scattered villages in the north were trying to survive on toxic seeds. Once these seeds were ingested, paralysis and death could result. To prevent this deadly outcome, these desperate people washed the seeds in a final, frantic attempt to survive. But many would not. That unimaginable choice, slow death from starvation or an uncertain chance at life from eating poison seeds, faced thousands in Darfur, just as it had in Afghanistan.

For those who died in the camps of Darfur, death had a certain quiet dignity. The body of the deceased was lovingly washed and wrapped in folds of fabric, then carried away from the camp living quarters and buried in a hole dug by the family. The body was then covered with rocks to prevent animals from tracking the scent. Dirt was piled on top and bits of thorn brush were thrown over the little mound. The spiky little bits of brush served as further deterrent to the foraging animals.

And there lay the remains of the once-loved person until the rains or the winds or the persistent animals finally removed all traces of the burial spot. Only memories would linger, and those, too, would soon grow dim.

A Return to Abu-Shok

———◆———

It was not until late October that I was able to return to Abu-Shok in North Darfur. I'd heard it had become a "show camp," but I still remembered it as a vast desert wasteland where small shelters dotted the bleak landscape and where our little clinic stood alone. I was stunned as I approached the camp and gazed upon a veritable village of some sixty thousand. So orderly and well organized was the camp that it even boasted a bustling little marketplace. Sturdy shelters had sprouted up everywhere, and this once dreary place was filled with life and hope. I asked staff in our clinic there about Hawa, the midwife who had suffered and lost so much in the carnage in Tawila, but she was nowhere to be found. No one could say for sure where she had gone. I asked at the other NGO facilities, but she had simply vanished. I asked, too, about Halima, the lady from Kabkabiya who had worked as our registrar, but no one knew her either.

Though Abu-Shok was an oasis amid misery, it housed only sixty thousand of the more than one and a half million displaced, desperate, and dying Darfurians. Babies were still dying needlessly of malnutrition and preventable disease. Starvation was an everyday occurrence for pockets of people trapped and hidden in Darfur's darkest corners. Insecurity made them inaccessible; our aid and food programs could not reach them, and they could not escape. As my assignment there ended and I packed for home, I couldn't help but wonder if any of us had really made a difference, and that persistent worry made my good-byes that much harder.

Saying good-bye to the people I've worked with has never been easy, but it was especially difficult in Darfur. I had been in Darfur for several months on this last visit, and I knew the region well. I knew how the sun sneaked up quickly in the morning and then disappeared just as swiftly in the evening. I knew the sounds of the call to prayer, the almost dreamlike melody of the chant. With my eyes closed even now, I can see the haunted, hungry eyes of the children there. I can hear, too, the sound of a dying baby's cry and a mother's wail of sadness. But I can hear, too, the unforgettable music that the laughter of Darfur's children creates. For even in their deepest misery, they somehow managed to find joy.

It is the staff and the displaced in the camps, too, that I will always remember. Their names and stories, like so many others in Afghanistan, Iraq, the Balkans, and Kakuma, flow through my memory like pearls on a string. In Darfur, there were Hawa and Halima, Talya, and Aliah. And Hossein, the little boy who finally received a soccer ball courtesy of the reporter who'd covered his story, and Mohammed, the tailor who'd been provided with money to help him learn a new trade, something that wouldn't require his hands.

And I will never forget the staff in our clinics, many of whom lived right there in the camp, and who, despite their own tragedies, trekked each day to the clinic to care for their neighbors with a quiet grace and steady hand that so often took my breath away. I wanted to be one of them—to have that unselfish, unfettered heart and mind.

To that end, I am a work in progress.

The people of Darfur continued to suffer. The region is vast, often remote, and frequently too violent to traverse. The situation is complex and requires far more resources than are currently available. The world's attention has moved on to other crises. I can't remember when Darfur last made the news.

In 2009, IRC and nine other aid groups were expelled from Darfur after the International Criminal Court issued an arrest warrant for President Omar al-Bashir for war crimes and crimes against humanity in Darfur. He retaliated by banishing the aid that was so desperately needed there.[1] And so, fifteen years after the madness and evil set in, Darfur is still under siege, still waiting for rescue, still praying that it will all end.[2]

And, despite the bureaucracy and the bullshit, I long to be there again.

Final Thoughts

And here we are, back to the beginning, wondering just who these refugees are that hold the world's attention. Are they sinners or saints? The reality is they are as varied as the tragedies that produced them, and most are probably a little bit of both. Many that I met wanted only to go home, not to flee farther away from the places they so loved. But there are others, as there always will be, who will greedily manipulate the system for their own gains. The difficulty is in knowing the difference, an almost impossible task.

For me, the refugees are often friends, people I've come to know and love. And in each village or camp where I've worked, it came to this—how could I ever say good-bye to these people, to those places? The truth is, I simply could not, and so, like precious gems, I carry their names and memories tucked safely into my heart.

These days, the scent of a wood fire or curry spices is enough to bring them all back to me. In an instant, I am there—a distant village, a crowded refugee camp, a deserted village where a mother cradles her starving child, a worn and weary family collapses, too weak to take another step in their journey to safety, a child closes his eyes to the sounds of gunfire and death. It has been my privilege to be a part of their lives, if only for a moment.

Though I've been paid little to go to the world's hot spots to provide desperately needed care, and will always have to work, to save my money and to count my pennies, the truth of it is, sappy as I know it sounds, I am truly the richest person I know.

And those people whose lives so enriched my own carry me forward even today. Though I've been asked again and again to work on one crisis or another, it hasn't worked out just yet, but as each new crisis is reported, I imagine myself packing up once again and rushing back into the festering turmoil that seems to chase so many. It was a tiny girl in Homs, a once thriving city in Syria, now reduced to rubble and tears, who articulated the crisis and her own needs in a way that was both heart wrenching and unforgettable. "I want cookies and milk," she cried into a television news camera, her eyes shining, her little arms wrapped around her equally hungry friends.

Her plea for cookies and milk went unanswered that day, but it is a plea that is universally understood, and as hard to forget as it is to imagine: cookies and milk—a simple request, but not so simple these long days and nights in Syria, and so many other dark places around the world. And, I know with certainty, just as I knew so many years ago, that I can help. The doe-eyed faces of starving children in South Sudan or Syria still make my heart ache, and it is only a matter of time. . . .

Until then, I hope you'll remember the stories written here of people who fight against the odds to live simple lives of dignity and grace. They are, in the end, just like us. You can join me on this journey to make the world's dark spots a little brighter, one child, one family at a time, for someone who, even as you read this, longs for a bit of food or water, or medicine for a dying child. Not everyone is able to volunteer overseas, but support for these programs is desperately needed. To learn and to help, if you are able, I hope you'll have a look at the following aid groups' websites:

Americares www.americares.org
International Committee of the Red Cross www.icrc.org
International Medical Corps https://internationalmedicalcorps.org/
International Rescue Committee www.rescue.org
Medecins Sans Frontieres www.msf.org
Mercy Corps www.mercycorps.org/
Save the Children www.savethechildren.org
UNICEF www.unicef.org
World Vision www.worldvision.org

GLOSSARY

—•◆•—

BBC British Broadcasting Corporation

CA Civil Affairs (military section dealing with issues relating to civilians)

CDC Centers for Disease Control and Prevention

CMOC Civil-Military Operations Center (military operation center providing information to NGOs involved in work here)

HACC Humanitarian Assistance Coordination Center

HOC Humanitarian Operations Center

ICRC International Committee of the Red Cross

IMC International Medical Corps

IRC International Rescue Committee

MSF Medecins Sans Frontieres (Doctors Without Borders)

NGO Nongovernmental organization; a private humanitarian aid group

ORHA Office of Reconstruction and Humanitarian Assistance

PPE Personal protective equipment

TBA Traditional birth attendant

Triage Literally to 'sort out': to determine who is sickest and requires immediate care, and who can wait to be seen

UN United Nations

UNHCR United Nations High Commissioner for Refugees: The UN Refugee Agency

UNICEF United Nations Children's Fund

USAID United States Agency for International Development

UXOs Unexploded ordnance

WFP World Food Programme

WHO World Health Organization

REFERENCES

—•—

Introduction

1.	UNHCR, *Figures at a Glance*; June 19, 2017, http://www.unhcr.org/en-us/figures
	-at-a-glance.html.

First Steps

1.	Ronald W. O'Connor, *Health Care in Muslim Asia: Development and Disorder in
	Wartime Afghanistan* (New York: University Press of America, 1994), 23–24.

Winter 1987

1.	CIA Report, Pakistan, *Coping with Afghan Refugees* (Sanitized copy approved for
	release, December 29, 2011) https://www.cia.gov/library/readingroom/docs/CIA
	-RDP88T00096R000600770001-2.pdf.

The Lost Boys

1.	Sief, Kevin, "The Children's War," (Washington Post, November 10, 2017) http://www
	.washingtonpost.com/sf/world/2017/11/10/they-were-rescued-from-war-now-south
	-sudans-child-soldiers-are-going-back/?utm_term=.3d84215cc1ae.

The Albanians

1.	AFP, "Ethnic Albanian gets life for 2015 Macedonia shootout," (Digital Journal,
	November 2017) http://www.digitaljournal.com/news/world/ethnic-albanian-gets
	-life-for-2015-macedonia-shootout/article/506697.

Waiting
1. WHO, *Afghanistan Statistics Summary* Global Health Observatory Country Views, (WHO, 2016) http://apps.who.int/gho/data/node.country.country-AFG.
2. UNFPA, *Dying to Give Life: Maternal Mortality in Afghanistan*, (News, 2005), https://www.unfpa.org/news/dying-give-life-maternal-mortality-afghanistan-0.

Last Days
1. Medecin Sans Frontieres, *Afghanistan: MSF leaves country following staff killings and threats*, (International Activity Report, 2004) http://www.msf.org/en/afghanistan-msf-leaves-country-following-staff-killings-and-threats.
2. AKDN, "New hospital facility brings world-class healthcare to Afghanistan's Bamyan province," (Press Release, April 24, 2017) http://www.akdn.org/press-release/new-hospital-facility-brings-world-class-healthcare-afghanistans-bamyan-province.
3. UNICEF, *Key Data on Women and Children*, October 2014, https://www.unicef.org/infobycountry/files/Key_Data_Afghanistan_Final_Oct2014.pdf.

Preparations for War
1. Physicians for Human Rights, *Health and Human Rights Consequences of War in Iraq* (A Briefing Paper, February 2003). http://physiciansforhumanrights.org/library/reports/iraq-health-human-rights-consequences-of-war-2003.html.

A Secret War
1. Human Rights Watch, *Darfur Destroyed: Ethnic Cleansing by Government and Militia Forces in Western Sudan*, (HRW Report on Darfur, April 2004, NY, New York). https://www.hrw.org/report/2004/05/06/darfur-destroyed/ethnic-cleansing-government-and-militia-forces-western-sudan.
2. UN, "Press Briefing on Humanitarian Crisis in Darfur, Sudan," (Press Release, April 2, 2004) https://www.un.org/press/en/2004/egelandbrf.DOC.htm.

Back to Africa
1. US Agency for International Development, *Projected mortality rates in Darfur, Sudan*, (USAID Situation Report, April 2004).

Mayo
1. ReliefWeb, *Sudan—Complex Emergency Situation Report*, (Report #2 FY 2004) https://reliefweb.int/report/sudan/sudan-complex-emergency-situation-report-2-fy-2004.

Meetings
1. ReliefWeb, *UNFPA Sudan Newsletter—Khartoum, Sudan,* May 2004, https://reliefweb.int/report/sudan/unfpa-sudan-newsletter-may-2004.

Hawa and the Terrors of the Janjaweed

1. U.S. Department of State, *Ethnic Cleansing in Darfur* (Fact Sheet Bureau of Democracy, Human Rights and Labor, NY, New York, April 27, 2004), https://2001 -2009.state.gov/g/drl/rls/31822.htm.

Tawila

1. Office of UN Resident and Humanitarian Coordinator for The Sudan, *Darfur Crisis, Sudan,* UN Weekly Humanitarian Roundup, Khartoum, Sudan, July 4-11, 2004.

Disease and Disaster

1. WHO/UNICEF, *Global Plan for Reducing Measles Mortality 2006-2010,* Joint Statement Pamphlet, NY, New York, 2010; https://www.unicef.org/media/files /globalplan.pdf.

2. ReliefWeb, *Sudan: Meningitis situation in the IDP camps, Greater Darfur, 19–25 Feb 2005,* Update, February 19–25, 2005, https://reliefweb.int/report/sudan /sudan-meningitis-situation-idp-camps-greater-darfur-19-25-feb-2005.

3. WHO, *Polio experts warn of largest epidemic in recent years, as polio hits Darfur,* Media Centre, Geneva, June 22, 2004 *http://www.who.int/mediacentre/news/releases/2004 /pr45/en/.*

Halima-Dignity and Desperation

1. ReliefWeb, *Report on Inter-Agency Mission to Kebkabiya, Saraf Omra and Tawilla Administrative Units, 23–26 Feb & 4 March 2004,*UN Resident and Humanitarian Coordinator for the Sudan, March 7, 2004; https://reliefweb.int/report/sudan/report -interagency-mission-kebkabiya-saraf-omra-and-tawilla-administrative-units-23-26.

The Continuing Genocide

1. United States Senate Committee on Foreign Relations, Subcommittee on Africa. *Hearing on Darfur and South Sudan,* June 15, 2004. 108th Congress, 2nd Session, Washington, DC (statement of Roger Winter, USAID Assistant Administrator, Bureau for Democracy, Conflict, and Humanitarian Assistance), https://reliefweb .int/report/sudan/testimony-roger-winter-usaid-dcha-assistant-administrator -humanitarian-crisis-sudan.

2. UN, *Rebels release abducted UN staff and aid workers in Darfur, Sudan,* UN News, September 1, 2004, http://www.un.org/apps/news/story.asp?NewsID=11803 #.WkaQ-3lG2M8.

3. UN, *Annan meets Sudanese officials and US Secretary Powell to discuss Darfur crisis,* UN News, June 30, 2004, http://www.un.org/apps/news/story.asp ?NewsID=11202&Cr=sudan&Cr1=#.WjvZOnlG2M8.

4. Amnesty International, *Amnesty International Report 2005—Sudan,* May 25, 2005, http://www.refworld.org/docid/429b27f42f.html.

Return to Darfur
1. CNN, "Powell calls Sudan killings genocide," Report September, 2004 http://www.cnn.com/2004/WORLD/africa/09/09/sudan.powell/.
2. World Health Organization, *Retrospective Mortality Study Among the Internally Displaced Population, Greater Darfur, Sudan*, WHO Report, September 2004, Geneva.
3. BBC News, "Eritreans in plane hijack drama," World Report, August 27, 2004, http://news.bbc.co.uk/2/hi/africa/3605184.stm.

Kalma Camp
1. ReliefWeb, *The comings and goings of Kalma Camp in South Darfur*, Report from World Vision, July 16, 2004, https://reliefweb.int/report/sudan/sudan-comings-and-goings-kalma-camp-south-darfur.
2. WHO, *Hepatitis E in Sudan*, Emergencies preparedness response, Disease Outbreak News, July 10, 2004, http://www.who.int/csr/don/2004_08_10/en/.

A Return to Abu-Shok
1. Human Rights Watch, *Sudan: Expelling Aid Agencies Harms Victims*, HRW Report, NY, New York, March 5, 2009, https://www.hrw.org/news/2009/03/05/sudan-expelling-aid-agencies-harms-victims.
2. Human Rights Watch, *World Report 2017: Sudan*, 2017, New York, New York, 2017, https://www.hrw.org/world-report/2017/country-chapters/sudan.

ACKNOWLEDGMENTS

—•—

In 1986, by the light of a flickering candle, I started writing this book, although at the time, it was meant only to be my memory keeper, a way to cherish and savor what I was sure would be special moments with refugees. And, for years, it was just that—a private journal. But in 2003, a reporter in Iraq encouraged me to "write a book," and the first of many drafts was born. I had no idea though how to create the story arc that publishers requested, so instead I wrote novels based on my own experiences. It wasn't until recently that my two beloved agents encouraged me to dust off these pages and bring the refugees and their stories to life. For that and so much more, I am enormously grateful to Cynthia Manson and Judy Hanson for their extraordinary guidance, their cherished friendship and their unshakable faith in my ability to craft a story. Without their encouragement, these stories would remain tucked away in my heart and the far corners of my closet, the pages and memories fading with each passing year. Instead, the people and their stories seem as vivid now as they did in those early days.

To Jessica Case and the team at Pegasus Books, many, many thanks for taking a chance on this story and bringing the warmth, spirit and resilience of these unforgettable people to life.

To the brilliant medical team who re-wrote my own story shifting what might have been an ending to a safe spot somewhere in the middle, I am so grateful. To Dr. Tyler Berzin, Dr Leah Biller, Dr. Vitaly Poylin, Dr. Benjamin Schlechter and the team at the BI-Deaconess Medical Center in Boston, my gratitude is endless. You are miracle workers.

And, finally to the refugees whose stories are printed on these pages and to those whose stories are imprinted on my heart, my deepest gratitude.

Thank you will never be enough.